T0339764

VITALITY

VITALITY

A Psychiatrist's Answer to Life's Problems

Richard Esser

Algora Publishing
New York

Library of Congress Cataloging-in-Publication Data —

Esser, Richard, 1925-
    Vitality : A Psychiatrist's Answer to Life's Problems/ Richard Esser.
        p. cm.
    Includes bibliographical references and index.
    ISBN 978-0-87586-618-5 (soft cover: alk. paper) — ISBN 978-0-87586-619-2 (hard
cover: alk. paper) — ISBN 978-0-87586-620-8 (ebook) 1. Mental health. 2. Vitality. I.
Title.
    RA790.5.E822 2008
    613—dc22
                                2007052059

Printed in the United States

For
Alexandra and Ingrid

I have spent my work life helping people who were at the end of their rope. My rewards have been three: first, my gratification on seeing individuals be rid of the distress that plagued them and seeing them get what they wanted most out of their living; second, the gratitude they showed me for the help they received; third, the lesson that this work has taught me about how to confront, understand and deal with difficulties in my own life. It seems to me that in this work I learned something new about the most difficult problems we all have in our living and about how to help both oneself and others deal with those problems. I wanted to share that new knowledge with others. I thought that others might benefit from what I learned. This book is the result.

I owe a special word of thanks to those who have helped me greatly on my way: Elvin Semrad of the Boston Psychopathic Hospital and Harvard University; Douglas Bond Sr. of the Pennsylvania Hospital and the University of Pennsylvania; Lawrence Kubie of the New York Psychoanalytic Institute and Columbia and Yale Universities; Kenneth Clark of the Northside Center and the City University of New York; Gunnar Inghe of the Karolinska Institute and the Swedish National Board of Health and Welfare.

One derives sustenance for our living primarily from the love of others. Thus this book is dedicated to my beautiful daughters Ingrid and Alexandra.

Table of Contents

Introduction. What Does a Psychiatrist Know About the Best of Living?

What does a psychiatrist know about the best of living? When I started out in psychiatry some fifty-odd years ago, the answer to that question would have seemed obvious to me: nothing. A psychiatrist's expertise concerned only the diagnosis and treatment of mental illnesses. Most psychiatrists today would be of that same opinion, even though the term mental illness has often been replaced by mental disorder. They would consider that psychiatry has nothing to do with living in general, let alone with defining the best of living and spelling out how to go about getting that best of living. That, however, is precisely how I came to see what was at the heart of my work. When I could help people get that "best" out of living, the severe distress that brought them to me completely disappeared. Put more pointedly, I found that what pulled people out of the difficulty they were caught up in was getting a clear idea of what the best of living for them was and how to go about getting that.

At the heart of *Vitality* is the idea that knowing what the best of living is and how to get that comes from knowing how to deal well with the worst of living or, more specifically, it comes from knowing how to turn desperation into vitality.

This perception stemmed directly from my efforts to help people in the worst of states. It came from my need to come up with a clear, commonsense, practical understanding of how to turn one's living completely around from the worst to the best. I came to see that there were four questions I needed good answers to if I were to help people be rid of the great distress that troubled them and get what they wanted most in their living. The answers I came up with lie at the heart of the message of this book. Here are those questions:

- What is it in a person's perception of living that leads to the worst of states, and what is it that leads to the best of states?
- If the different forms of severe distress that can cripple people are not mental illnesses or mental disorders, how can one make common sense of them so as to be completely rid of them and bring forth the best of living?
- What determines success or failure when one person would help another in severe distress?
- Is it possible to pinpoint one single resource all individuals possess that is essential to getting the best out of living and to dealing with the worst of living?

Here are my answers to those four questions:

WHAT IS IT IN A PERSON'S PERCEPTION OF LIVING THAT LEADS TO THE WORST OF STATES AND WHAT IS IT THAT LEADS TO THE BEST OF STATES?

I came to see that those people in the worst of states were caught up in the pursuit of false rewards in their living. What helped them — and what made for the best of living — was a realization of what the real rewards in living are and how to get them. Such rewards are to be found in six different spheres of our living: loving, friendship, learning, work, idealism and a private life.

When a person I would help got a clear idea of what he or she ought to be getting out of a given pursuit — its real reward, that person became filled with a great new enthusiasm for that aspect of living. They then talked about meaningful work, meaningful studies, a meaningful marriage, a meaningful friendship, meaningful leisure.

In contrast, the usual situation that drove people to seek help was a sense of meaninglessness in living. They experienced their daily life as empty, superficial, devoid of any real reward and of any wonder. I set forth what I see are the real rewards in each sphere of living, those that bring a sense of fulfillment, and contrast them with the false rewards, those that undermine our living. I make clear why, by far, the most difficult sphere of our living invariably is loving.

The details of my answer to this question are spelled out in Chapter 8, "The Real and the False Rewards of Loving, Friendship, Learning, Work, Idealism and a Private Life."

IF THE DIFFERENT FORMS OF SEVERE DISTRESS THAT CAN CRIPPLE PEOPLE ARE NOT MENTAL ILLNESSES OR MENTAL DISORDERS, HOW CAN ONE MAKE COMMON SENSE OF THEM SO AS TO BE COMPLETELY RID OF THEM AND BRING FORTH THE BEST OF LIVING?

People do move from the best of states to the worst of states and also from the worst of states to the best of states. It was imperative for me to make sense of what underlies that movement. Many individuals who came to me in the worst of states were fearful that they might be locked into an irreversible, debilitating mental illness, be that psychosis, neurosis or some other psychiatric diagnosis. I had to offer them optimism. When difficulties seem overwhelming in our everyday living, we move towards increasing desperation in our living; when we deal well with those difficulties, we move increasingly towards vitality in our living. I saw that there is a sliding scale in our living between desperation and vitality, depending upon whether things are going well or poorly.

It became increasingly apparent to me that the very worst of desperation is a mixture of six elements in different degree: craziness, rage, panic, violence, hopelessness and self-destructiveness. As we deal well with our desperation, each of those elements is turned into a corresponding element of vitality: we turn craziness into creativity, rage into courage, panic into initiative, violence into dynamism, hopelessness into achievement, and self-destructiveness into self-fulfillment. I set forth the sliding scales between those extremes. For example: craziness — eccentricity — originality — creativity. It is the middle two elements — in this case originality and eccentricity — that tie together what appear as the extremes of the worst and best in living.

To turn desperation into vitality it is necessary to see that each element of desperation is not something to be feared but serves as an essential resource that we need in our efforts to turn the worst of living into the best:

- underlying the creativity–craziness linkage is *imagination*
- underlying the courage–rage linkage is *power*
- underlying the initiative–panic linkage is *self-mobilization*
- underlying the dynamism–violence linkage is *self-assertion*
- underlying the achievement–hopelessness linkage is *ambition*
- underlying the self-fulfillment–self-destructiveness linkage is *self-gratification*.

This perception offers several significant advantages: 1) It makes clear just what the best of living is and how to get that, 2) It offers a way of discarding intimidating and stigmatizing psychiatric diagnoses of mental illness and replacing them with an optimistic, commonsense, alternative, 3) It enables us to see that concealed behind the worst appearing of psychiatric difficulties are the most admirable of qualities, 4) It dispels the fear associated with the worst states of living.

This question is answered in detail in Chapter 9, "Where Creativity, Courage, Initiative, Dynamism, Achievement and Self-Fulfillment Come From."

WHAT DETERMINES SUCCESS OR FAILURE WHEN ONE PERSON WOULD HELP ANOTHER IN SEVERE DISTRESS?

All of us need help from another person at times when things are going poorly in our lives. There are also times when we would offer such help to another. In my work I felt an over-riding need to boil down to its bare bones what works and what doesn't work when I — or anyone else — would help a person in severe distress. That boiling down took the form of my answers to three questions: What kind of relationship ought to exist between me and the person I would help? Where does one find answers to the many difficult questions central to helping? How do I know what to say and when to say it?

These were, respectively, the answers I came up with: *affection* between the helper and the person needing help; *the ability of a helper to put himself or herself in that person's shoes*; and *the asking-for-help-and-giving-of-help*. I set forth what I see as the critical significance that each of those seemingly simple principles has for success or failure in helping. Such a perception lies at the heart of my distinction between what is good helping and what is bad helping — regardless of whether the helper is a professional or a nonprofessional.

The details of my answer to this question are spelled out in Chapter 5, "The ABCs of Successful Helping."

IS IT POSSIBLE TO PINPOINT ONE SINGLE RESOURCE THAT ALL INDIVIDUALS POSSESS THAT IS ESSENTIAL TO GETTING THE BEST OUT OF LIVING AND TO DEALING WITH THE WORST OF LIVING?

This question increasingly concerned me when I tried to make sense out of what we need to tackle the difficult problems in our living. The answer that made the most sense was how we use our imagination. And out of that answer came the perception that at the crux of our living is the ability to turn craziness into creativity. I spell out a new perception of a craziness — or wildness and bizarreness — within all of us that is the wellspring of our imagination.

In our living, we test out our craziest ideas to see whether or not they work in getting what we want for ourselves. When they work, we experience a special creativity within ourselves. That testing-out is the central challenge in our living.

What psychiatrists and people in general view as craziness can be understood as a last-ditch effort to utilize one's wildness and bizarreness to stay alive, to stave off suicide. I set forth a commonsense understanding of such bizarreness. I came to see that my task was to help people utilize that selfsame craziness to get what they wanted most out of their living. Seeing such a linkage between craziness and creativity was the key to developing one's sense of self-confidence and self-pride.

This question is addressed in Chapter 10, "The Crux of Living: Turning Craziness into Creativity."

My answers to those four questions stemmed from what I experienced over the course of my career that was unexpected, that contradicted what I had taken for granted about psychiatry, and that was from the very start a continuous journey of discovery.

I tell the story of that journey in several early chapters, because I see that those who would utilize the ideas set forth in these pages ought to have a clear idea of just how the ideas were arrived, of just how they filled a practical need in my striving to know what works and what doesn't work in helping and living. That story began with my training in psychiatry, psychotherapy and psychoanalysis. More specifically, it began with my training in general psychiatry, child psychiatry and psychotherapy at Harvard Medical School institutions and my three years of psychoanalytic training at the New York Psychoanalytic Institute. It began with what drew me so powerfully to those pursuits.

I was drawn to psychiatry because of its idealistic character: it was that specialty most specifically concerned with helping those with the severest problems in living. Psychiatrists are generally acknowledged as being the last resort in helping those who are worst off, those considered crazy, those totally incapacitated, those nearest to suicide.

I was drawn to psychotherapy and psychoanalysis because they epitomized a "listening to–talking with" approach in helping people, an approach that seemed both humane and sensible. However, I soon ran into difficulties in my attempts to utilize such specialized knowledge in my helping efforts.

What increasingly troubled me during those training years was that the psychiatric, psychotherapeutic, and psychoanalytic concepts that I was exposed to did not help me in my own helping efforts.

I was dismayed to find that, contrary to my original expectation, psychiatric diagnosis was far from precise; such diagnosis was an inexact matter of finding a descriptive category that fit a person's most prominent troubling symptom. Furthermore, psychiatric diagnoses seemed to have an inbuilt pessimism; diagnoses of different psychoses, neuroses and character disorders invariably implied conditions that were never completely reversible. People acquired derogatory, stigmatizing, labels — such as schizophrenic, manic-depressive and obsessive-compulsive — that seemed to sum up the whole of a person. Medication, at best, offered some relief but had to be continued indefinitely, at times with serious side effects.

I looked to psychotherapy and psychoanalysis for a better understanding of the difficulties I was dealing with — and found myself up against another kind of problem. Most such specialists sidestepped the matter of whether or not people were suffering from a mental illness or mental disorder. To compound that difficulty I came to see that what had initially impressed me as so profound in many psychoanalytic and psychotherapeutic theories was of little help when I was sitting with a desperate person and searching for the right words to say, how to say them, and when to say them. Most such theories were far too complex to utilize in practice.

Those problems I had with psychiatry, psychotherapy, and psychoanalysis came to a head during the ten years I worked in Harlem. Those years, when I was Associate Clinical Director at the Northside Center, were a turning point in my career. They profoundly changed how I saw my work. That experience crystallized a pressing need to get to the root of how to help people. Those years were the prime source of the ideas I set forth in this book.

A common complaint of my colleagues was that people in Harlem were poorly motivated for psychotherapy. After an initial contact, they rarely returned for further visits. I came to see things differently.

I recognized that in my very first contact with a person, I had to make clear just how coming to me would help that person with the pressing problems confronting him or her. Right at the start, I had to be able to instill a newfound sense of optimism and enthusiasm for living. I had to overcome a marked wariness and skepticism about seeing a psychiatrist. I had to be able to put my ideas into clear, commonsense, everyday words. If I could do all that, people would come back. If not, they wouldn't.

I thus experienced a great pressure to simplify and clarify how to help people turn their living around, a way that made good sense to both me and the person I would help. When I succeeded in an initial contact, I felt a continued pressure to help a person find practical ways to follow through on changing his or her everyday life until that person got what he or she wanted most in living.

My training in psychiatry, psychotherapy, and psychoanalysis hadn't prepared me for that kind of pressure. That became clear to me when I compared my work in Harlem with my work outside of Harlem

In my private practice outside of Harlem, people would usually keep coming back. It was easy to deceive oneself that discussions about insight into a person's past experiences was progress — even if a person's everyday life did not change noticeably for the better. Self understanding easily became not a means to an end but an end in itself. Applying what I learned in Harlem was of great help in avoiding that pitfall.

As a result of that Harlem experience, I became critical of what I saw underlay a great deal of psychotherapy and psychoanalysis.

It was often assumed that helping is extremely complicated and complex. People who came to me for help usually assumed that such helping was a process beyond their own comprehension and only understandable by the experts. They were all too willing to accept the authority and word of the professional helper unquestioningly. They did not press such a professional for answers as to just how he or she worked. The professional was rarely criticized, even if the person felt criticism was merited. If one disliked the professional, such dislike was kept to oneself. People kept coming back because it was assumed that such dislike or criticism was unjustified, an expression of one's own inadequacy or immaturity or personal problems.

I spell out the difficulties I had with psychiatry in Chapter 3, "Searching for Optimism in the Wilderness of Psychiatry."

It was my work in Harlem that taught me to think and talk in plain language. It was my work in Harlem that forced me to have a clear idea of what the best in living is and how to get that and also what the worst in living is and how to deal well with that.

I spell out the great impact of my experience of working in Harlem had for me in Chapter 4, "Learning Basic Lessons in Harlem."

I wrote this book in the hope that a great many people may benefit from such clarity.

* * *

Many readers might find it hard to accept the assumption that conclusions stemming from my work as a psychiatrist have a central relevance to the living of people as a whole. Such an assumption would seem to fly in the face of a commonly accepted perception of what psychiatry is and what psychiatrists do.

One might well wonder whether people in general need an insight into the inner workings of psychiatry. I see that such an insight is essential. For psychiatry has a profound — and almost completely unrecognized — harmful effect on how we live our lives. I thus see it as necessary to deal with people's perception of psychiatry and psychiatrists.

Most people believe that psychiatric difficulties concern a relatively minor portion of populations — and not themselves. A remarkable, thorough, wide-scale survey done in New York in 1962 brought strikingly home to me just how untenable that perception is. The Cornell Midtown Manhattan Survey revealed that 81% of those surveyed had out-and-out clear-cut psychiatric symptoms and that only 19% were symptom free (see Chapter 13). The survey's results have been confirmed repeatedly by other similar surveys.

That result coincided with how I saw the living of people. I found that I could not draw a line between what psychiatrists deal with and what other helping professionals deal with, nor between what were considered psychiatric difficulties and problems in living that people in general experienced.

In my work I had to help individuals who were caught up in almost every conceivable difficulty, from craziness to narcotics abuse. Between those two extremes I helped individuals with a wide range of difficulties: marital strife, family disintegration and divorce, severe child-rearing problems, overeating and obesity, the abuse of alcohol and tobacco, crippling psychosomatic handicaps, paralyzing tension or fear, middle-age burnout, gambling away one's livelihood, a resort to prostitution and the sex market, outbursts of violence, attempted suicide. Underlying the effectiveness of my helping efforts was my idea of helping a person turn desperation into vitality. Those helping efforts with a wide range of difficulties convinced me that great numbers of people simply lived with their desperation and ended up seriously handicapped by psychiatric difficulties.

That conclusion was a striking finding in the Cornell survey mentioned above. That survey found that only a miniscule number of those with psychiatric difficulties had any contact with psychiatry; they did not seek help or get help; they lived with their difficulty. That matter went largely unrecognized and that need was largely unmet. And psychiatry was largely responsible for that state of affairs.

For psychiatry has shut its eyes to the scope and nature of the problem of psychiatric difficulties in society. That blindness can be traced back to thinking in terms of mental illness. Such thinking is an attempt to narrow the concern of psychiatrists and delimit it from the broad sweep of difficulties people in general experience. Psychiatrists need only concern themselves with those who come or are brought to psychiatry, those who are considered *ipso factor* to be suffering from a mental illness or mental disorder.

That idea of mental illness is just what gives rise to many people's reluctance to seek psychiatric help. For the idea of mental illness reflects a popular image of psychiatry as being incomprehensible to ordinary people, laden with pessimistic diagnoses and, it bears repeating, stigmatizing individuals with such labels as schizophrenic, manic depressive or neurotic. In the public mind, seeing a psychiatrist is often associated with being a hopeless psychiatric case, with being mentally ill. It is understandable that one would live with one's difficulties as long as possible rather than face such a confirmation. As long as one didn't come to psychiatry, one could see oneself as being among the mentally healthy, the normals.

It became clear to me that people in general need an insight into the inner workings of psychiatry — for their own good. For, psychiatry has a far-reaching, profound — and almost completely unrecognized — harmful effect on how we live our lives.

That harm stems from psychiatry's role in society.

Psychiatrists are generally considered the ultimate experts on the worst of psychological states. They define those states as mental illnesses or mental disorders, abnormalities of the mind, permanently handicapping conditions that cannot be completely eliminated. Such a definition, as noted, is permeated with pessimism and stigmatization. What builds such a negative perception of the worst of states into society is that famous writers, journalists and highly-educated persons accept uncritically the expertise of psychiatrists to make such a definition. They use the different diagnoses of mental illness when they want to derogate a person. And it is just that widespread acceptance of the diagnoses of mental illness in society that brings a disabling futility into the living of people.

For people are not immune to crazy thoughts, feelings of, rage, panic, violence, and hopelessness, and impulses to self-destructiveness. Those reactions arise when living is going poorly. When those reactions do arise, one might fear that one is losing one's mind. I have heard that fear expressed by many who came to me for help, people who outwardly seemed as well balanced as anyone else. That fear is usually so threatening that people would try to put it out of their minds rather than looking at what might underlie such fear. The result is that they deal poorly with the problems facing them in their everyday living; they don't come to grips with the desperation in their living.

Such desperation is largely hidden because people are loath to show that aspect of their living to others. That is the reason why the widespread problem of desperation in society goes unrecognized and people live with their desperation instead of getting help. That avoidance of dealing with desperation underlies, to my mind, such difficulties as the widespread abuse of alcohol, tobacco and psychopharmaceuticals.

It is important to understand why people have a great apprehension for the severe desperation they experience and why they avoid dealing with that desperation. Those reactions stem from the belief that there are such things as mental illness and mental health; desperate people fear that they might be mentally ill, not mentally healthy. That, to my mind, is belief in a myth.

In the 1960s, when an idealistic movement within psychiatry attempted to offer an optimistic counterweight to mental illness, serious attempts were made to define mental health. That effort is almost completely absent today, and it is important to know why.

The reason lies in how psychiatry defines mental illness. That definition is solely a descriptive classification based upon which symptom of a person's distress is most prominent. There is no common underlying definition of mental illness. The result is that mental health has become, in practice, simply the absence of mental illness. There is consequently no clear borderline between mental health and mental illness — and the result has had serious consequences for people's living.

A person who is seriously troubled is left not knowing whether he or she is crossing a line from health to illness. And, conversely, there is no clarity in knowing how one can move in the opposite direction, how one goes from illness to health. The mythical character of mental illness and mental health leaves people up in the air, not knowing what is central to living. This paralyzes people in dealing with living, in being able to turn desperation into vitality.

For the myth that there is a clear dividing line between mental health and mental illness instills fear in people when they are extremely desperate, that fear stands in the way of understanding what underlies their desperation.

That myth has been brilliantly exposed by Thomas Szasz in his book, *The Myth of Mental Illness*. It has been further amplified by several penetrating works including: *The Selling of DSM*, by Stuart A. Kirk and Herb Kutchins, *Mad in America: Bad Science, Bad Medicine, and the Enduring Mistreatment of the Mentally Ill*, by Robert Whitaker, and *Blaming the Brain: The Truth About Drugs and Mental Health*, by Elliot Valenstein.

It is essential for people to know how to make common sense of — and deal with — the scariest aspects of one's living. That matter is dealt with in Chapter 12, "Coming to Grips with the Scariest Part of Ourselves."

There is a great need to replace the pessimism and incomprehensibility characteristic of most of today's psychiatry with optimism and common sense. That is what my book offers.

* * *

Seeing living in terms of turning desperation into vitality led me to the question of how to tackle the sweeping problem of widespread desperation in society. It seemed to me that my perception of living and helping might open up a new approach to that problem. The idea I came up with was crystallized in an idea of psychiatric prevention. That idea resulted in a concrete preventive psychiatric project.

The idea at the core of that project was that personnel outside of psychiatry and psychology could offer effective helping to people who were troubled early on — before they might need to come to psychiatry — if they received backup supervision from me in how to do that.

Over seven years in Malmö, Sweden, I had forty supervisory groups that included neighborhood police, social workers, immigrant counselors, teachers, judicial referees in child custody disputes, recreational center leaders, outreach workers in delinquency, and workers in the areas of narcotics and alcohol abuse. What made that project a success was my having a clear idea what the essentials in helping and living were. That clarity enabled me to put ideas into everyday language that personnel in other fields could easily understand and utilize.

The details of that project are found in Chapter 13, "The Key Question of Prevention."

* * *

The ideas set forth in this book are very personal ones. They are one psychiatrist's attempt to answer questions he sees as central to our living. I cannot offer proof of the validity of those ideas. I can only offer examples of how I have helped people get what they wanted most out of their living. I can only tell the story of how I came to those ideas.

Despite that qualification, it is important to make clear that there is an excellent precedent for deriving from my helping efforts as a psychiatrist ideas about the living of people in general. That is precisely what the early psychoanalytic pioneers did. One need only look at some of the titles of Sigmund Freud's books: *Beyond the Pleasure Principle*, *The Psychopathology of Every-*

day Life, Totem and Taboo, Thoughts for the Times on War and Death, Civilization and Its Discontents.

When all is said and done, this work stemmed from my fascination with my work as a psychiatrist. Perhaps a word about that fascination is in order. At a social gathering not so long ago a young academic asked me what I did for work. When I said I was a psychiatrist, her reaction was, "Your work must be extremely difficult and extremely discouraging." That assumption — that a psychiatrist's work is onerous, offers a minimum of either success or gratification, and demands a great deal of forbearance — is common. She was surprised when I replied, "Quite the opposite. I see my work as one of the most optimistic, the most rewarding and the most fascinating pursuits imaginable."

What gives me optimism is that people whom I have helped have had a great desire to be rid of the difficulty oppressing them. The motivation and energy to do something about their situation was clearly there — even if many felt nearly ready to give up completely. The task facing me was to help them put that motivation and energy to work. To do that meant helping them clarify just what they wanted for themselves in such areas as loving, learning, work, friendship, recreation and parenting — and then helping them find a way to go about getting those ends. More than half the battle is won by simply having a good clear idea of what one wants and how to get that.

When an individual arrives at such clarity and gets the encouragement to try to reach such ends, his or her difficulty usually disappears in a short time. Such helping does not need to take a long time, as is commonly supposed — even with the severest appearing of psychiatric difficulties.

The acid test of the worth of my idea of the best of living and how to get that was that it served to turn a person's living completely around from the worst of living to the best of living. That is the ultimate test of the practicality of these ideas. Examples of that turning around are in Chapter 2, "Turning Living Around, Eight Thumbnail Sketches."

There is an enormous sense of gratification in seeing such a process at work. It is the same great gratification we experience when we can help someone close to us who is deeply troubled: our child, friend, wife, husband, co-worker, student. Such gratification is even greater for psychiatrists, for often we are the last resort. Others have failed. It is up to us to make such helping work. The optimism I find in my work comes from seeing that most of those whom I have tried to help have, indeed, gotten the help they wanted from me.

My work in helping people opened up a whole new world for me: the world of our inner life. When people trusted me, they opened up about their most private selves, about their hidden dreams, hopes, fantasies, imaginings, fears, doubts, secrets, failures. Those were things that they usually did not open up with others — even those very close to them — for fear of criticism, derogation or condescension. Hearing those aspects of other people's most private selves gave me just that sense of being an explorer on a journey of discovery in trying to understand more and more of that vast world of our inner life.

The greatest challenge came from helping those who were almost ready to give up on living, those closest to suicide. Such a confrontation with death, the possible taking of one's life, brought me face to face with the questions of what is truly meaningful in living, what is really important in living, what is basic in our living. Or, if you will, what vitality in living is. The answers to those questions go to the very heart of our living.

CHAPTER 1. GETTING A KICK OUT OF LIVING

We know immediately and instinctively what getting a kick out of living is. We feel great. Everything is just rolling along in our lives. There is a pithiness and succinctness in that expression which captures the qualities of enthusiasm, zest and high spirits in living. That is how most of us would want our living to be. How to get that kind of living is the central theme of this work.

When we get a kick out of living, there is a special character to the beginning and end of each day. We get up eager to meet the new day, eager to see what new experiences and new rewards that day will bring into our living. We go to bed at night with a sense of satisfaction that the day was well spent, that it brought just those new experiences and new rewards which added to the enrichment of our living.

One might well object that living simply cannot be that way all the time, that such a description makes sense when life is going great and everything is clicking, but what about all the other times? One can't live on Cloud Nine every day. What about all those other days when one may feel overwhelmed by problems, setbacks, frustrations and all the other agonies in living?

Putting that objection in a somewhat different light leads to a different answer: How does one get a kick out of living in the face of all the severe problems that can and will crop up? The answer to that question pinpoints what is at the heart of getting the best out of living and the wonder in doing so.

The answer, in a nutshell, is to see all such problems as challenges to our ingenuity — and not as oppressive burdens to avoid or to bear. Since, indeed, severe problems are indisputably part and parcel of living, the path to getting a kick out of living lies in how we tackle those problems. If we see them as a test of our mettle, as something to sink our teeth into, there will be an eagerness to come to grips with them and overcome them. Although it may sound strange at first, it can be fun and stimulating to tackle the hardest problems in living.

The reward for tackling and overcoming such problems is an enormous sense of pride in oneself. It seems that the more severe the problem is, the greater the challenge is — the greater the reward. Overcoming small problems brings only small rewards. The heart of living, in this light, can be seen as a never-ending series of new problems, new challenges, new tests of one's ingenuity, and new and greater rewards in living. That is the direct opposite of stagnation. One avoids getting stuck in the stagnation of a routine in living. Let me spell out how I see that opposite alternative — for doing so ought to give an appreciation of why it is so easy to wind up in a complete paralysis of living.

In that opposite alternative what is paramount is smooth, problem-free living. Major problems are seen as oppressive and insurmountable burdens to put off, bear with, or avoid as best one can. Those problems are not seen as a test of ingenuity. Rather, they are seen as being caused by circumstances beyond one's control. One is consequently powerless to deal with them. One doesn't look inside oneself for better ways of tackling those problems. Instead one is content to find fault everywhere else. One blames one's husband, wife, children, parents, friends, boss, co-workers. One blames whole peoples who are different from oneself. One blames society. One blames fate. One blames heredity. One blames teachers, police, schools and universities, industry, politicians. It is not that those other instances are blameless, for such blame may well be justified — but when one see things that way, one cripples oneself.

One can easily end up with a life dominated by bitterness at one's lot, by cynicism, hopelessness or suspicion. There is little sense of accomplishment or self-pride. Every day is the same as the previous one. There is a deadening routine in living. One constantly feels worn out. One alleviates the routine by a whole gamut of instant pleasures: eating, drinking, buying sprees, gambling, passive entertainment. I see nothing wrong with such pleasures. We need them; we need breathing room; we need time to forget all the difficulties in our living; we need pleasures to renew ourselves. What I mean is that if those pleasures are central in our living, there is something seriously missing.

Why make such a stark contrast between those two ways of looking at living? It is not to put down the need for routine, problem-free times, security, happiness and pleasure. Rather, it is to make clear why far too many people live out their lives without getting any real kick out of living, without any enthusiasm, without experiencing any wonder.

Seeing major problems as challenges to ourselves means, in concrete terms, how we set priorities in our daily living. We ought to tackle those major problems, the ones that trouble us most, first off. Our major energy should be directed there. We shouldn't get hung up on minor issues, as it is far too easy to do. That, of course, is easier said than done. And that is what brings me to what I see is the great wonder in our living.

The wonder lies in finding out that we do, indeed, have the ingenuity, creativity and other resources within ourselves to deal with and overcome all the problems we face.

Finding those resources within oneself, bringing them forth and making the most of them, are what I see as the great wonder in our living. That is what makes living fascinating, what makes each day a new adventure, what is the key to getting a kick out of each successive day, what brings a sense of perpetual discovery to the whole course of one's living. My aim in this book is to make clear just how to get that wonder in living.

One might question whether living can be like that for all of us. I am convinced that it can. After working intensively over so many years to help people deal with the severest problems in living, it is the only way I see that makes good sense. That is how I see my own living. Such a perception of living is eminently practical. It works. It works by doing two things simultaneously: It brings us the best out of our living and it deals effectively with the worst in our living. It does so by making crystal clear what is important in living and how to get that. When we see things that way, we can turn our living around completely.

Chapter 2. Turning Living Around, Eight Thumbnail Sketches

People who came to me for help wanted to turn their living around. My aim was to help them do just that. In the following eight stories, I set forth in capsule form some of the helping problems I have had to deal with and how I did so. They are an attempt to give an idea of what I have found so challenging and so fascinating in my work.

Tom, Cus, Floyd and Me

He was 16 but looked 22 or 23. Big, well over six feet, powerful and, most characteristically, with a ferocious scowl on his face that said loud and clear, "Don't cross me." I'll call him Tom (all the names in these stories are fictitious). I was working at a psychiatric center in Harlem at the time we first met. He had been referred by the school because of violence; he had been in dozens of fights. He had had a fistfight with an assistant principal and had once threatened the principal with a knife. Even though he was a loner, because of his size and anger he was sought after in gang fights.

We hit it off well from the start. He started right off with what seemed like a question but was really a challenge, "What can *you* do for me?" I said, "I can help you get the school off your back, if that's what you want." He began to open up. He had vivid fantasies of blowing up buildings and killing people. Nevertheless, I liked him. When he dropped his super-tough mask I saw a warmth, openness, and honesty in him. I learned that he had a strong mother, no father, and four older, domineering sisters. He then confided to me that he could not read. He had managed to cover that over in school by simply not doing any work or by cheating. But I found him smart. I put him together with a remedial reading expert at the Center and he began making strides in his reading.

We met once a week. He seemed eager to come and tell me what was going on in his life — even at times asking for my advice. His fighting stopped, even though his fantasies about violence continued. In the early spring I asked him what he was going to do during the summer. I was concerned because when school stopped for the summer, there was invariably a marked increase in gang fighting and violence in the streets. He mulled that over and then said he thought that he'd try and get a job. He worked for a short time at Yankee Stadium followed by a short stint sweeping floors at a karate hall. But those jobs just bored him. We sat and puzzled the problem together. Then I had a brainstorm. I had heard that Cus d'Amato had a great interest in helping boys from Harlem. Floyd Patterson was world heavyweight champion at the time and d'Amato was his trainer. I suggested that Tom call down to see if he could train at d'Amato's gym. I was surprised when Tom was taken by a sudden shyness. He said, hesitatingly, "You call." And I did. I told Cus d'Amato who I was, and that I was working with a fine fellow who wanted to learn boxing. His answer was short and fast, "Send him down."

Tom trained regularly. It wasn't so easy for him because, despite his size, he was always pitted against others who were much older. During this time his fantasies of violence disappeared completely. He was doing better in school. We were almost ready to stop at the end of that December. Then I got a beautiful Christmas card. It was signed Floyd Patterson, but obviously came from Cus d'Amato. I showed it to Tom and his eyes grew large. I asked him whether he would like to have the card. He exclaimed, "Can I really have it!" I said, "Of course." What a thrill for a sixteen year old!

We stopped. A year later I got a telephone call from Tom. He asked whether he could come and visit me at the Center. He looked quite different when we met, dressed in a suit, tie, and white shirt. He was self-confident and self-assured. We exchanged small talk. It later became clear to me why he had come. He was proud of himself and what he had accomplished. And I was inordinately proud of him.

TURNING POINT

It was during my earliest years as a psychiatrist that I came to know Carol. She was in her mid-thirties, highly intelligent, well-dressed and a skilled professional. We had met previously at a child guidance center when I had helped her with her seven-year-old son. Now she wanted help for herself. However, it was extremely difficult for her to pin down what was troubling her. She felt tense, was dissatisfied with her life, and often argued with her husband. She found fault with him; she thought he wasn't involved enough with the children and was rather passive — even though he was kind and a hard worker.

I felt that there were things bottled up inside her that she simply could not get out. Nothing I said or did worked. The techniques I had learned of psychotherapy and psychoanalysis did not help. There were often long silences where we sat together. She would sit tense, intent, speechless, often glaring at me. My hope was that she would finally bring forth what was troubling her so deeply. I felt that there was simply no progress — yet I knew that she desperately wanted to continue coming. She saw hope in that. I think she sensed how much I did want to help her. I felt that stopping her visits would kill that hope. She was obviously in some kind of torment. So we kept on, well over a year.

I am not sure now, so many years afterwards, just how the turning point came up — but I do remember what it was. I had asked her whether she thought she was attractive. She said that she didn't think so. I asked, "Why not?" She felt that she was overweight. I said that I thought she had fine features and agreed that she would look much more attractive if she lost weight. She was eager to do that, and I gave her advice on how to do so. She went at it with a steadfast determination.

I still remember vividly how, after she had lost a good deal of weight, she came for a visit one day, extremely pleased with herself. She had visited her hometown and met some old friends she hadn't seen for some time. They exclaimed spontaneously, "Carol, we wouldn't have recognized you! You look simply wonderful!" She had found a new pride in herself and, more specifically, in herself as a woman. There were far fewer arguments with her husband. Their life together was decidedly happier. She was radiant. We had reached an endpoint. Before we stopped, though, her husband also wanted to come to see me to express his thanks personally for how much better their life together had become.

There is a sequel to that story. Many years later, after I had moved from the States to Sweden, I received a visit from her son, now a university student, bearing greetings from Carol. How touched I was!

DETECTIVE WORK

I was working in the child and youth psychiatric department of a large general hospital in Sweden. Bengt, then 18, was referred from the internal medicine department because of severe stomach pain that had persisted for months. Extensive studies could find no reason for his difficulty. It was important to rule out a possible psychosomatic causation.

He was a tall, good-looking youth, well dressed and well spoken. It was immediately clear that he did not want to see a psychiatrist. He was tense and answered questions reluctantly and as curtly as possible. He came because his parents had urged him to do so. He said his stomach distress was constant throughout the day, that nothing seemed to make it better or worse. He felt his life otherwise was perfectly fine. It was clear to me that what I had to tackle first off was his extreme guardedness.

I asked a number of questions about less charged matters: his school, his friends, his outside interests. We found a common interest in guitar playing. That was his great passion. Since at the time I was doing a bit of guitar playing myself, it was easy to draw him out about the kind of music he liked best, the guitar he had, the one he would like to have, the friends he played together with. During this discussion he became increasingly more relaxed and freer in talking. I then went back to the question of his stomach difficulty.

He said he was convinced it was something physical and not due to tension. He was completely puzzled as to why it was present. He could not find anything wrong with his life. I said that that might well be so but that it wouldn't hurt if we tried to pin things down somewhat better. What followed seemed to me like a trail of detective work. This is what I found out: His distress began early in the morning; it intensified as he sat on the school bus; it persisted during school hours; it abated on the bus ride home; it was never present over the weekends. I then asked him how he felt about school. The following story gradually came out.

He was in his last year of *gymnasium*. He did not really want to go on to university but he felt he had to. Both his parents were academics and, although they never put any pressure on him, he felt it was taken for granted by them that he also would pursue an academic career. I asked him what he would like to do instead. He said he would like to try and play music professionally. I said that I thought that was a good idea, worth trying out. I encouraged him to discuss the matter with his parents.

It seemed that that bit of encouragement was just what he needed. He did so and was pleased by their response. He decided that, if he were to go on to university, it could be put off for a year. He was completely surprised when his stomach distress disappeared almost immediately. We kept on for a total of four more once-a-week visits to make sure that there was no recurrence. The whole matter might seem extremely simple and straightforward — but only in hindsight.

CALL IT MAGIC

I had just started working at a child psychiatric center in a nearby suburb of Stockholm. A fellow child psychiatrist asked me whether I might be able to help a family she had worked with unsuccessfully over a number of years.

Gustav was 11 years old. He wet and soiled himself and had always done so. He could not go to sleep at night without the light on and without the radio going next to his ear. He was fearful of animals. He had no friends. He did little school work. He seemed quite immature in comparison to others his age, his play interests being much more common to a boy years younger. Despite those features he was not taunted, as he may well have been, for he was large and strong. Most troubling to his parents was that he insisted almost every day that his mother divorce his stepfather. There were constant arguments between Gustav and his stepfather.

As was my custom when working with families, I first saw Gustav alone. He proudly showed me how strong he was when he squeezed my hand. He told me about his favorite foods. His favorite toys were airplanes and he proudly drew me a picture of a bomber. We played Chinese checkers. During this time he talked freely about his mother, stepfather and school. It seemed clear to me that he wanted to be friends with me and that such a friendship was forming.

I next saw his mother alone. She gave an impression of being gentle, well intentioned and completely at a loss as to what to do. She found herself hopelessly caught between a son who repeatedly said that he hated his stepfather and a strong husband whom she wanted and needed as a support.

Next I saw Gustav's stepfather Karl alone (I see parents separately, at first, because I want them to feel free to talk uninterruptedly about personal and private matters, which is often not so easy to do when one's wife or husband is present). He was a short, vigorous, intense man, a craftsman. He seemed distinctly on guard, as though he might be criticized for not taking his full responsibility as a father. He told me, with only little prompting, that he was doing his very best to teach Gustav what is right and wrong in such things as manners, how to talk respectfully to his mother, his duties at home, being punctual. I listened for quite a while and he seemed to ease up, in part because I acknowledged how much he did care about Gustav and in part because he got no criticism from me. Indeed, I said that it seemed to me that he had tried his very best to do all he could for Gustav.

I then asked him if it would be alright if I asked him a question. When he said I could, I asked, "Would you say that you and Gustav are friends?" He had to answer what was patently obvious, that they were not friends at all. I suggested that that might be a good way to try and make things better between them. He told me that he had never been friends with his own father and neither had his three brothers. His father was a strong person and, like him, emphasized emphatically what was right and wrong and the importance of not spoiling a child. He wanted my advice as to how to make friends with Gustav.

From my conversation with Gustav, I knew that he liked the idea of fishing. I also suspected that, despite his supposed hatred, he looked up to his stepfather just because Karl seemed so strong. I suggested that Karl ask Gustav whether he would like to go fishing together on the weekend, just the two of them. They had never done anything like that before. I cautioned Karl not to lecture Gustav on how to fish, just to encourage him and praise him for his efforts. Also to bring along some good food that Gustav especially liked. The one and only point was to have a good time together and do only what Gustav would like to do. Karl ought to treat Gustav the way he would have liked to have been treated by his own father.

I waited with a great deal of anticipation for their next visit a week later. I wondered whether Karl could pick up on the ideas I had thrown out and whether Gustav would respond. Imagine my great pleasure when I heard from both of them that it had gone splendidly. They were both enormously proud and pleased. It was as though Gustav had found a father and Karl had found a son.

Suddenly there was no more talk of kicking Karl out of the house. Rather, they did things together. Within a few weeks his wetting and soiling stopped completely and he could go to sleep without the light or radio on. What was most striking were the comments Gustav's grandmother and teacher made only a few weeks later. Both were amazed. They remarked spontaneously to Gustav's mother that Gustav seemed like a completely changed boy, self-assured, able to make friends, no longer childish, doing his school work. It was as though some kind of magic had taken place. We stopped after ten weeks, continuing a longer time just to see if the progress which had taken place held.

Such is the stuff of wonderful times experienced when one's helping efforts click.

DAMAGE DONE

Karin was 30 when she came to me. One of the first things she was quick to say was, "Don't pay any attention to how fast I talk, that's just the medicine." She also explained that the medicine made her overweight. She had been taking that medicine for years, ever since she was placed on it during a first admission to a psychiatric hospital. She had come to me after reading that I had a psychiatric practice in which I did not use drugs, only talked with people.

She was right on both accounts. When she stopped taking medicine, her speech lost the former great pressure behind it and she slimmed down greatly. She had been admitted to that hospital years before because she caused a great deal of trouble for those around her. She had become infatuated with a fellow, but whatever attraction he might have had for her soon disappeared. They shared adjoining rooms at a university dormitory. She began to hear his voice talking to her through the wall — even when he wasn't there. She entreated their common friends to intercede with him on her behalf. He moved away to a different city but she did not give up. She wrote a stream of letters over the years; she pleaded with friends to help her. The fact that she often heard his voice talking to her was a constant source of encouragement for her. Her friends finally persuaded her to seek help at the hospital. On medication, she did become appreciably calmer but her life seemed on hold. She lived on social welfare supports. Thoughts of suicide persisted.

When I first saw her I was struck by how bright and charming she was. She had graduated from the university with top grades. She was remarkably quick in her thinking and was clearly seeking help from me. One development which seemed most promising was that the city had a support program in which individuals could get practical experience in a given field. Since she was accredited in accounting, she was placed in a small firm which needed such services. She was greatly pleased with her work, and felt she did it quickly, accurately, competently. Each week that she visited me she remarked about the spontaneous compliments she got from her boss. He saw her as a distinct asset. He told her that there was no question in his mind that when she finished the trial period he would offer her a permanent position.

It seemed clear to me that she would not let go of her thoughts about the fellow she had been enamored with — and her hearing his voice — unless and until she began seeing other fellows. I encouraged her to do that. I thought she was attractive and told her so. She began — tentatively. It also seemed to me that the new sense of self-confidence she experienced in her work would help her greatly on that score. And then the roof fell in.

She came to me almost in tears. Her boss had said that before he could hire her he had to have a green light from the city's rehabilitation program. When he talked to the administrator she was shocked and exclaimed, "You can't hire her; she's schizophrenic!" I was furious. I offered to call up both her boss and the administrator. But Karin would not let me. She just wanted to back away from any confrontation. She did not want to cause any trouble and possibly make things worse for herself. I did not feel I could go against her wishes. That was the end of our contact.

I've often thought about her. I wondered if I could have done anything different and better. I wonder where she is now and how she's faring.

CLEAR-SIGHTEDNESS

Robert was greatly troubled by blurry vision. Medical examinations showed that there was nothing wrong with his eyes. The assumption was that his problem was psychosomatic — and he agreed with that. But he could not come upon any underlying reason.

When he came to me he was in his mid 40s. He was a highly successful businessman and accomplished in sports. He was tall, handsome and well spoken. He felt his marriage was rather good even though he had had a number of affairs with other women from time to time. But he did acknowledge that there was little enjoyment in his life. It was dull, a monotonous routine. He was constantly tense, worn out.

He seemed to be very much on guard with me. If I asked a question about his life, he wanted to know why I did so. If he asked for my opinion on a matter, I had to make perfectly clear just why I answered the way I did. He was constantly ready to challenge me. Even though he often did that in a rather irritated tone, I liked that quality about him. I saw two distinct advantages in it. First, it forced me to make crystal clear for him what I meant. When he did get such clarity and saw logic in it, he would act upon it directly. Action was his strong suit. Second, my accepting his right to challenge whatever I said put us on an even footing. I was not a superior psychiatric expert whose opinions could not be questioned. I was simply a fellow human being doing the best I could to help him. It became easy to establish a dialogue between us. His original defensiveness quickly disappeared. He could open up about his personal life.

It then became clear that what troubled him most was his marriage. He was extremely fond of his wife. He saw her as trustworthy, loyal, and a good mother to their children. But there was almost no fun in the marriage for him. Sex was absent. That was a major reason he sought the companionship of other women. He felt he could not bring up that problem with her, that she might easily be offended. Sex was a difficult subject for her. I encouraged him to do so. I gave my opinion that it made little sense to put sex in one compartment and marriage in another; that such pleasure together ought to be important for both of them.

He did try. He did so with all the hesitancy, gentleness and tenderness he possessed. But he met up with a stone wall. He felt that she saw her marriage as doing the acceptable and responsible thing but not as being the source of great fun together. The security of the marriage was enough for her. It became clear to him then that he either had to accept his marriage on those terms — which meant, in his eyes, continued extramarital affairs — or to bring up the question of divorce. That was extremely painful for him because, despite an outward toughness, he was highly sensitive and hated the thought of possibly hurting her.

In the end he came to the conclusion that, regardless of his fondness for his wife, he had but one life to live and had a right to enjoy that as best he could. Being married and having a series of extramarital affairs did not make sense to him. He saw such affairs as a betrayal. He then fell deeply in love with another woman, one whom he felt could give him the pleasure and kind of companionship he sought. Needless to say, his blurry vision and tension disappeared quickly during this time. He seemed far happier with his life.

A HEAD FULL OF NUMBERS

Leif, who was in his late 30s, was desperate. He felt he had been helped greatly by me some years back. Now he was so distraught that he wanted to see me as soon as possible. He was enormously troubled, for he could not stop counting numbers. Incessant counting preoccupied him almost constantly, but it was most severe when he was alone or at work. He found that he could not work at all; he could not concentrate. That had been going on for well over a week.

When we met, the following story came forth. Leif thought that outside of that incessant counting his life was going splendidly. He had a fine job. Most importantly, he was head over heels in love with a young woman who was just as enamored with him as he was with her. They were to be engaged in a few weeks and married in a few months. As we talked he suddenly brought out what appeared to be a deep-lying concern. He wondered whether he was as mature as she was, for she had had sex far more often than he. He was completely baffled as to the reason for his incessant counting and had no idea of what to do about it. Those were the two questions he put to me. I shared my ideas with him.

I said, in summary, that sometimes seemingly meaningless thoughts can preoccupy us constantly because we are greatly troubled by what is going on in our lives. We are troubled to the degree that we have no idea of how to deal with that situation. Those seemingly meaningless thoughts serve to keep our mind off what we don't want to think about. In this instance it seemed to me that, despite the great love he felt, he was troubled about what would happen. Getting married is a major event, a turning point in life. He was concerned whether or not he was prepared for it. I said that in my opinion the number of times one has had sex has nothing to do with how mature a person is. What matters is that both of them, for the first time, could combine sex with a wonderful and rare sense of intimacy and partnership. It was just such a combination that, to my mind, brought with it a true sense of maturity.

Leif listened intently. He felt greatly relieved and said so. We had another appointment four days later. He said his counting had almost completely disappeared. He felt so confident of himself that he felt he did not have to come back again. Some months later I received a Christmas card from Leif and his future wife expressing their thanks for my help.

Helping usually seems easy in retrospect. When I first heard Leif's complaint, it seemed like a complicated phenomenon which wasn't easily understandable. I had to ask myself when I might have had a similar experience and what was its cause. That is the knowledge I shared with Leif. That it worked so successfully was a confirmation for me that, to help another person who was desperate for my help, I had to look for answers in my own life.

What Worked

Ronald called me on a sudden impulse. He had seen an article about me in the local newspaper with an accompanying photograph. He liked what he read and saw. He felt he simply had to see a psychiatrist. He was deeply depressed, thought constantly about taking his life.

He was in his early thirties, had a good-paying, highly skilled technical job, a faithful wife, and three children he was proud of. What had thrown him completely off balance was a torrid love affair with a young woman in her early twenties. It was heaven when it lasted and a catastrophe when it ended. He could barely function at work or at home.

We hit it off well. He said afterwards that coming to me was like finding a new friend he could confide in. He wanted my advice about many aspects of his life and I did my best to answer his questions. He had a splendid voice and I encouraged him to act in an amateur opera company. He did so with great success and with obvious pride. He was an accomplished sportsman and found a renewed interest in competition. After several months he felt his life was going splendidly. He was pleased with himself, his family, his interests. His love affair was a thing of the past.

At our last meeting I asked him, as I usually do just before stopping with someone, what he felt had helped him most in our contacts. He answered quickly and spontaneously, "When you told me how crushed you were after your own disastrous love affair and how you managed to come out of it."

In selecting the above eight stories and cutting them down to their bare bones, I have taken a certain risk. It might be wrongly assumed on reading them that the helping I have described is not particularly difficult or demanding. It might, furthermore, be wrongly assumed that the kinds of difficulties described were not particularly severe; otherwise they would not have responded well to such helping efforts. Thus a word of explanation is needed to make clear why I have taken such a risk, why I have set forth these stories at this point and why I have done so in such skeletonized form.

All the ideas set forth in this book are based upon my work in helping people. It is important, at the very start, to give as clear, concrete, and succinct an idea as I can of what that helping is like. Later on I shall set forth what I see is the understanding needed to help another be rid of the severest of psychiatric conditions. I shall also set forth what I see is particularly difficult and demanding in such helping.

An important word of explanation: I describe my work as "helping" for a very specific reason. There are simple and basic principles in how professional helpers do their job effectively. Those principles, elaborated in the chapter, "The ABCs of Successful Helping," are basic to any situation where one person, professional or not, wishes to help another who is in severe emotional distress. That includes a parent and a child, a husband and a wife, two friends, a teacher and a student, a work supervisor and a subordinate, a sports coach and an athlete. Seen this way, "helping" is just the right word both for what I was doing as a specialist and what people in general do. There is a common core in all effective helping.

Since such a perception stemmed from my work as a psychiatrist, that is where this book begins. My thoughts on what works in helping — and what does not work in helping — evolved over a long stretch of time, from those particular experiences I had in psychiatry, child psychiatry, psychotherapy and psychoanalysis. Out of those experiences my ideas emerged about how people plagued with the severest of difficulties can turn their lives completely around and get the best out of living. To understand what underlies those ideas it is necessary to see how they developed. That is the story I tell in the next chapter.

Chapter 3. Searching for Optimism in the Wilderness of Psychiatry

When Bill, as I shall call him, came into my life, he was a troubled and threatening man. I was in my first year of specialty training in psychiatry. Bill looked just like the professional football player he was, outsized-big and formidable. He said almost nothing but glowered ominously as if daring anyone to cross him. People kept their distance. It didn't help matters that he was the only black person in that private mental hospital. Bill was convinced that his wife was trying to poison him. He was admitted to the hospital because his family felt there was a serious risk he would kill her.

I liked him. We played tennis together. We talked together a great deal. He progressively opened up and tried his best to answer the host of questions which I, in my eagerness to understand what was going on, asked him. Over the following weeks he improved markedly. His menacing attitude disappeared as did his suspicion of being poisoned. He was moved successively from the closed ward to the middle ward to the open ward.

That is clearly not the end of that story. But I cite that episode from long ago because it taught me a lesson. Fumbling to learn something about psychiatry, I realized that I could, even in my innocence, reach and help someone in the throes of craziness if we could first be friends. That experience was my first inkling that calling craziness the mental illness of psychosis was a gross oversimplification

Over the next fifty-odd years, up until now, I have tried to sort out what works and what doesn't work in helping people in the worst of states, those situations when they wind up seeing a psychiatrist. That sorting out took many unexpected turns. It led me to perceive the living of all of us in a far different way than is usual.

I came to see that every negative aspect of living — craziness, rage, panic, violence, hopelessness, self-destructiveness — contains a kernel of something positive; if, that is, one knows the trick of turning the worst of living into the very best. I came to see that my job as a psychiatrist was to help those who came to me That ability to turn the worst of living into the very best was the key to preventing getting stuck in a permanent psychiatric disability.

In the 1950s, remarkable events were taking place in American psychiatry. Those events set the foundation for all that happened later on in my career. At that time it was as though a completely new kind of psychiatry was being created from scratch, a specialty that was visionary, wondrous and exciting.

Before then psychiatry had, for the most part, the character of a dumping ground. People languished year after year in mental hospitals. A whole battery of physical and medication treatments were utilized, but to little avail. All of that effort seemed like trial-and-error guesswork. Psychiatry right through the 1930s was clearly the lowest rung on the ladder of medical specialties. There was little vision, wonder or excitement in the specialty.

That changed dramatically after the Second World War. Four developments affecting American psychiatry brought with them a striking new optimism.

Psychoanalysis. The influx of eminent psychoanalyst-psychiatrists who had fled from Europe brought a new, highly promising, psychological element into psychiatric thinking. It suddenly seemed possible to explain the cause of even the worst of psychiatric conditions in terms of what had happened during a person's earliest years. Psychoanalysis, furthermore, offered the prospect of being able to correct that causation solely by psychological means. Psychoanalysis vastly expanded the scope of psychiatric concerns. Psychiatrists were no longer concerned only with those who were almost totally disabled but also with many who did not appear to be psychiatric cases at all. That scope was even further extended by the fact that many of the early psychoanalytic pioneers considered that their knowledge was central to the living of human beings in general. They wrote extensively about different aspects of human nature.

The social sciences. A great burgeoning within academia of sociology and anthropology concerned itself in good part with issues of psychoanalysis, psychology, and psychiatry. Those efforts were aimed at adding to our understanding of such issues by putting them into the wider perspectives of society and culture. It was psychoanalysis, with its focus on matters of human nature in general, which served as a direct coupling-point for such social scientific application. Such application offered the prospect of being able to significantly better the living of people on a widespread scale.

The mental health movement. A combination of lay, psychiatric, and governmental agencies forwarded the concept of mental health as a basis for the prevention of mental illness. The focus of psychiatry was thus not exclusively on mental illness as it had been but also on what was positive in the living of people in general. That movement greatly broadened the scope of psychiatric concerns and brought to them a new optimism.

Social welfare. Idealistic national welfare programs during the economic depression of the 1930s had as their objective the providing of help on a widespread scale to the poorest in society. It was out of that initial concern that a parallel concern developed, after the Second World War, about the mental health of those who were poorest. That concern was prompted in no small measure by markedly increased rioting and protest within the poorest, black communities. It was felt that such unrest might be caused in part by mental health problems. As a result, in the 1960s Congress passed legislation establishing comprehensive community mental health centers throughout the country. Of equal importance in such a social welfare context was a growing concern about the welfare and well-being of the family and, most particularly, of children. Such a focus fit well with the concern of a number of prominent psychoanalysts working in child psychiatry. As a result of those developments, the new subspecialties of community psychiatry and child psychiatry came into being. It seemed at that time self-evident that psychiatrists had a right and responsibility to concern themselves with social and societal matters.

These, then, were the factors which exerted such a profound influence upon me and upon many others of my medical generation. They brought to psychiatry a new, powerful attraction. Psychiatry became, for the first time, highly popular. It went from the bottom rung to the top rung of medical specialties.

Those factors combined for me both a fascination and a trepidation. The fascination lay in how to put all those factors together into one whole of a new psychiatry. The trepidation lay in the great difficulty of doing just that. That fascination and trepidation followed me throughout my training in psychiatry and child psychiatry and, after that, through three years of psychoanalytic training and three years of doctoral work in sociology.

Psychoanalysis had a great attraction for me because it provided the foundation for a listening-to and talking-with, one-to-one kind of psychiatric helping. It offered the prospect of making sense of human behavior that for ages had seemed mysterious and almost totally unfathomable. Its detailing of unconscious processes underlying a good deal of the trouble people experienced in living was tantalizing. Equally tantalizing was the idea of getting at such unconscious processes through free association, letting one's uncensored thoughts and feelings pour out. However, the reality of psychoanalysis soon began to trouble me — just as did the reality of psychiatry itself. My initial fascination stayed with me but the trepidation increased greatly as I became more and more confused by what I encountered in psychiatry. What I experienced didn't fit well with the way I expected things to be.

Six questions in particular troubled me greatly. After struggling with those questions I came to see that I would have to come up with my own answers if I were to make sense of my work as a psychiatrist. I see these as the six basic problems of modern psychiatry today.

1. Why was it almost never possible to make a hard and fast psychiatric diagnosis?

When I started out in psychiatry, I thought that most of the problems I met up with would fall into clear-cut, classic, diagnostic categories, categories which seemed as sharply defined as in the psychiatric texts which I had read. That was the way things were, for the most part, in the rest of medicine. That wasn't the case in psychiatry. The elements of tension, fear, depression, over-activity or under-activity and even bizarreness could be found in almost every form of psychiatric distress. I found that experienced psychiatrists very often did not agree among themselves on a given diagnosis, even the diagnoses of schizophrenia and manic depression, the seemingly most clear-cut of psychiatric diagnoses. It was as though the different diagnoses of neuroses, psychoses and personality disorders were all mixed together. Making a diagnosis seemed arbitrary. One could only weigh the severity of different symptoms and make a diagnosis according to what was most bothersome or most prominent. Making psychiatric diagnoses was like trying to force the square peg of a person's distress into the round hole of a given diagnosis.

A further trouble was that psychiatric diagnoses did not, to my surprise, have much bearing upon who would respond to my helping efforts and who would not. It was not unusual that those who functioned fairly well in their everyday life — and presumably had a less severe psychiatric diagnosis — ended up taking eternities to improve. In contrast, others who seemed almost totally incapacitated — those with a presumably severe psychiatric diagnosis — might show a quick and dramatic response.

The difficulty with psychiatric diagnoses caused me a great deal of trouble. If diagnoses were not clear cut, how could treatment be clear cut and specific? If diagnoses did not hold up, what was the nature of my expertise as a psychiatrist? In my need to help those in severe distress I was faced, in the end, with this question: *If psychiatric diagnoses were so inexact and arbitrary, how could I explain what underlay or caused the different pictures of psychiatric distress and their overlapping symptoms?*

2. What was mental health?

The concept of mental health seemed like a wonderful idea. Here was something that psychiatry could offer to people in general which they could utilize in everyday living. A mentally healthy way of living would prevent the development of mental illness. That concept gave promise of a new, optimistic, line of psychiatric thinking that could serve as a counterweight to the pessimism usually associated with mental illness. Unfortunately, I found that the reality of psychiatry did not live up to that promise.

Psychiatrists were almost totally concerned with defining different kinds of mental illness and almost totally ignored mental health. Mental health, in practical terms, meant simply the absence of mental illness. The few definitions of mental health I could find seemed to equate that state with some form of "leading the good life." There was nothing in such a definition that made clear just how that good life prevented the development of mental ill-ness. That matter troubled me greatly. For without a specific definition of mental health there could clearly be no idea of how people could live their lives so as to prevent the development of a crippling psychiatric condition or even whether that might be possible.

In the end, then, I was faced with this question: Could I find out if there was a way of living which prevented the development of psychiatric conditions and, if so, make clear just how that worked?

3. *Why was it sometimes so difficult to draw a clear distinction between psychiatric prob-lems and problems of social deviance or crime?*

I originally thought that such a distinction would be obvious. Psychiat-ric problems were medical illnesses which could be diagnosed on the basis of characteristic psychiatric symptom-pictures. Problems of social deviance — such as drunkenness, narcotics abuse and prostitution — were character-ized by behavior markedly deviant from what was generally considered ac-ceptable. Criminal problems — such as stealing, robbing, assault, rape, and murder — were those in which a person deliberately broke the law.

My trouble in making such a distinction was magnified while I was work-ing in Harlem. For there, in the black ghetto, I found a great overlapping of those three kinds of problems. People who came to psychiatry with marked psychiatric difficulties also often had marked social or criminal problems. Likewise, those who came to the attention of authorities because of marked social or criminal problems often had distinct psychiatric problems. Living under the ghetto conditions of massive unemployment, poor schools, inad-equate housing, extreme poverty, single-parent families, and prejudice was mainly responsible for the conspicuousness of such overlapping. Given such conditions, some forms of social deviance or crime were more often the rule than the exception. It was as though such means were different forms of survival for many. In addition, people were often forced to live with their psychiatric problems — until they became almost totally incapacitating — because resources for getting psychiatric help were so few. Psychiatrists and psychologists working in impoverished areas were a scarce commodity.

I contrasted that situation with my parallel psychiatric work with indi-viduals living outside of Harlem. It seemed clear to me that those who were better off had far less need to resort to socially deviant or criminal actions. They also had the means to get help for psychiatric difficulties before such difficulties were incapacitating. Psychiatric help was more readily available. I reasoned that it was those factors that made it appear that there was a clear distinction between psychiatric difficulties, on the one hand, and social and criminal problems on the other hand. Psychiatrists, for the most part, were concerned with the difficulties of those who were better off and thus were more likely to see such a clear distinction. I came to see, though, that such a distinction was superficial.

For even if those who were well off had far less need to resort to socially-deviant or criminal means, their psychiatric difficulties were, nevertheless, not seldom combined with such problems as drunkenness, narcotics abuse, prostitution, theft, sexual abuse, assault, and murder. This combination, without an impoverished ghetto existence to explain it, seemed to be an even more compelling reason to learn why and how psychiatric, social and criminal problems could overlap.

It troubled me greatly that this mixture of psychiatric, social and criminal problems made it almost impossible to home in on the causation in my helping efforts. I found myself face to face with this question: *Could I explain the overlapping of psychiatric, social and criminal problems as a result of a single underlying factor, thereby making it possible to focus in on a common causation?*

4. Why was it that the great promise which the use of medications brought with them invariably ended in disappointment?

In the 1950s, when I began my psychiatric training, new medications had been recently developed which seemed to offer nothing less than a cure for some of the most difficult of psychiatric conditions. Among the first were Miltown and Thorazine. They had a remarkable effect. The most troublesome symptoms appeared to disappear completely. Individuals could be discharged from mental hospitals. The use of insulin shock treatments for schizophrenia was abandoned. The use of electroshock treatments for severe depression was cut down greatly. Those medications seemed like miracle drugs. It was felt by many psychiatrists that they attacked the very cause of such severe conditions. They went under such designations as antipsychotic and antidepressive drugs. Lithium was seen by many psychiatrists as a specific cure for manic depression. Tension could be markedly reduced, some thought eliminated, by the use of tranquillizers. In more recent years, Prozac has been seen as a new miracle drug. I expected that such psychopharmaceuticals would lead to some specific cures. That, however, was not what I found.

Those medications did not in fact eliminate psychiatric difficulties. Even though people usually could function better, an underlying problem of bizarreness, depression, fear or tension remained. Those difficulties were still troubling and troublesome even though to a lesser degree. At times such difficulties burst forth again in great intensity leading to the need for readmission to a mental hospital. Less often, despite being on such medications, people committed suicide. In addition, serious, sometimes disabling, side effects were almost always associated with the long-term usage of such drugs. Not the least of such side effects was apathy, a loss of drive and enthusiasm. Furthermore, it became clear that such drugs were not specific for a given diagnostic condition. They were used interchangeably — on a clearly trial-and-error basis — regardless of diagnosis. It seemed hardly likely that such drugs targeted the cause of a given condition.

The use of medications in psychiatry followed a recurrent pattern. First, a new drug was introduced which offered the promise of a splendid, almost miraculous, effectiveness without serious problems. After a time the serious shortcomings of that drug were generally recognized. Then a brand new drug came on the market once again bringing with it a new hope of cure. And then the cycle was repeated once again.

There was no denying both the benefit and the harm in the use of psychopharmaceuticals. Many psychiatrists felt that such use made it much easier to reach and help people in psychotherapy. They felt that such use reduced troubling symptoms so as to make a dialogue easier. My own experience was that such use made helping more difficult. The drugs greatly reduced the drive and motivation that individuals needed to change their lives for the better.

In the end, this question remained: *Could I come up with a way of completely eliminating psychiatric disabilities through a listening-to/talking-with approach without the need for using psychopharmaceuticals?*

5. *Why was it impossible to know which children would later on develop a serious psychiatric disability and which wouldn't?*

At the start of my career it seemed to me that such predictability ought to be possible. Psychoanalytic and psychological theories usually maintained that severe psychiatric conditions had their origin in early childhood. It seemed reasonable to expect that serious adult psychiatric difficulties ought to be readily discernible very early in life. Non-psychoanalytic psychiatrists usually maintained that severe adult psychiatric conditions had a genetic origin. It seemed equally reasonable to suppose, if that were so, that such a genetic defect would be apparent in early years — rather than to appear first in adulthood after a symptom-free childhood. In sum, I thought that the diagnoses made by child psychiatrists ought to lead to the diagnoses of specific adult psychiatric conditions. The great problem for me was that I could not see any such connection.

The severe difficulties of children do not necessarily develop into the severe psychiatric conditions of adulthood. Likewise, severe psychiatric conditions of adulthood can develop out of what seemed like an apparently trouble-free childhood. Thus, for example, marked eccentricity in a child does not necessarily lead to craziness — such as schizophrenia — in adulthood. I found it impossible to classify the problems of children as different and discrete neuroses, psychoses, character disorders and the like. It seemed to me that the diagnoses used in child psychiatry had nothing to do with the diagnoses used in adult psychiatry.

Equally troubling were the research approaches to predictability. It was common to make some general assumption about probability. Thus, one might maintain that there was a probability that such-and-such a childhood difficulty would lead to an adult psychiatric condition or to predispose to an adult psychiatric condition. Such generalization did not help me in my work. Such childhood difficulties might also *not* become serious. It seemed that understanding the development of psychiatric conditions required being able to say that a given child would, almost without question, go on to develop this or that specific adult psychiatric condition. That was not possible.

I found myself left with no good idea of the early development of adult psychiatric difficulties. That caused distinct practical problems. When working with adults, I had to make good sense to them in explaining how their problems had developed in early years. When working with parents, I had to make good sense about the future course of their children's development.

I was left, in the end, with the challenge of coming up with a good explanation of *what happens during childhood years which either makes for or prevents the development of later psychiatric difficulties.*

---

6. *Why were psychoanalytic and psychotherapeutic theories so difficult to make use of in the practical work of helping a person in severe distress?*

When I started off in psychiatry, the different psychoanalytic and psychotherapeutic theories struck me as dazzlingly profound. It was as though such theories offered not only a brilliant new insight into the severest difficulties of people but also an effective way of dealing with those difficulties. It seemed to me that with enough intelligence and with enough diligence I ought to be able to master the techniques needed to apply such theories. I tried my best to absorb as much as I could. I read all there was to read. I listened to lectures with wide open ears. In psychoanalysis I learned about the id, ego and superego, transference and counter-transference, mechanisms of defense, libidinal stages of development, Oedipal and Electra complexes. I read extensively about other approaches.

However, when I was sitting with another person who was in desperate need of my help, those theories did little to help me find the right words to say, the right time to say them, and the right way to say them. What at first had struck me as brilliant and impressive had very limited application in my practical helping work as a psychiatrist.

My confusion increased when I saw how members of one school of thought often bitterly attacked the theories of another school of thought. It was as though each school was basically sound in the eyes of its own adherents and the others' theories were basically flawed. I was left with the difficulty of trying to make sense out of what in those different approaches was valuable and what was not.

That was no easy matter. I found most such theories to be far too intellectual, too complex, too confusing. Most depended upon newly-coined technical words and phrases which were hard to make sense of. It seemed to me that many such theorists were far more involved in refining a grand theory or science of behavior than in spelling out how to help a person in need. I could not find the clarity to differentiate between what was "good" helping and what was "bad" helping. Sometimes my efforts succeeded and I didn't know why. At other times, my efforts failed — and once again I didn't know why.

I needed good answers to those questions. People who wanted my help depended upon my ability to know what was good helping. I felt a pressing need to be able to put my way of helping into words they could understand. I felt I ought to be able to give a clear answer to the questions, "How do you work? How will my coming to you help me?" They had a perfect right to ask such questions.

In the end, the question was: *Could I come up with a clear, easily understandable, idea of what makes for success or failure in helping a person in severe distress, an idea which made it clear what to say, when to say it and how to say it?*

Those six unanswered questions, one piled on top of another, left me more and more dismayed by what I was experiencing in my specialty.

That dismay stemmed, first of all, from what I saw was a rigidity, if not dogmatism, in both psychiatry and psychoanalysis. It was as though there were two mutually antagonistic camps. On the one hand there were most mainstream psychoanalysts who regarded the ideas of Freud as almost sacred tenets that could not be questioned, only elaborated upon. On the other hand, there were most biologically-oriented psychiatrists who considered psychoanalysis as a kind of great psychological fraud which clouded the true genetic and scientific basis of psychiatric conditions.

Even more dismaying was the almost complete disinterest in both camps in studying and tackling social factors that contributed to people's severe distress. There were some psychiatrists who were notable exceptions to that disinterest but they were considered far out on the fringe of the psychiatric specialty. The primary, if not exclusive, concern of psychiatry seemed to be to turn out highly-skilled technicians who were expert in either psychoanalytic or biological methods.

The dismay on that score was undoubtedly intensified when I began working at a psychiatric center in Harlem. There the effect of such social factors in causing psychiatric difficulties seemed glaringly self-evident. It seemed untenable to think that social factors should not be a major concern for psychiatrists.

What dismayed me most of all was the public perception of psychiatry. Most people I met, including those who were highly educated and well-to-do, still regarded the work of psychiatrists as something mysterious, beyond the comprehension of laymen. Such incomprehensibility would be acceptable if psychiatry was seen as a highly optimistic specialty. The trouble was that psychiatry was instead regarded with suspicion and pessimism. One did not turn readily to psychiatry for help as one did with other medical specialties. "Shrink" was a popular epithet for psychiatrists and was clearly uncomplimentary.

My vision of psychiatry as a wondrous and exciting specialty had begun to fade. If I were to maintain the great enthusiasm which had first attracted me to psychiatry, I would have to find my own way out of that wilderness of pessimism. I would have to make my own good sense out of what I was experiencing. Two factors were of great importance in helping me to do that. First was the influence of several exceptional psychiatrists who provided me with fine examples of the best in psychiatry. Second were the ten years I worked in Harlem.

Most of that time I worked at the Northside Center, which for years was the only psychiatric facility in Harlem outside of Harlem Hospital (a general hospital which offered only emergency psychiatric services). In addition I was at various times a consultant to a number of other agencies: the Domestic Relations Court of Manhattan (which dealt with court-related problems of children, youth and parents), the Wiltwyck School for Boys (a residential program for young boys deemed to be pre-delinquent by the courts), the Brooklyn Psychiatric Centers (which served the Bedford-Stuyvesant area), Speedwell Services (a large adoption service) and the New York State Rehabilitation Center (a facility for 800 women referred by the courts because of narcotics abuse). During that time I also had a private practice in Manhattan and for a short period served as Instructor in Child Psychiatry at the Cornell Medical College where I supervised the work of psychiatrists in training.

During those ten years I gradually found good answers to the six questions about psychiatry that troubled me so.

CHAPTER 4. LEARNING BASIC LESSONS IN HARLEM

My colleagues in psychiatry and psychology who worked outside of Harlem usually wondered whether it was possible to work effectively with those who lived in Harlem. It was often taken for granted that people who had least education, who lived in near poverty and who knew little about modern psychiatry and psychology would be unmotivated and unsuitable for such helping. That was not what I found. The people in Harlem with whom I worked were highly motivated. There was, however, one striking difference between my work there and my parallel work with those who lived outside of Harlem and were better off. That difference — and the lesson it taught me — was epitomized in how people reacted to an initial contact.

During that very first meeting people in Harlem needed a crystal-clear idea of just how coming to see me would help them get out of the troubled or troubling state they were in. It was difficult to recognize that need because it was almost never put into words. When dealing with authorities and experts, people usually kept their mouths shut; they kept their feelings and thoughts to themselves. It was only when they were convinced that a person was truly interested in helping them and would welcome possibly challenging questions that they would open up and voice their questions. Because that was rarely the case, they were often seen as sullen or passive, a perception that reinforced the idea of their supposed lack of motivation.

What made matters worse was what happened after such an initial con-tact. Professionals who did not recognize the need for such clarity repeatedly found that people would agree to a second appointment and then would not come back. This was usually interpreted as a sign of lack of motivation. I came to see it as a reflection of the helper's inability to offer effective help in the first contact. When people did get such clarity right at the start about how helping would work to help them, they invariably latched onto it, they came back repeatedly and improved both dramatically and rapidly.

A child who was in constant conflict with his teacher could understand that his problem was how to get along with the worst teachers, not the best ones, and that he could learn ways of doing so to get them off his back. A mother complaining about her child's rotten school could understand that that situation was not going to change overnight and that she herself, de-spite having a job and a big family, would have to spend an hour each evening tutoring her child; if she didn't know how, we three would do that together. A youth, heroic in repeated gang fights, could understand how empty such status was and that if he wanted to make something out of his life over the next ten years he ought to redirect his energy. True, such problems did not appear at first glance as classic psychiatric ones. But that first impression was deceiving. For behind such aggression — in the private lives of such children, youth and adults — there were, indeed, classical psychiatric prob-lems: tension, desperation, psychosomatic symptoms, drinking problems and the whole host of other psychiatric difficulties.

People wanted results. They wanted to get rid of the problem bothering them and they wanted their living to go well. They were quite willing to work hard to change their situation — but only if it was perfectly clear to them just how that effort would help them get what they wanted in their liv-ing. That demand for down-to-earth clarity was just what I needed. It forced me to clarify in my *own* mind just how helping worked.

I was forced to express myself in simple, clear commonsense words. Be-hind those words I had to have simple, clear commonsense thoughts. I had to see a clear line in how my efforts would actually work to help people get what they wanted and be able to put that idea into everyday words which would convince blunt-thinking, highly skeptical people. That demand great-ly helped me in my work outside of Harlem. It helped me separate for myself the wheat from the chaff in knowing what is basic in helping people in distress.

In Harlem I learned how to think and talk in plain language. In my work outside of Harlem I could easily hide behind professional jargon and imagine that I was helping people when, in truth, I was only adding to their difficulty. I increasingly became aware of how the language and theorizing of psychiatrists, psychologists, psychoanalysts and psychotherapists could easily conceal a professional helper's own clumsiness, insecurity and ignorance.

Both helping professionals and the people who came to them for help were often handicapped by their very education, intellectual orientation and social sophistication. Those who came for help had often read extensively about psychiatry, psychology, psychoanalysis and psychotherapy. They took many things for granted, things that were by no means certain. And professional helpers often encouraged that by sharing the same intellectual orientation.

Both often assumed that helping was extremely complicated and complex. People who came for help imagined that it was beyond their own comprehension and only understandable by the experts. They were all too willing to accept the authority and the word of the professional helper unquestioningly. They did not press such professionals for answers as to just how they worked. They did not criticize the professionals, and if they disliked a professional, they kept it to themselves. They kept coming back, and assumed that their dislike was unjustified, an expression of their own inadequacy or immaturity or personal problems.

Both often used technical terms to describe difficulties as though the meaning of such terms was obvious and precise — even though such meaning was invariably complex and far from obvious or precise. One might, thus, characterize a person's difficulty as being neurotic, obsessive, narcissistic, phobic, aggressive, an inferiority complex or an oedipal one — without making clear what that meant specifically for just that person. In the same vein, one might talk about the helping process in such technical terms as establishing a therapeutic relationship, gaining insight, working through deepseated personality problems or through the transference. One assumed that many sessions were to be devoted exclusively to the individual's describing in detail the trouble he or she needed help with. Much later on the professional helper might offer some comment on the underlying reason for such trouble. It was common for such professional helpers to discourage direct questions. For example, if asked, "What do you think is the reason for my difficulty?" the answer would be, "What do *you* think is the reason for your difficulty?" Or if asked, "What should I do to deal with my situation?" the answer would be, "What do *you* think you should do?"

Most importantly, when working with those who were more knowledgeable about psychiatry and psychology, it was invariably assumed by both professionals and those in need of help that helping must take a long time. Results should not be expected at the very beginning. The reason for that was a mutual assumption that the problems of the individual stemmed from deeply rooted and highly inaccessible factors. It would require a great deal of time and effort, first to uncover such factors and then to deal with them. That point of view was a major reason for the ineffectiveness of such helping efforts.

Far too often psychotherapy or psychoanalysis went on and on interminably without any noticeable improvement. I saw this happen with many friends and acquaintances who had sought professional help. What took place was an endless rooting into the individual's past. Many individuals, after years of such psychotherapy or psychoanalysis, talked of having gained insight into themselves — but at the same time acknowledged that their life had not changed noticeably for the better in any respect. In such instances people only imagined that they understood themselves better. The only true measure of insight is whether or not such new understanding leads to a significant change of one's life for the better. The aim of helping is not mere intellectual understanding but a new knowledge of how to apply such understanding so as to markedly improve one's life. Otherwise, there could be no end point to such a dialogue; it could go on endlessly. This is an intellectual trap.

Working in Harlem helped me to avoid just such a trap, for such endless intellectual discussions were impossible there. People who needed help needed results right from the very first meeting. It was my job to make that happen. I came to see that people had a right to get clear, unambiguous, answers to a number of important questions during that first meeting. If they did not ask those questions, I had to help bring them forth. Here are some of the questions people put to me — when I encouraged them to do so:

- How do you help people who come to you?
- How long will this take?
- How do I know if I'm getting better?
- When do we stop?
- How do I get rid of this difficulty that plagues me (suicidal thoughts, panic attacks, persistent tension, fear, drinking, obesity, drug abuse......)?
- How should I handle the great trouble I'm having (with my love life, marriage, friendship, work, studies, children......)?
- How do I know whether my somatic difficulty is really caused by my personal problems?
- What's wrong with me (Am I schizophrenic, manic-depressive, paranoid, neurotic, an alcoholic...)?

Such questions were usually not asked because people thought that they were too simple, or that they reflected naiveté, or that they could not expect direct answers to such presumably highly complicated questions, or that they were not supposed to put the psychiatrist on the spot. Sometimes the questions were not asked because people were afraid of the answer they might get ("Yes, you are schizophrenic").

The way I answered those questions would convey in unequivocal words my own clarity and my own optimism about what I was doing. If that came through — as I hoped it would — the helping situation would be off to a great start. Such answers would reflect concrete know-how on my part. There would be a clear expectation of success for both of us. That is what I felt people had a right and a need to expect at the very start.

To find good answers to those questions, I had to start from scratch. That meant looking at what takes place between two people, one desperately in need of help and the other doing all in his or her power to offer such helping. I had to forget my role and status as a psychiatrist. If I had learned anything during my specialty training, it had to funnel down into just such a basic relationship. I had to listen carefully, try to make my own sense of it, and then test out the different ideas I came up with to see if they would or would not help the person.

That meant that I had to simplify in my own mind what helping was and how it worked. I would have to have a clear idea of the beginning, middle, and end of helping, one which ordinary people could understand. I would also have to have a clear idea of what was good helping and what was bad helping. In that endeavor I had to keep constantly in mind the sole aim of what I was trying to do: to help people get the best of living that they wanted and deserved.

In the end, then, I was faced with having to pare down to its bare bones my idea of what works in helping.

Chapter 5. The ABCs of Successful Helping

The bare bones of helping meant coming up with good answers to three questions: What kind of relationship ought to exist between me and the person I would help? Where do I get my answers from to the many difficult questions a desperate person has? How do I know what to say and when to say it?

My answers to those questions are summed up in the following three terms: Affection; Putting-Oneself-In–Another's-Shoes; The-Asking-For-Help-And-The-Giving-Of-Help.

Those terms are the ground conditions or basic principles for effective helping. They are reference points which I could turn back to when I felt lost or failing in my efforts and needed to find out why. I see them as the elements that make for success or failure, not only in my own efforts but in the efforts of those whose work I supervised and in the efforts of my colleagues. I also see them as the basic elements for successful helping in *any* situation where one person would help another who is in sore need of help. I call these three terms the ABCs of successful helping.

Affection

Affection is a liking for another person which is so strong that that person becomes someone very special for oneself. Mutual affection between a helper and the person he or she would help is the bedrock for all effective helping. Such affection must come first of all from the helper. Affection from the helper usually brings forth a corresponding affection from the person he or she would help. Here is the reason why I see things that way.

The people who have come to me were desperate for help. They had almost all tried repeatedly to help themselves — but in vain. Often others had tried to help them, with the same fruitless result. In almost every instance the difficulty I faced at the start was to help that person bring forth and discuss matters which were extremely private, extremely painful, and extremely sensitive. That is what he or she wanted and needed help with. But such matters are not easily revealed to others, sometimes not even to oneself. What is easy to talk about has usually been discussed many times before. The central difficulty in bringing forth those matters is that doing so is highly embarrassing, for they reflect a side of oneself which one sees as one's inadequacy, one's failing, one's possible incompetence as a human being. Bringing forth such matters puts one at risk for possible condescension, condemnation or ridicule. It is natural to feel extremely guarded at the outset.

One knows logically that one ought to bring forth such matters to a psychiatrist, psychologist, psychoanalyst or other helping professional. But such knowing is only in one's head, not in one's heart. For one also knows that that other person is a human being, that there may well be both good and bad helping professionals, that such persons are not immune from condescension, condemnation, or ridicule. So one treads lightly. One remains guarded.

In getting us to let down our guard, logic has its limits. It is not enough to reason with ourselves, to remind ourselves that we must expose ourselves to a stranger in order to get help, that that stranger's professional competence and ethics insure against possible condescension, condemnation or ridicule. What if one takes an immediate dislike to that person? What if one senses that that other person is some unfeeling expert who will treat one's desperation as only a technical problem? What if one feels that that other person sees one's difficulty as reflecting some deep-rooted and basic human failing? Such apprehension has been expressed to me many times by people who have gotten that impression on meeting other professionals.

The basic issue here is trust. Trust in this situation is solely a matter of feeling and conviction. People who come for help ought to have, right at the start, the feeling and conviction that the helping professional sees admirable qualities in them; cares deeply about what happens in their lives; would never, even inadvertently, ridicule, condescend to or condemn them. When such conviction is present, there is no need for defensiveness. I see only one path to such trust. It is for the helper to show his strong and genuine liking for the person he would help. One usually cannot help but have a strong and reciprocal feeling of liking for such a helper. Seen this way, trust is inseparable from affection.

When such trust is present the individual can open up about his or her innermost feelings, can reveal his or her craziness, fears, childishness. Those matters can then be looked at together. It is taken for granted that those features are not the whole of a person but are only his or her troubled and troublesome side. Furthermore, when such trust is present the words of the helper will be listened to with great attentiveness and, if they make good sense, will be taken to heart and acted upon. Not least important, when such trust exists a person in need will excuse the helper's poor ideas, mistakes and shortcomings, knowing that all those failings are, nevertheless, well intentioned.

The paramount importance of affection in helping is most apparent when working with children and youth. One must first become good friends. Only after that will they open up about themselves. If there is no such affection, they will simply close up. There is then no possibility of carrying on a discussion about what deeply troubles them. The adults who have come to me seem to have just as strong a need to be liked by me but usually do not recognize that need.

Repeatedly, when helping has been successful, those who have come to me have said, at the end of our work, that they saw me as a special friend. That meant that they saw me as someone completely outside the rest of their life, someone who had nothing to gain other than seeing their lives go better, someone who could give them a better, more objective, view of what was going on when their own reactions might be distorted, someone who cared deeply about their personal welfare. In my working with children and youth, that need for a special friend came forth almost without fail. They said that they often wished for just such a special and understanding friend when their difficulties seemed crushing. They could not turn to their parents, at times because their difficulties concerned their parents and at other times because they were fearful of their parents' critical reaction.

If one is aware of that need for a special friendship in the helping situation, it is far easier to bring it about than with other kinds of friendships. For its sole focus is, on one side, the need to confide in another and, on the other side, the need to honor such confidence. Other friendships are more difficult and demanding because friends who live a significant part of life together expect a deep sense of gratification in being with one another, and because one expects such a friendship to last indefinitely. Since none of those conditions are a part of the professional helping situation, it is much easier for the helper to show his or her strong liking for a much broader range of people.

This point of view about the importance of affection was instilled in me primarily by Douglas Bond, when I was in my first year of psychiatric training at the Pennsylvania Hospital. He was one of my supervisors. It was not his words that I remember so well but what he was as a person. He radiated a kindliness, warmth, liking and strength. I felt instinctively that he liked me and cared personally about me. I felt that I could trust him, that I could reveal the mistakes I had made without fear of condescension, condemnation, or ridicule. I felt that this is the way that a good psychiatrist ought to be.

One might think that for a helper to show affection for someone needing help is natural, obvious and uncomplicated. It is none of those things. For when people are desperate for help — and particularly when they come to a psychiatrist as a last resort — they invariably put their worst foot forward. They may come across as clinging, demanding, passive, long suffering, frantic, or hopelessly pessimistic. Desperation often brings forth the worst of a person, which makes it easy to dislike, to be irritated with, or to feel superior to such a person. Indeed, that is often the response of others one has turned to for help. People who are desperate are often rebuffed by those around them. And professional helpers are not immune to such feelings of dislike, irritation and superiority.

The good professional helper sees beyond those surface negative features that put other people off. He or she can like and admire people whom others find almost impossible to like and admire. Such perceptivity is essential. For it is just those fine, admirable, features which are the resources a person must mobilize to get what he or she wants most out of living. It is the helper's job to help that person do just that.

It is not difficult for a helper to show affection if he or she is aware of the need to do so. That is what one does when one tries to make friends with another person. It shows in one's eyes, smile and manner. One listens attentively, shows a keen interest in what the other person has to say, draws forth that person's ideas and sentiments without any hint of criticism. Most importantly, one is able to voice a word of honest praise. There is no over valuing the importance of the helper's show of affection.

The person in need then usually thinks to himself: Here is a person, an expert in psychiatry or psychology who knows all about the hang-ups of people, yet who nevertheless actually likes me and sees admirable qualities in me. Such praise is unexpected. The person is usually prepared for criticism, for a concern solely with how poorly one has acted. Thus, when one gets a word of honest praise, one feels a pride in oneself. I have found repeatedly, strange as it may seem, that such a word of honest praise is the only open expression of affection a person may get in his or her daily life. It is as though a husband, wife, parent or friend never thinks such a word is necessary.

During my early years in psychiatry, when I was floundering in my efforts to make sense of what I was doing, I think that the only thing that really helped people was the fact that I liked them and cared deeply about them.

Bill was cited as an example in the introduction to chapter 3. Then there was Jean. She was in her early 20s, a highly talented music student. She had been brought to the Pennsylvania Hospital by her parents because she was mute, seemed consumed with anger, and refused to leave her room. I sat with her often. At first, I did all the talking. I can't remember now what I said. Later, she could speak in monosyllables. One day I was called by the nurses in the middle of the night because she appeared violent. She was standing naked in her room and glowering. She had broken everything she could get her hands on and the floor was littered with bits and pieces of glass. I was angry with her and said so, in no uncertain words. She became quiet and calm. I think she listened to my reprimand solely because she trusted me. On another occasion she ran away from the hospital. Later that day we got a call from a distant church saying she was there. I went in a police car to get her. On the way back, she suddenly hugged me, presumably because she felt I cared so much about her. During those months I saw her parents once a week. I think they listened to me because they knew I had Jean's confidence. What had come forth was that they strongly disapproved of a fellow music student she was going out with, solely because he was of a different religion. I felt that in their well-intention efforts they put an unbearable pressure on

Jean and could not see the need to let Jean live her own life. I told them just that. There was a reconciliation. Jean improved markedly and was discharged from the hospital. When I look back now at what helped, it seems to me that I was simply following my instincts, that it was the obvious caring and affection I had for Jean that was the deciding factor.

Two years later, I was working at the Children's Hospital in Boston during my specialty training in child psychiatry. Paul, who was five, was brought there, I think because of temper tantrums. I recall that he seemed intensely interested in playing games with me. He was a bright, quick, likable boy. But when I tried to get him to talk about what was going on at home, I got nowhere. He ignored me. My helping efforts seemed to be futile and I was ready to stop. I was taken completely by surprise to hear from his mother, whom I also saw once a week, that Paul looked forward so much to coming to see me. She felt that that was the major reason why he had improved so dramatically during that time. It occurred to me that I was substituting for what Paul wanted from his father. I suggested to his mother that Paul's father might profitably spend a lot more time with Paul. He did; and there was then no need for further visits.

The year before, in 1954, during my second year of psychiatric training at Harvard's Boston Psychopathic Hospital, I had an idea for a kind of experiment. As part of that training we residents went out to Metropolitan State Hospital one day a week. Metropolitan State, in contrast to the Boston Psychopathic Hospital, was a psychiatric institution for those who needed long-term care. I was assigned responsibility for one male ward. Almost all the men on that ward had been there for many years. My idea was to get a group of college students to come out once a week and see what effect that might have on the twenty-odd men who were there. Those men were representative of the most serious of psychiatric cases at that time. I contacted an acquaintance at the Harvard Divinity School and explained my idea. There were about twenty volunteers. I met with them and told them what I had in mind. I said the only thing they should do is to sit with one person and talk with him, the same person each time. The idea was to draw that person out about his previous life. The effect was remarkable. The nurses told me that the men looked forward so eagerly to that one day a week. There was a marked lifting of spirits on the ward. For me, that little experiment was evidence of how powerful an effect a simple show of affection can have, even on those who seem almost beyond hope.

Years later, when I worked at the Northside Center in Harlem, I had a colleague who was extremely effective with adolescent girls. I felt that her great strength was that she cared so much about them, that she was like a substitute mother. Her affection was openly apparent to us all. They re-sponded well to that.

The above are a few anecdotes drawn from many which made a lasting impression on me. I have cited them to give a more concrete idea of what I mean by the power of affection in helping.

The major problem most professional helpers have in their work, as I see it, is that they see a show of affection on their part as not only unnecessary but actually harmful. Before explaining the reasoning that underlies that point of view, I feel it important to make clearer what I mean by affection and, even more to the point, what I don't mean.

I do not mean caring. I take it for granted that most professional helpers care about those they would help, just as most physicians care about their patients. That term is far too mild in my eyes. It is simply one small step beyond indifference. One may well care about the well-being of a troubled person without necessarily liking that person. Affection, to repeat, is such a strong liking for another person that that person becomes someone special in one's own life. The person I would help becomes someone very important in my own life. I think often about that person; I take his or her predicament home with me. I derive a great sense of gratification when I see his or her life going better. If I am a special friend to those who come to me, so they are special friends to me.

The reason why most professional helpers see such affection as unneces-sary and harmful is that in their training they are usually taught that there is a paramount need for neutrality and objectivity. One must keep a distinct emotional distance, a neutrality, so as to insure objectivity. It is assumed that such neutrality and objectivity is essential if the professional is to be able to perceive how the individual is acting irrationally and ineffectively. A strong feeling of affection is seen as blocking such objectivity. The think-ing behind that assumption is that the helper has identified so closely with the person so as to be blind to that person's poor, inadequate or irrational responses. The helper then takes the part of the person even when he should not do so. Such reasoning stems directly from one of the central tenets of psychoanalysis.

In psychoanalysis, the analyst is supposed to maintain a strict neutrality, to not reveal any personal feelings or personal experiences. He or she is supposed to be something like a blank card, showing neither positive nor negative feelings. The idea is to wait until the individual projects strong feelings of like or dislike onto the analyst. Since the analyst has maintained a strict neutrality, those feelings are seen as irrational. Such irrationality is assumed to reflect the distorted feelings towards one's parents stemming from one's early childhood. Those distorted feelings are seen to be central to the person's current difficulty in living. Such feelings are "transferred" on to the analyst and are termed *transference*. The irrationality of such a reaction is then made clear. The individual gains insight into how his reactions are irrational not only towards the analyst but towards others. When the analyst cannot maintain such strict neutrality it is assumed that his or her own early distorted childhood feelings interfere with the psychoanalysis. Thus the term *countertransference*. That term means that the personal problems of the professional helper interfere with his or her ability to see the personal problems of the person who needs help. One's perception is distorted. One is unable to maintain neutrality and objectivity.

There have been many variations in psychoanalytic and psychotherapeutic concepts over the years but such an idea of neutrality and objectivity, with the above rationale, has remained central to most of them. The reason for that central concern stems from a search for a scientific approach to helping. One is searching for reliable methods which can be applied successfully regardless of who does the helping. One is looking for techniques that could be applied that were not influenced by the helper's personal beliefs, feelings, convictions and way of living. Such a standardized technical approach could then be both taught to trainees and evaluated in research studies.

The great problem with that approach is that it is impossible for a helper not to be influenced by his feelings towards the person he or she would help. Whatever a helper says or does in the helping situation reflects his or her personal beliefs, feelings, convictions and way of living. Psychoanalysts are no exception — even if one sits out of sight behind a couch. Certain statements are questioned, other go unquestioned. Lying on a couch one can still hear sighs, abrupt movements, changes in breathing, furious writing and other signs clearly indicating the analyst's impatience, satisfaction, interest, disinterest and a host of other feelings. I certainly did. For me, it is completely unrealistic to assume that a helper can be neutral in his or her feelings.

The result of such an attempt is that the helper takes on a role that undermines effective helping. One sees oneself as an authority on what's wrong with people, on why they behave inadequately and irrationally. The person in question is expected to take the word of such an authority without questioning it. Such questioning is written off as a mark of that person's inadequacy, irrationality and lack of insight. The resultant image of the professional helper is that of a distant, aloof expert, one beyond reproach.

There is no conviction on the part of the person needing help that the expert sees admirable qualities in him or her and takes a very personal interest in his or her well-being. The person feels like simply another case to be diagnosed or analyzed and treated. In such a situation trust, if it exists at all, exists solely in that person's head, in the knowledge that one is consulting an expert. It does not stem from a conviction that this expert truly cares about oneself as a very special person. That is hardly a good basis for taking to heart the helper's words and utilizing them to make the very difficult changes in one's life that are necessary. Whatever dialogue takes place is solely on an intellectual level. Such dialogue is sterile. It can go on endlessly without any significant improvement in the individual's life. It is, to my mind, a pretense of helping, because the mutual affection — which I see as the bedrock of helping — is lacking. In my opinion that is a major reason for the great decline in psychoanalysis. That is also a major reason why so much of psychotherapy is ineffective.

It is important to make clear that I have met many fine psychoanalysts and psychotherapists. It took me a long time to realize, however, what made them good — and what made others bad.

What made them good was that they radiated a deep affection for people and particularly those people they would help. I could not see the importance of that quality when I began in psychiatry. The emphasis in my training had been on techniques to apply in various situations. Almost all of the professional literature concerned itself with such techniques. Much later on, I could see clearly that some professionals did not have any particular liking for those they would help. Rather, they felt superior, even if they would deny that.

There was a sense that those with personal problems needed the expertise of a person without personal problems. Such superiority was, in my opinion, unwittingly combined with condescension and often even dislike. It was as though such professionals were put off by the same things that irritated other people. They made a clear distinction between the job that they had to do and their feelings for the person needing their help.

That attitude was apparent with a number of my supervisors during my training. They were super-critical, unable to offer a word of praise and, on occasion, had an actual dislike for me as a person. They expected me to respect their words because of their superior position. I could hardly confide in such a person. I could not see how a desperate person who came for help could do so either. Those, then, were the ones whom I came to realize, later on, were poor at their specialty. They could keep their distance and rationalize such superiority and dislike under the guise of objective professionalism.

Psychiatrists, psychologists and others whose helping efforts I supervised often asked, "But what if I don't like the person needing help?" My emphasis on affection was something new for them. Up to that point, it invariably had not occurred to them that affection might be important in their work. My answer, in summary, was, "There must be some fine qualities discernible which you can admire and praise. You don't have to like everything about a person but there ought to be more to him or her than simply disagreeable faults. It's the faults he or she needs help with. But if your dislike of that person is so strong, I don't think you ought to work with him or her. You will only engender a reciprocal dislike. There will be no trust in you or your words. The problem is far more serious if you find that you don't like most of those who need your help. You should then ask yourself why you are in a profession which deals with individuals who often arouse the worst of responses in others. It is your job to see fine qualities in a person when others are blind to them. After all, that person is simply a suffering human being and needs, above all, a word of honest praise from you. If you cannot manage that, you should ask yourself whether you are in the right profession."

I had long ago made up my mind that if I found myself with someone for whom I had no strong liking, no admiration and no word of praise, I would say right out that I was not the right person to help him or her. Fortunately, that has never been the case. That, however, does not mean I have not failed on this score. I have. There were times when, no matter what I did, there were some whom I could not reach. There was not the strong trust — and strong liking — which I saw was necessary to make helping work. That, to my mind, was at the bottom of most of those failures I have had in my helping efforts.

In those instances it seemed that I could not create a situation in which the person I would help could open up about his or her most private, most sensitive and most embarrassing feelings and thoughts. They kept a distance from doing so in different ways.

One young man became almost paralyzed when I asked him to respond spontaneously to some innocuous questions; he was constantly tied up in knots. A young, highly intelligent woman seemed totally preoccupied with a perpetual and fruitless search for the single and sole cause in her childhood for her present difficulty; she wanted some expert to tell her what that cause was, but she found a reason to reject every possible explanation. A middle-aged man likened coming for help to going to a dentist, necessary but extremely painful; he was thus constantly on his guard. A middle-aged woman who was troubled by difficulties in her marriage did not come for sessions which might be difficult but sent her husband instead.

I failed in those instances. It seems to me that in each instance the person I would help was extremely fearful of being hurt or wounded by me if he or she did open up. Nothing I said or did could dispel such a fear. I felt that the problem lay in my inability to bring forth the trust and strong liking that is essential to overcome such fear. The explanation for such inability seemed clear.

Even if the special friendship in the helping situation is less difficult and less demanding than other friendships, it nevertheless still follows the same rules. One simply cannot be friends with everyone. Call that a matter of personal chemistry, if you will. Affection doesn't always bring forth a reciprocal affection. Try as I might, I could not always overcome such guardedness. In such instances, the only possible conclusion for me was that another person might do a better job than I had done. Fortunately, such failures were uncommon. If they were common, I would have been forced to either radically change my way of helping others or look for another line of work.

The affection between two people is such a powerful force for helping that it makes no sense not to recognize its importance and to utilize it as a resource. Not doing so is like trying to help with, figuratively, a blindfold on and both arms tied behind one's back. One deprives oneself of one's major means for helping another. It is just such affection that dispels a person's defensiveness. That is what makes a person receptive to new ideas which otherwise might meet with great resistance. One is willing to test out such new ideas — even though such testing out may appear extremely difficult — because of the trust engendered by affection.

If there is mutual affection, where does one go from there?

Putting-Oneself-in-Another's-Shoes

A person needing help has, in essence, only one question for the helper. It is this: How do I get out of this awful morass I'm in? To answer that question the helper should be asking himself or herself this question: What would I do if I were in that person's shoes? That is the source of a helper's answers.

Such a conclusion is far from being obvious or acceptable within psychiatry or psychology. Indeed, it is the direct opposite of most psychiatric and psychological thinking. It was certainly foreign to my own way of thinking when I started off in psychiatry.

There was then — and there is now — an incredibly wide variance in how psychiatrists, psychoanalysts and psychotherapists found and find answers to how to help a person. Despite such variance, though, I have come to see that one fundamental assumption — and fundamentally *flawed* assumption — underlies almost all of those different approaches. That assumption is that there are special techniques or procedures that are applicable to correct a given difficulty depending upon just what kind of faulty functioning is present. It is assumed that a given technique or procedure is more or less specific for a given faulty functioning. The nature of such faulty functioning might be seen as either biological or psychological or a combination of the two. The great variance in psychiatric, psychoanalytic and psychological approaches is due to the wide theoretical diversity in how one explains or understands such faulty functioning.

When I started out in psychiatry I did my best to utilize such theories. However, I soon ran into trouble. One problem was that there were so many approaches that it was easy to get lost among them. And they didn't work as I thought they ought to work. They didn't help me very much in finding the right words to say, the right time to say them and the right way to say them.

They were far too intellectual, at least in my hands. I was confused. I had to do mental contortions to make some sense of them.

One of the first inklings that an effort to make sense of such theories involved futile mental contortions came to me when I was in psychoanalytic training at the New York Psychoanalytic Institute. The Institute had a series of lectures for members, trainees and invited guests. The auditorium was always filled. The lecturers, most of whom were among the most prominent American psychoanalysts, presented the results of their most current work. I tried my best to follow their line of thinking, to make good sense of the special language of psychoanalysis. It was usually difficult. The ideas presented usually seemed extremely complex. At that time I attributed my difficulty to inexperience. When I talked this over with my fellow psychiatrists in training they admitted they had the same difficulty as I did. I came to think that any new, valuable, ideas should be those that made such helping efforts clearer and easier to utilize. Most of what I heard did the opposite.

Such an impression applied to most of the theories I had studied. During that time, parallel with such confusion, something else was happening to me which set me off in another direction.

It was common when medical students studied an illness to imagine that one suffered from that same illness. When one had a problem with coughing, headache, stomach distress, pain or other medical symptoms, it was easy to imagine the worst. A similar experience happened with me when I began studying psychiatry. And it was scary.

When I worked closely with people, it seemed that all the problems they had, I had too. I could see inside myself the makings of schizophrenia, manic-depression, paranoia, hysteria, obsessive-compulsion, alcoholism, violence, irrational fear, narcotics abuse, brutal crime and all the rest of psychiatry's diagnoses. Even if I didn't show it, I could see the impulses that might lead there. What was scary was that I had thought that those conditions were abnormalities, illnesses, disorders or some other aspect of psychopathology. I had imagined that I was at least normal and healthy, not abnormal, ill or disordered. Feeling the way I did seemed to go against everything I had learned. It took me some time to realize that what I was experiencing could be a great asset.

I had to ask myself how I dealt with those different impulses. Working almost every day with people who were greatly troubled forced me to confront that question, to look at how I could deal in a better way with the most troubling aspects of my own life. It was that need which led me to find my own good answers to how to deal with such frightening and threatening impulses. In the end I came to see that in trying to help another person what I had to offer was — plain and simple — only how I had handled in my own life the same difficulty which troubled that person. I found that my sharing that knowledge was, without exaggeration, of tremendous importance.

The person seeking help thought: "He knows; he's been there too. I can't be such a hopeless case." When I spoke from within myself, my words carried believability and conviction. My personal answers had a good probability of being right on the mark since they come from what had worked for me. My words had the advantage of being concrete, practical, and easily understood. At the very least the person I would help would be willing to try out my ideas of how to deal with the desperation in his or her life — and that's all I could ask for. For I saw it as a great step forward for a highly troubled person to simply be willing try out a markedly different way of dealing with his or her life.

My ability to help another in this way developed over time. I didn't always succeed. Sometimes what I offered was rejected. Sometimes it didn't work. Each such failure forced me to look once again inside myself, to ask myself once again what I would do if I were in just that particular person's shoes. Each of those failures forced me to confront a different aspect of the same problem. It was as though there was a special aspect to each of those frightening and threatening impulses depending upon just whom I was working with. It was also as though my having to confront such problems in my helping efforts was of great help in my being able to better my own life.

Over time, after seeing many people, I found that I had sharpened my ability to put myself in another's shoes. I had weeded out what worked for most of them and for myself too. The probability of my own answers being of significant help increased accordingly.

Looking back now I can see where that "Putting-Oneself-In-Another's-Shoes" idea came from. There were two major sources. It came most tellingly from Elvin Semrad.

In 1954, when I was a resident at the Boston Psychopathic Hospital, Elvin Semrad was undoubtedly the most popular of our Harvard professors. Most striking for us were his interviews with people who had been newly admitted to the hospital. Those interviews took place at our staff meetings where there were about forty people present. Despite that large gathering, Semrad had a way of making immediate contact with the other person, as though the two of them were holding a private conversation. Without any apparent clue, he seemed to be able to divine what the person was thinking or feeling. Thus, for example, if a person said nothing at all and appeared indifferent, Semrad might make a statement such as, "You are furious with me, aren't you." It was as though he could discern, when we could not, a person's inner rage, terror, martyrdom, self-glorification, isolation, self-hate and the other most private elements of another's innermost life. I recall the effect his words had on both the person being interviewed and upon the staff. Most of the time the person being interviewed was left astounded, amazed at how Semrad could know such things. We residents in training were equally amazed. It was as though his words came out of a clear blue sky.

I didn't know how he could be so perceptive. It seemed incredible. Long afterwards it came to me that he could do what he did because he was so sensitive to his own inner feelings, to his own inner craziness, depression, and what have you. He was speaking from inside himself. The person he was sitting with aroused in him a finely-tuned ability to put himself in just that person's shoes.

The second major source was what I experienced the prior year during my first year's specialty training in psychiatry at the Pennsylvania Hospital. The hospital had two sections, one a hospital section, the other for psychiatrists' consulting offices. That first year was spent in the hospital section working with seriously troubled people. I remember vividly what happened on our very first day. Each of us was given a list of some forty names and told to talk with each person. I felt shaken.

I imagined that we would start off soft and easy, that there would be introductory lectures on how to talk with those needing help, how to understand their difficulties, and how to help them. There was no such preparation. So we just plunged in. That experience was a great boon even though I did not realize it at the time. I saw each person as a very special human being — and not as a psychiatric case. That experience taught me to rely upon myself, to try to draw my own conclusions from what I was experiencing. When I look back now, I can see that experience as the beginning of my ability to put myself in another's shoes. And for that I have to thank the two psychiatrists who ran that hospital section, J. Martin Myers and Harold Morris.

I think it fair to ask: Is it really possible to see within oneself all the great number of psychiatric afflictions, including some which appear so incredibly bizarre and incomprehensible? What about such things as schizophrenia, paranoia, manic-depression, violence, heroin addiction, sexual abuse? Given that people differ so markedly I think it fair to also ask: Can one really feel in one's innermost self what it is to be aged, black, destitute, a prison inmate, an unschooled, foreign-speaking immigrant and all the other greatly varied aspects of the human experience?

My answer is this: That is precisely what fine writers and actors do all the time. They have a finely-tuned sensitivity to the inner self of other people, to what's going on deep under the surface. That sensitivity comes from their being intimately in touch with their own inner selves. They feel what it is to be that person. They can put themselves in another's shoes. That is why their portrayals of people are so vivid and convincing; that is why we know without questioning that such portrayals ring true. Those people come to life for us. We too can, then, put ourselves in their shoes.

Look, for example, at the characters of Shakespeare, at Macbeth, Lady Macbeth, Hamlet, Ophelia, Othello, Iago, Richard the Third, Cassius, Falstaff. They live for us because they go to the heart of the extremes of torment, hatred, brutality, treachery, suicide, bizarreness and the rest of the worst elements of our living. I see that the professional helper must develop the same kind of artistic sensitivity. That is what is needed to make the same kind of intuitive sense out of the great variance of the human condition he or she must deal with.

All of which raises another question: Given such a view of the source of a professional's answers to helping, what, then, is the role of textbooks, learned articles and supervision by more experienced professionals?

Those factors are important — but not in the way they are usually seen. It is not a matter of studying different theories, techniques and procedures so as to apply them. Rather, it is a matter of taking from those sources what helps in one's own living. If such learning feeds into how to deal with one's own life it will be utilizable in helping another. It also means looking critically at every idea from those sources and rejecting those that one cannot utilize in one's own living. That kind of learning, in my eyes, is what is truly important, that is what is remembered without effort; that is what comes forth spontaneously in one's own living and in one's own helping efforts.

Underlying putting-oneself-in-another's-shoes is the idea that all of us share a common core in our inner life. That common core consists of the same impulses that can drive us to the worst of living when we are at our wits end. It likewise consists of the same gratification or reward we seek in our loving, friendship, learning, work, idealism and private moments. That commonality of inner life is the bond that unites people despite vast differences in the outer circumstances of living.

That is what makes it possible for us to understand and respond to the lives and living of those in nations and cultures far different from our own. That is what makes it possible for us to value artistic contributions in literature, art and films from such widely varied sources. That is what makes it possible for a helper to help people who come from vastly different backgrounds and circumstances.

When I meet someone I would help, I draw forth, during our first meeting, the details of that person's life until it becomes so vivid in my mind that I can imagine myself being that person and being in his or her present situation. That takes a great deal of time and patience. Such time and patience may seem extremely demanding and burdensome. It is not that way at all — provided, that is, one has an intense interest in the life of just that particular person. If there is a groundwork of mutual affection, it is easy to do. The person I would help realizes what I am trying to do. He or she will do all that is possible to help me put myself in his or her shoes.

There are two main aspects of that person's life which I need to know about. First, I want to be able to acutely feel the pain of his or her desperation and sense what feeds into that desperation now and what fed into it from earlier in his or her life. During that drawing forth I am asking myself only one question: What would I do if I were or had been in his or her shoes. Second, I want to get as clear a picture as possible of that person's strengths: admirable qualities, talents, skills, special interests, accomplishments, what he or she is proud of, what others like about him or her. I see those strengths as the resources one can mobilize to deal effectively with his or her present life situation. They are sources of self-confidence and self-reliance.

It is important not to get sidetracked in drawing forth such a story. I have done so often in my earlier efforts and have seen others do so. The difficulty is that when some particular detail of a person's actions is brought forth there is the temptation to deal with it at that moment. For example, I have asked, "Why did you do that?" with an unwitting, rhetorical, criticism implied. Or I have asked, "Did you think of alternatives to what you did?" with the implication that this is what should have been done. Or I have suggested, prematurely, a course of action. Or I have gone into a detailed discussion of an issue that is not central to the person's difficulty or strengths or concerns. Another potential sidetrack is when one is asked early on, and with a good deal of urgency, "What would you do if you were in my shoes?" My answer is, "That's a good question. I will try to answer it. But first I must get your whole story so I can put myself in your shoes." That answer invariably makes good sense to the person I would help.

Going about helping in this way can be of inestimable value. Taking the time to go into the details of a person's life conveys an impression of one's deep personal interest in just that person. He or she thinks, "He understands me, he understands the chaos and desperation in my life; he is not only interested in my hang-ups but sees admirable qualities in me." Such an impression imbues the helping effort, right at the start, with a powerful measure of optimism.

That is not the way most professional helpers see their work. Putting-oneself-in-another's-shoes is rarely part of their understanding of how to help a seriously troubled person. I think that most psychiatrists and psychologists would see that idea as naive, if not an impossibility. They would think that imagining they have within themselves such elements as the weirdness of craziness, the brutality of violent crime, the terror of fear, the murderousness of hatred and the repugnance of self-destruction would be absurd.

The reasoning goes like this: Those who need help are suffering from a deleterious condition. Depending upon one's theoretical orientation condition, that condition might be described as a disturbed functioning, a particular form of disorder, an impaired personality, a mental illness, a psychopathological condition. Implicit is the assumption that the professional helper does not suffer from such a condition. Thus, the idea that he or she could put himself or herself in that person's shoes — feel what that person feels and think the way that person thinks — is simply not credible.

I certainly felt that way when I started out in psychiatry. My own initial assumption was that I — being neither ill or disordered or disturbed

— could not share the same thoughts, feelings and experiences of those who suffered from a mental illness or mental disorder or mental disturbance. Even if I now disagree with that point of view, I see it as understandable. For to put oneself in the shoes of a person trapped in the worst possible aspects of the human state brings one terribly close to one's own inner chaos.

That is frightening. It is frightening for two reasons. First, it brings one so near to one's own helplessness in dealing with that chaos. Second, if helping another means revealing one's own way of dealing with such chaos, as I see it does, then the helper risks exposing his or her own clumsiness, naivety, immaturity, mistakes or uncertainty in doing so. One would keep a great distance from all that. Most people do. Living every day with such a constant confrontation is too much of a burden. But that is just what I have come to see that the good professional helper cannot avoid. That is precisely what makes him or her a good professional. Perhaps such a demand to face one's own inner chaos and how one deals with it is the reason why suicide has been unusually high among psychiatrists.

Professional helpers have a special way of keeping a confrontation with their own inner chaos at arm's length. Instead of looking inside oneself for answers to how to help a person, one looks for answers in textbooks, learned articles, research studies, the words of well-known authorities. Or, in other words, in the vast literature of psychiatry, psychoanalysis and psychotherapy.

Those sources reinforce the idea that people who need psychiatric or psychological help are suffering from conditions which do not afflict professional helpers. Professional helpers have at their disposal a wide array of special, complex, professional techniques and procedures that can be applied to deal with such afflictions. Such authoritative sources can be cited as justification for the utilization of such means. The end result is that one has no need to look inside oneself for answers.

Looking back now at my own early years in psychiatry, I can see why I found that approach particularly attractive. I could observe people as though they were subjects of study. I could develop theories as to why they were afflicted the way they were. I could test out different techniques and procedures. I could, in all that, keep an emotional distance from those needing my help. Whatever problems I had in my living had nothing to do with the ones they had in their living. The trouble with that approach was that, although good for writing learned articles and academic advancement, it did not help those whom I would help.

I felt that I was often talking like a textbook. My words, though possibly sounding profound, seemed somehow artificial, sterile, even to me. Later, on reflection, it seemed that my problem was that I was trying to apply knowl-edge learned from others rather than learned from my own experience. My words did not bring with them a reaction of immediate comprehension from the person I would help. I came to see that such an approach was not what such a person needed. I could, of course, resort to the use of medications to relieve their distress but that seemed like a cowardly way out. I would then be avoiding the problem of my own inadequacy in helping another.

It took time, courage, and experimentation to come to terms with that inadequacy. I had to find things out for myself. I came to see that what peo-ple wanted from me was an example of how to change one's own life from the worst to the best and not simply words divorced from my own personal experience. For that task of changing one's life meant pulling together all the resolve they were capable of, certainly a momentous and critical turning point in their lives. For me to help others do that, my words had to bring forth a spontaneous reaction, one that did not need to be pondered over. What I was saying had to make good common sense. That was what was needed to help others make such a formidable effort. Given such a percep-tion, it seemed clear to me that I should not be afraid of revealing myself. That is what I came to see would carry conviction and believability.

This way of looking at helping was particularly valuable when I, at times, found it impossible to put myself in a person's shoes. I had no clue what to say that might help. At those times, I had to tell myself, "Something is missing in the story I've gotten up to now. I have to go back and find out what that is." Usually, that something missing was a matter that had been passed off as trivial or ignored but which was highly sensitive. It might have been something like bitter feelings in one's early life towards an extremely important person, or cheating during school years, or a single highly embar-rassing sexual encounter. When such experiences came forth, I could relive them in my own life. I could put myself in that person's shoes. I could see the importance of those missing elements. I could offer, hopefully, a better way of dealing with them.

Having the opportunity to put myself in another's shoes — to experience the most intimate, personal and private of that person's life — has brought with it a priceless reward.

It has been like a travelogue of the inner world of the human experience. I have learned the fine details of how people experience different occupations, different cultures, different ideological orientations, different family constellations. I have had a chance to refine my own way of seeing living in those various contexts. My life has been incalculably enriched.

If Putting-Oneself-In-Another's-Shoes is the source of answers to how to help another person, the next questions that need to be answered are: How does one put those answers to use in the actual dialogue of helping? What words does one use? When does one say those words? How does one deal in words with difficulties that arise in the helping situation? My answers to those questions are in the next section.

THE ASKING-FOR-HELP-AND-THE-GIVING-OF-HELP

The-Asking-For-Help-And-The-Giving-Of-Help sums up my view of what underlies all the words spoken between two people in effective helping. It defines the roles of those two people. It pinpoints concisely what each must do to make such helping work well.

The person who needs help puts into words the questions for which he or she has not been able to find good answers. Those questions concern how to deal with what is so deeply troubling him or her. The person who would help puts into words his or her answers to those questions. If the first person thinks those answers make good sense, he or she tries them out, puts them to use. If not, new answers must be found and tested until they arrive at what will make that troubled state disappear.

Although that Asking–Giving phrase may seem so elementary as to be self-evident, it took me a long time to see matters this way. It was not because I hadn't read what was written about psychoanalysis and psychotherapy. It was probably because I had read too much. It took time for me to wade through the confusion I experienced, to come to grips with what I was doing every time I opened my mouth and to arrive at what I saw was the essence of the dialogue in helping.

I saw a great advantage in thinking about what was being said in terms of The-Asking-For-Help-And-The-Giving-Of-Help. It helped me deal with three difficult problems: 1) What to do when the dialogue went on endlessly without any improvement or any end point in sight; 2) How to deal with a tug-of-war situation which paralyzed helping; 3)What to do when nothing seemed to work despite my best efforts. The problem of talking endlessly without improvement was by far the commonest one I faced.

1) The problem of what to do when the dialogue went on endlessly without any improvement or end point in sight

In some of my helping efforts I felt that our conversations were on an un-ending treadmill. Even though neither of us wanted to stop, it seemed clear that there was no progress being made. It took some time for me to realize that a major reason for that difficulty was that I had a seriously flawed, vague, idea of the end point in helping. That vagueness was captured particularly well in a discussion early on in my psychiatric training with a professor of mine, a prominent psychoanalyst.

I asked him, "When does one stop?" His answer was, "When the transfer-ence is worked through." At the time that seemed to me like a profound an-swer. However, since I had little experience in "working through the trans-ference," it left me not very much wiser. This typified my confusion about the goal and end point of helping efforts. It was as though the essence of helping was to get a person to understand himself or herself, that being what "working through the transference" meant to me. The problem that I came to see in such an approach was that the need for such self-understanding was a never-ending need; it was something we all need throughout our lifetime. There was thus no clear end point or goal to my helping efforts. Lacking such a clear end point and goal in my mind, I was left with only a vague idea of what I was doing every time I talked with a person. Here, then, is the way such a faulty understanding led my helping efforts askew.

My idea of how to help a troubled person was, first of all, to get as de-tailed a picture as possible of what had gone wrong in his or her life. Out of that picture would emerge an idea of the cause of his or her present trou-bling difficulty. The invariable cause was a faulty relationship with one or both parents. Given such a faulty relationship as an example of causation, I would at some later point make clear to that person how such a faulty re-lationship lay behind his or her present difficulty. Such a step would cor-respond to what psychotherapists call an interpretation or analysis of what had gone wrong. Hopefully that knowledge — or insight — would result in a more balanced, more realistic, perception of one's parents and a resultant improvement in one's current situation. Sometimes that helping effort *did* work — but more often it did not. In those latter instances it was as though, in session after session, we were endlessly rooting around in that person's early life in a futile pursuit after insight. There was never sufficient insight to result in any noticeable improvement. It was as though such a hope was always just around the corner.

It took some time to see that in such situations we had become enmeshed in a futile, harmful, mutual dependency. We were both deceiving ourselves. The person needing my help imagined that somehow, as long as we continued talking, he or she was being helped and that complete relief would eventually emerge. I imagined that as long as we kept on talking, I was somehow being effective as a psychiatrist. That person *did* find it helpful to ventilate to a sympathetic ear the troubled aspects of his or her life past and present. That is what kept us talking with each other. However, such a dialogue, although seeming to make a person wiser about what had gone wrong in his or her past life, had almost no effect on improving his or her present life. Whatever improvement there was was all in our heads.

I had to face the fact that in such instances my explanations were not directly utilizable by the person I would help. I was not able to put the theories about causation into words that could, in turn, be put to use directly by that person. My words and the understanding I would convey came out as being too far removed from his or her everyday needs; they were too theoretical. It eventually became clear to me that I was going in a diametrically wrong direction. I came to see that what was needed were words that were so simple, so straightforward and so obvious that they could be utilized directly by a person in his or her everyday life and show immediate results. There should be no need for reflection to understand what I was talking about.

I could pinpoint my problem as lying in the way that I and many professional helpers thought of insight. There was no difficulty in defining insight itself: Insight is an individual's new understanding of his or her difficulty which explained that difficulty in a way that made good sense and could be utilized to improve his or her condition. The problem came with my understanding of the source and verification of such insight.

I saw the source of such insight as being the knowledge found in one or another of the widely accepted psychoanalytic or psychotherapeutic theoretical approaches. Since that knowledge was the result of the thinking and researches of leaders in those fields, I saw such knowledge as being fundamental to understanding the cause of the difficulties I was dealing with. I saw that my task was to bring such an understanding to bear on the troubling difficulty of the person I would help. The problem lay in how I interpreted a person's acceptance or rejection of the understanding I was offering.

If the person needing my help accepted and agreed with that explanation, he or she was seen as having gained insight — whether or not such insight improved that person's everyday living. If a person rejected that explanation, he or she was seen as lacking insight. It was even common among professional helpers to characterize a person who rejected repeated attempts to convey understanding as lacking a basic capacity for insight. That was considered a legitimate reason for breaking off the helping effort.

The result of such a perception of insight was that, whether intended or not, a professional helper's explanations had the character of being infallible. Such explanations were buttressed by the accumulated wisdom of psychotherapy and psychoanalysis. One could hardly interpret a rejection of such presumed insight as due to something wrong in either the helper's explanations or the explanations found in such theories. The fault must lie with the person needing help. For me, there was an obvious falseness in such an idea of insight.

For my understanding of what underlay a person's troubled state could be equally wrong as right. That wrongness or rightness applied equally well to the knowledge found in learned works. The definition of insight had become, in actual practice, what one thought one knew about a person which that person did not know about himself or herself — whether or not that person agreed with such presumed insight. I saw that if a person could not accept my explanations and utilize them to better his or her living it was wrong for me to imagine that I was offering insight. I came to see that the only true criteria of insight was that such new knowledge brought with it an immediate crystal-clear clarity on the part of the person I would help which led to unequivocal improvement.

To get such clarity, I had to start from the beginning. That meant defining a much clearer end point in the dialogue of helping and a much better idea of what I and the person I would help ought to be saying in such a dialogue.

In the introduction to this book, *What Does a Psychiatrist Know About the Best of Living?*, I made clear how I came to see the goal and end point of helping. That goal and end point is to help a person get what he or she wants and should be getting out of one's loving, friendship, learning or work. When one gets those rewards, one's troubling psychiatric condition disappears. Looking at the goal and end point of helping this way shifts the emphasis on what each person should be talking about.

The person needing help, instead of only setting forth the details of his or her troubled life and troubling symptoms, must say what he or she wants most in those areas of living. That is usually not easily done. Often such a person has been so preoccupied by troubles or symptoms that he or she has not thought about what is missing and how to go about getting that.

On occasion, when a person has come to me for help about a troubling symptom such as tension, a somatic difficulty, depressing thoughts, or a sleep disturbance and I have tried to explore personal areas of that person's life, I have been asked, "Why is it necessary to go into that?" My answer was, "Because, in my experience, when a person has a clear idea of how one's life ought to be and goes about getting that, one's difficulty disappears. It is not simply a question of getting rid of what is negative in one's life, it is a question of knowing what is positive and getting that." Sometimes a person is still skeptical as to whether such an effort will make his or her troubled state disappear. In answer to that skepticism I say, "You have nothing to lose and everything to gain. At the very least you will get what you want so much in your loving [friendship, learning, work]. If it works as, I think it will, your difficulties will also disappear." That reasoning is usually convincing.

There are two reasons why putting into words what one wants most out of living is difficult. The first is that when one reveals to another person what is so seriously lacking in one of those areas of living, it is easy to imagine that that person sees one as have seriously failed in one's living. That other person might see such failure as being a mark of one's inadequacy as a person. That is highly embarrassing. What a person needs to counteract such thoughts is this kind of encouragement, "We all have at times severe difficulties just as those troubling you. That is not a mark of incompetence on your part. We will work together on how to get just what you want."

The second reason why it is difficult to put into words what we want so much in our living is that we then face the prospect of trying to get that missing element, a prospect which may well be so formidable that it appears beyond our ability. We may have faced that prospect before and either failed in the attempt or backed away from an anticipated failure. In contrast, if we confine ourselves to describing in detail our troubling symptom or situation, and expect that understanding the cause of that difficulty will make it disappear, we aren't faced with doing something hard — and failing at it. It is as though one could better one's life without much effort other than talking and thinking. Given such apprehension, a person seeking help needs encouraging words such as these: "I realize that you have not succeeded so well in getting what you want most, but I am convinced that if we two work on that together, you will do so. You have, in my opinion, all that it takes to succeed."

This way of looking at what a person needing help ought to be saying ends up with that person asking, "What would you do if you were in my shoes?"

Usually there is a reluctance to put the helper up against the wall with such a point blank question. One might think that that is rude or naive or embarrassing. Yet that is what The-Asking-For-Help-And-The-Giving-Of-Help boils down to in the end. For that person does not have the answers to what he or she might do. Otherwise there would be no need for help. It is perfectly alright to try and draw forth what a person thinks he or she might do — and then encourage him or her to try that out. But in my experience there almost always comes a point when that person cannot think of any good answer to what to do to get what he or she wants out of living. At that point, that person deserves an answer from the helper. When a person is ready to ask such a question, he or she is ready to make use of the answer gotten.

To get a person to ask that question, after drawing forth what he or she wants most out of living, I ask, "What questions do you have for me? You have a right to get an answer to any questions concerning you, even those that might appear to you as perhaps simple or foolish." That usually works, but if it doesn't, I ask, "Would you like to hear what I would do if I were in your shoes?" Putting such an answer into words pinpoints, to my mind, what is the main responsibility of the helper in the dialogue of helping.

The helper will be ready with such an answer if, while drawing forth a person's story, that question has been constantly in his or her mind. Looking at the helper's role in this way shifts the helper's main responsibility from analyzing what went wrong in a person's life to sharing one's own highly personal ways of dealing with that person's difficulty.

That was no easy matter for me to do when I first came to such a realization. Neither is it easy to do for most professional helpers. It demands revealing oneself and one's own possibly poor ways of thinking about and dealing with living. Doing so can be seen as highly embarrassing. However, there is a much more serious barrier to doing that. Most psychotherapeutic and psychoanalytic approaches contend that doing so is unprofessional and unethical.

It is maintained that doing so unfairly influences another person to live one's life as the helper has lived his or her life. One is steering or dominating a person, taking unfair advantage of a person's dependence on the helper. One is impressing on another person one's own values in living. One is taking away from an individual an independence to live as he or she would. It is maintained that putting helping into such a highly personal context is unprofessional since professional conduct demands impartiality and neutrality.

My answer to such an objection is that the person seeking help sets the goals of what he or she wants to get out of living — not me. That is not only his or her own free choice but his or her responsibility. My task is to help that person find an effective means to attain such goals. I make it clear that that individual is free to reject such means if it doesn't make good common sense to him or her. From the very start, the person I would help is working with me in every session progressively towards an end point of complete independence, towards a situation in which that person does not need my help any longer.

Perhaps most importantly, it seems that professional helpers deceive themselves if they imagine they can be impartial and neutral, or can prevent their own values from influencing their helping efforts. I have already touched on this matter in the section on Affection. This is a central difficulty in the helping efforts of many professional helpers. They reveal their own way of living, albeit unintentionally. They do so in selecting certain topics for discussion and overlooking other topics. They do so by their uncontrollable expressions of satisfaction, exasperation, indifference or distaste at what is being said. They do so by offering an analysis or interpretation which can never be free of their own personal perception of living. Since I find it impossible in any helping situation for the helper not to influence another person with his or her own perception of living, I think that it makes good sense to use such influence deliberately and wisely rather than to deny that it exists.

I had come to the conclusion that the essence of my helping efforts lay precisely in my ability to put into words my own personal answers to the "how" of living. All my knowledge about psychiatry and psychology, in the end, had to funnel down into such words. With that perception as a point of departure, I found a way of putting into simple words just how I go about helping a person.

Sometimes I have been asked: "What [psychotherapeutic or psychoanalytic] school do you belong to?" My response has been, "It seems to me that you really want to know how I work in helping people. Is that so?" The answer has always been, "Yes." I then go on, "You have told me what you want out of living. I will do all in my power to help you get that. We will work on that problem together. I will share all my knowledge with you about what works and what doesn't work. If my answers make sense to you, then you can try them out. If not, we'll come up with other ideas until we find one that does make sense."

Such an explanation goes to the heart of the great benefit in The-Asking-For-Help-And-The-Giving-Of-Help: It translates thinking into direct action.

This is how that translation works: If a person feels that the answer about what to do to get what he or she wants in loving (or friendship, work, or learning) makes good and practical sense, then it must be tried out, put to the test. Such action might involve, for example, getting a boyfriend or girlfriend, dealing with arguments with one's wife or husband, enjoying sex, finding enthusiasm for one's work or studies, making a good friend. If that action succeeds, in the next session whatever new problems that may have arisen are discussed and a new way to tackle those problems is set forth. If that action hasn't succeeded, the discussion concerns why it hasn't and the possible need to find a new, better, way. If the person could not put such an answer to the test despite wanting to, it is necessary to look into what blocked such action so as to remove such a block.

It is important that I set forth my opinion that even though such action may seem extremely difficult before an attempt is made, the individual I would help will succeed. A person trying something new needs a good deal of encouragement. He or she needs to know that one has a perfect right to fail in such an attempt, that the helper is there to help him or her deal with that possibility until one succeeds. There is a constant demand on the person to try out what makes sense and a constant demand on the helper to come up with good ideas to help that person get what he or she wants. Seen this way, each conversation is a step forward towards the end point that was set at the very beginning.

A person knows unequivocally when that end point is reached. One has gotten what one wanted. One is pleased with oneself. Life is going great. There is nothing left to talk about. It is just this approach to the dialogue of helping — with its constant movement towards such an endpoint — which is the key to making the duration of helping as short as possible.

2. The problem of how to deal with a tug-of-war situation which paralyzed helping

There were times when I felt that the dialogue of helping had become a tug-of-war with me trying to get a person to do something I thought would improve his or her condition or situation and with that person resisting whatever effort I made.

In my early efforts such a tug of war arose because I thought a person was asking for my advice when he or she was not doing so. A person would talk at length about difficulties that were extremely troubling and I assumed that that person wanted my opinion about how to deal with such difficulties. When I gave my opinion, it was not listened to and acted upon. There was usually no outright rejection of my opinion but, in essence, it was ignored. During session after session I would try to think of some new advice that might help. Such situations finally brought me to the realization that in the very first session I had to ask, towards the end, "What do you want to hear from me?"

I was greatly surprised that on some occasions the answer was, "Nothing." When I asked the reason why, the response was that that person only wanted someone to listen to his or her difficulties. In such a situation I either had to accept the precondition that my opinion was not wanted or make clear that I saw that there would be no improvement unless that person wanted to hear what I had to say.

More usual was a response of confusion. The idea of putting into words what a person wanted to hear from me had not occurred to the person needing my help. That person had assumed that if one's difficulties were set forth I would, at some point, offer my opinion about what could be done to deal with those difficulties. In such a situation my opinion was usually ignored, because that person was not prepared to accept it and utilize it. I came to the conclusion that there would be no such acceptance and utilization unless a person had put into words just what he or she wanted to hear from me. I had to say something such as, "It is important that you think about just what you want to hear from me. You don't have to accept my opinion, but without having a clear idea of what questions you want answers to, I don't think you will get any help. The more specific a question you have, the more specific an answer you will get and the quicker you will get what you want for yourself." Such an answer invariably made good sense and got helping off to a good start.

Another problem which gave rise to a tug-of-war situation was a person's talking at length about a difficulty which was not his or her primary concern. For example, such a person might go on at length about arguments with his wife and not bring up a deep-lying fear of possible homosexuality. In such an instance I would wrongly assume that that person wanted my opinion about how to deal with those arguments. Such discussion would lead nowhere. It was as though I was trying to get that person to better deal with his or her marriage and he or she was resisting every effort I made. I came to realize that when that happened it was invariably because I had not asked what that person wanted to hear from me and, consequently, I could not deal with his or her fear of bringing up such a deeper-lying concern. I had to say something such as, "We are not getting anywhere in our discussions. What is it that you really want to hear from me? I feel that there is something more important troubling you which you have not brought up yet. I realize that some subjects are very difficult to talk about but unless I hear just what you want to hear from me, I won't be able to help you get what you want most out of your living." If a person trusted that I would not influence his or her life in an undesired, possibly threatening way, such words were usually effective in bringing forth that deeper-lying concern and dealing with it.

What is central in the above tug-of-war examples was my wrong assumption that a need for help was the same as an asking for help. I wrongly assumed that my opinion was wanted, even though it was never requested. Looking at the dialogue of helping in terms of The-Asking-For-Help-And-

The-Giving-Of-Help corrects such a wrong assumption. It sums up what I have come to see as one of the primary rules of helping: *Do not give help until it is asked for*. Otherwise, such help, no matter how well meaning, will be ignored or rejected.

A more difficult tug-of-war situation has arisen when it seemed to me that I wanted more for a person's bettered living than that person wanted. It was as though I was caught up in a constant effort to encourage a person to try out a way of bettering his or her life and that person, although agreeing with the logic of such a suggestion, seemed blocked in utilizing it. We would discuss in session after session why such a course of action appeared almost impossible — but never arrive at any explanation that did away with that barrier. In such instances it was often as though the person I would help had become emotionally dependent upon me in a way that was deleterious. Not infrequently that meant that the person I would help read sexual implications into what was taking place between us. I saw that my problem was that I had lost sight of The-Asking-For-Help-And-The-Giving-Of-Help principle.

In such instances I had to return to what I saw was basic in our dialogue. I had to say something such as this, "The sole reason for our talking with each other is for me to help you get what you want out of your living. When we have reached that point we will stop. It seems to me we have reached an impasse. I very much want to help you better your life but I do not feel I have been successful in doing so. I feel we have to think about the possibility of stopping." The idea of confronting the possible need to stop was often effective in getting the helping situation going again in the right direction.

3. The problem of what to do when nothing seemed to work despite one's best effort

One of the most difficult problems I have had to face as a psychiatrist has been how to deal with situations in which I had run out of answers. Since I clearly could not help all those whom I wanted to help, confronting such a problem was inevitable. In such situations it became clear to me that there was nothing more I could do and that we would have to stop. How to do that troubled me greatly, for I felt that I handled such situations poorly.

In time I came to understand why I handled such situations poorly. I had relied upon generally accepted explanations that such failure was usually due to some deep-seated problem in the make-up of the person I had tried to help which made him or her inaccessible to helping. Such problems would include a lack of sufficient motivation, a character defect, an incapacity for insight, or a gravely flawed early childhood. What troubled me so greatly with such explanations was that they did harm to a person I had tried to help. They assumed that that person was beyond helping. I came to see that such an appraisal was fundamentally wrong. I came to see that such explanations blamed that person for a failure which was solely my own. It stemmed from my inability to blame myself.

After all, it was solely my responsibility to find a way to help a person. Otherwise, he or she would not be in need of my help. Explaining a failure of helping as due to some flaw in a person needing help was akin to shifting the responsibility for success in helping on to that person.

My need to do so could be traced back to a problem that was described above, when I set forth my perception of what was wrong in the way insight is perceived by many professionals. I wrongly saw my role as applying the theories and techniques which psychiatry had developed. If a person was not helped, his difficulty was considered as being beyond such theories and techniques. The fault could not be attributed to my own lack of expertise. In looking at helping this way I could avoid the problem of my own fallibility. I could hide behind a false idea of what a psychiatrist's expertise is. Thinking in terms of The-Asking-For-Help-And-The-Giving-Of-Help corrected such a flawed perception of my own role and my own expertise. It helped me deal with my failure in helping in a way that did no harm to the person I had tried to help.

For The-Asking-For-Help-And-The-Giving-Of-Help makes helping a highly personal matter. It takes away any inference that the helper's words ought to be accepted because they are authoritative. The final determinant of the rightness or wrongness of the helper's words is only whether the person in need can make common sense out of them and put them to use. Otherwise, those words should be rejected. Seeing helping this way gave me a right to fail. For my words, despite all my knowledge and effort, might not provide the answers a person needed. I had to accept the fact that I was only human and did not have the answers needed to help all those I would help.

Before I saw helping in this way I thought I had to have all the answers to how to help a person. Giving up left me suffering a guilty conscience. I saw giving up as a threat to my expertise. After seeing helping in this new way I realized that after I felt I had done everything I could think of to help, I could not ask more of myself or the person needing help. I would not give up easily but I had a right to give up. Sometimes I had to realize that someone else might do a better job of helping than I had done.

I had to be able to say, "I think we have come as far as we possibly can. Things are not getting better. I don't feel that I have been able to help you as I should have been able to do. I think that someone else might do a better job than I have done. It is important that you realize that it is my fault that you have not gotten what you want, not yours. It has been my responsibility to give you the help you needed and wanted — and not yours." Those words have almost always been effective in relieving a person of blaming himself or herself.

It took some time to realize that before I could voice such words I had to possess one specific attribute. That attribute was a sense of humility. I was simply one human being trying to do the best I could to help another human being about whom I cared very greatly and who was temporarily stuck in his or her life. I had good resources for doing that since I had made a specialty of helping those in distress and had found ways of doing so which often did work. But, I was far from infallible. I saw that all I could offer another person was what I had learned about what works in living from my own experience in helping others and in helping myself. There were important gaps in that knowledge. Furthermore, my life was far from problem-free. Just because I made a specialty out of helping others did not mean that I was devoid of the same problems and the same desperation of those I would help.

Seeing myself in such a light brought with it a new way of looking at helping. The person I would help was working together with me on a joint project. I was trying to come up with good answers and that other person was testing them out. A sense of camaraderie and equality in that joint work was essential to making the dialogue of helping work.

There is a special value in looking at helping this way. For many people who seek help feel that their severe distress makes them inferior as human beings. They feel that they are failures in their living and that asking for help is a sign of weakness. That negative self-evaluation is reinforced by a common public opinion about those who seek or have sought help from a psychiatrist. It is assumed by many that such persons suffer from a mental illness, a condition with such serious consequences as, for example, to make that person unfit for responsible political office or for full medical insurance.

To complicate that matter further, such people often have an image of a psychiatrist as being free of such severe problems as they have, never in need of help, and thus somehow superior as a human being. Illogical as such a perception of human inferiority and superiority might seem, I could see the root of such a false perception even within myself. For when I started off in psychiatry I felt that way, too — even if I wouldn't admit it. I imagined that those needing my help were suffering from a condition that I was totally free of. I imageined that I could not be so desperate in my living as to have to ask another person for help. I later realized that such was not the case at all; this had a great influence on what I could say in the dialogue of helping.

I could say, "Many people see asking for help as a sign of weakness. I see it as a sign of strength. It takes courage to ask for help about a deeply troubling personal difficulty. If one doesn't ask for help, one has no chance of getting it. Far too many people don't get what they want out of their living because they are afraid to ask for help. Help from another person is something all of us need during our lifetime — me, too. That is nothing to be ashamed of. You are temporarily stuck in your life and we will work together to get things unstuck."

A person hearing such words usually gives an inner sigh of relief. Those words dispel a derogatory self-image which has been a severe burden. They convey an idea that that person is just as good as me and anyone else — and not a pathological case. They are central to stimulating a new sense of self-confidence. They offer the great encouragement one needs to come to grips with one's life.

There was another great value in seeing helping as a joint project between two equals. It helped immeasurably in bettering my expertise as a psychiatrist, for the person I was helping was testing out my ideas to see whether they would work. Oftentimes that person succeeded better than I would have done. Thus with each new helping situation I was adding to my own knowledge of what worked, how it worked and what ought to be rejected in my thinking. Seen this way, I was getting back from the person I was helping just as much as I was giving.

Underlying my perception of The-Asking-For-Help-And-The-Giving-Of-Help was a sense of equality between the asker and the giver. This perception originated in my early years from several persons far more knowledge-able about helping than I was who, nevertheless, treated me as an equal.

I think of Lawrence Kubie, an eminent psychoanalyst and a president of the American Psychoanalytic Association. We had met when I took a residency in neurology at Columbia before going into psychiatry. He lectured to us. I remember well when we drove up together in his car to New Haven, where he gave a seminar at Yale. He set a splendid example of how I imagined a psychiatrist should be: competent, warm, accessible. His influence was a major factor in my decision to go into psychiatry and to seek psychoanalytic training. I think of Franz Alexander, a seminal figure in psychoanalysis. During my first year in psychiatry, he and I spent two hours walking along the boardwalk at Atlantic City during a convention of the American Psychoanalytic Association. I remember even today how impressed I was that such a famous person would take the time to discuss with me, a pure beginner, professional matters which greatly concerned me. I think of Martin Gerson, my supervisor at the Psychotherapy Clinic of the New York Psychoanalytic Institute, whose confidence in me helped greatly in developing my own sense of self-confidence. I think of Nancy Staver, chief of social work at the Judge Baker Guidance Center in Boston where I trained in child psychiatry. She had a wonderful ability to put into concrete, practical, words what was needed to help another.

I can see now that when I talk with a person I would help I am trying to bring to our discussions the same qualities I admired in my discussions with those professionals. They listened to my questions with patience and did their best to answer those questions. They offered me encouragement by being able to give me a word of praise. They projected an idea that I might have something valuable to say despite my inexperience. They treated me as an equal.

That is how I came to see things, but only in retrospect. It took time for such an impression to sink in by some sort of emotional osmosis. What greatly complicated such awareness was another side of that coin. There were other psychiatrists and other supervisors who projected a different image. Their words came out as authoritative. They appeared totally self-assured. They projected an air of unerring expertise. They were polite and solicitous but also, as objective medical professionals, impersonal and detached. They saw helping in terms of applying proven methods and techniques to treat

psychopathology. For me, as a beginner psychiatrist, the sum of those characteristics brought forth an image of psychiatric expertise that seemed both
definitive and persuasive. But it increasingly left me in a quandary.

The quandary came from a growing realization that that image was the
direct opposite of the one projected by those whom I admired so much. The
two images were irreconcilable. One epitomized the best attributes of a psychiatrist, attributes essential to helping people in severe distress. The other
epitomized the worst attributes, those that did unintentional harm. That
contrast was exemplified by the two kinds of supervisors during my psychiatric training. There were those who left me with an encouraging sense of my
own increasing competence. There were others who left me with a crushing
sense of my own inadequacy.

That latter state was clearly not the intention of such supervisors. They
saw their efforts as being helpful. Nevertheless, that was the result of three
characteristics that went hand in hand with their self-image of a psychiatric
expert: They could not muster a word of the praise and encouragement that I
so much needed; They saw supervising as solely the exposing and correcting
of the serious mistakes I had made, a perception which came out as constant
critical fault-finding and which left me with an impression that nothing I
could do was right or would ever satisfy them; They assumed that their opinions were beyond questioning, an attitude which came across as an air of
superiority and left me with a sense of my own inferiority and a resentment
at their condescension. They were intimidating and I felt intimidated.

Looking back now, I see that they lacked the ABCs of helping. They could
not express any affection for me; they could not put themselves in my shoes
as a beginner; they could not accept any give and take in our discussions and
could not treat me as an equal. It became abundantly clear that, if I came
away from those encounters with such a negative reaction, the effect on individuals desperate for help from such psychiatrists would be even worse.
However, during my early training years I was taken in by the self-assured
image such psychiatrists projected.

I was unsure of myself and could not see what lay behind that self-assured
image. It took time to realize why I was so intimidated by it. That realization came out of my helping efforts with individuals who also projected such
a self-assured image. They did so because of their own marked insecurity.
They assumed an all-knowing attitude with others to reassure, first of all,

themselves. They were unable to deal with the uncertainty and serious lack of fulfillment in their work. A dogmatic, assertive, all-knowing posture had its rewards. Not only was it effective in avoiding such a confrontation but other people, insecure and unsure of themselves as I was, were easily taken in by it and looked up to such figures of authority. Such iron-clad certainty offered an easy path to follow within psychiatry.

It offered the reassurance that if one followed the dictum-like assertions of such psychiatrists, one would be successful in one's work. One would not have to deal with one's own uncertainty. One would not have to find one's own personal way to deal with the helping problems one was faced with. One would only have to learn the fine points of diagnosis and treatment. Such an approach was particularly attractive in psychiatry, where there was such great uncertainty in both understanding the difficulties one was dealing with and in knowing how to deal effectively with such difficulties.

What was dismaying about that image of the psychiatrist was its pervasive and increasing influence in setting the course of the entire specialty. Psychiatric academia was almost totally preoccupied with searching for proven, scientific, ways to assess and deal with psychiatric difficulties. The image of the authoritative psychiatrist fit in beautifully with such academia. Professorships were increasingly filled by such psychiatrists. Psychiatrists in training tried to emulate their attitude. Psychiatric journals, which set the standard of what was respectable and desirable in the profession, would increasingly publish only articles which buttressed such a scientific base of the specialty. Indeed, publishing such articles became the primary path towards academic advancement. I saw that even in other helping professions, such as clinical psychology, there was an identical trend. The sum of that perception left with me convinced that psychiatry was increasingly turning in on itself and increasingly unresponsive to the needs of people in severe distress.

For there was next to nothing in that authoritative, scientific, approach which fostered the development of a good helper. There was next to nothing which dealt with furthering an understanding of the basic elements of helping, the ABCs of helping. Instead, increasingly helping professionals were being produced who saw themselves as objective, distant, highly skilled technicians, expert at the techniques of their profession. I felt that the general public was being grossly shortchanged. People in distress who needed help in getting the very best out of their living were getting something far less than that. Any thought of how to go about getting the great wonder out of living was simply absent from such an approach.

This led me to raise several questions which go to the very heart of successful helping. Little in the literature dealt with those questions. But the answers I eventually came to crystallized the difference between the good and the bad in helping. People in general sorely need clarity on that score. My perception of the ABCs of helping gave me good, clear, and concise answers to those questions.

Chapter 6. Nuts-and-Bolts Questions People Need Answers to About the Good and Bad in Helping

At times in our efforts to get the very best out of our living we get hopelessly stuck. We need help from someone else. Many consider turning to a psychiatrist, psychologist or other professional helper. We assume that such professional helpers are far more skilled in helping people than nonprofessionals are. We assume that they have refined the art of helping to a high degree so as to help us get the wonderful life we want. All of which may or may not be so.

The questions raised and answered in this chapter concern the nuts and bolts of helping. They are questions which ordinary people ask. They are eminently practical questions. People in general need good answers to these questions, because the answers are crucial for making clear how to sort out the good from the bad in what the professionals of helping actually do.

Some of the issues dealt with here will course through the rest of this work since they concern central elements in how we live our lives.

These, then, are the questions:

1. How does one choose a psychiatrist, psychologist or other professional helper?
2. What should one expect from a professional helper, at the start, middle, and end of a helping contact?
3. How long should helping take?

4. Can everyone be helped to turn one's living from the worst to the best?

5. Should medicines be used in such an approach?

6. Is there any advantage in seeking help from a psychiatrist as compared to other professional helpers?

7. How does one help a person who has not voluntarily sought help such as those forced into a mental hospital, correctional institution or prison and those coerced into seeking help by courts, schools or probation authorities?

8. What is psychotherapy?

How DOES ONE CHOOSE A PSYCHIATRIST, PSYCHOLOGIST OR OTHER PROFESSIONAL HELPER?

People who have asked me this question were those whom I felt I could not take on for help because I was personally involved in their living as a close friend. Because the problems they needed help with were so central to their living, they wanted some way of judging whether a given professional would be good for them. My first suggestion was that they ask friends who had received such help and would highly recommend their own professional helper. That approach sometimes worked but too often there was no recourse except to turn to an agency or professional that appeared to have a good reputation. Regardless of which approach one took, I saw that the decision ought to be based on one's impression during the very first meeting. For, in my opinion, that initial impression would either set a firm platform for further success or would stand in the way of such success. There were three cardinal criteria for deciding whether one ought to continue working with a given professional helper.

The first criterion was this: Do I like him or her, and does that person like me? As the discussion progresses, one's impression on that score ought to become increasingly unequivocal. If there is no sense of a clear liking, it makes no sense to continue. It is futile to expect such liking to develop over the course of time. One can always revise one's opinion downward later on, but for me that initial liking is essential to being able to reveal one's highly sensitive innermost self, precisely what I see that one needs help with.

The second criterion was this: Is the professional willing to answer all my simplest questions, and do his or her answers make good common sense to me? Those questions should concern all the uncertainties one has about one's current troubled state. Probably the most important question to ask is how the professional goes about helping. I see that the professional's willingness to answer such questions is essential for the joint work the two will be doing together. I feel that if the professional avoids giving such answers or if his or her answers don't make good common sense one should not continue.

The third criterion is this: Do I feel that the professional has experienced just what I am going through? One's impression should also be unequivocal on this score. This is how one knows one is turning to a professional who has found some good answers to one's thorny questions. Such an impression will come through clearly as a reflection of the questions the professional asks, his or her statements and manner. If one gets an impression that the serious troubles in one's living are foreign to the professional's own life, or that he or she regards one as a disturbed or mentally sick person, there will no good basis for an effective helping dialogue.

These three criteria are intuitive and subjective. One must trust one's own judgment on each of them. No one else can make such a decision. There are no objective criteria that can substitute for them. It makes no sense to continue with a professional because of his or her reputation or because he or she comes highly recommended, if a person does not like the professional, if one's questions are avoided or if one feels that the professional doesn't really seem to understand what one is experiencing.

WHAT SHOULD ONE EXPECT FROM A PROFESSIONAL HELPER, AT THE START, MIDDLE, AND END OF A HELPING CONTACT?

Almost all who have come to me have had little idea of what to expect during the course of helping. There are certain central elements that should be present at each stage of successful helping. People ought to have a clear idea of those elements in trying to evaluate the kind of help they are getting. The answers to this question came from what I saw that those whom I have helped wanted and needed to hear from me at each stage.

At the very start almost everyone who has come to me is apprehensive as to what will happen. If I see that there is so much guardedness and so much difficulty in stating what a person wants from me I say something like this, "It is not easy to talk about highly sensitive and personal things. I can only assure you that my only intention is to help you get what you yourself want out of your living. Many who come to me are apprehensive at the beginning that they will be criticized, condemned or judged. I promise you that I will not criticize, condemn, judge or otherwise hurt you. If you feel that I am doing so you must let me know how you feel so I can correct that."

I have already dealt with the great importance of bringing forth just how a person would like the best of his or her living to be if it could be that way. I encourage that expression by saying something like this: "We will play a little game, just between the two of us and just here in this room. We'll do it just for fun. I'd like you to let your mind go free and imagine the wildest, craziest ideas you might have about what kind of life you want for yourself. Saying such things is not committing yourself to anything." The idea is to give free rein to one's fantasy. It is to get one started in thinking freely. So I get from a hard-working youth a wanting to buy a supercharged motorcycle; I get from a 40-odd-year-old successful businessman a desire to start in medical school; I get from a tradesman a desire to be an opera singer, I get from a Harlem youth ready to drop out of school a wish to be a doctor . . . along with all the other ambitions in one's loving, friendship, learning, work, idealism and private life. My point in this approach is to encourage a person to try and get those things, to test out whether or not that is what she or he wants, to realize his or her dreams.

All of which brings me back to a central element of that first meeting: a word of honest praise. While I am drawing forth a person's story I am asking myself, "What is it I like about this particular person, what attracts me?" After that person has said what kind of life he or she would like to have, I say something such as, "I think you have a fine chance of getting just what you want. I see admirable qualities in you. You have good resources to draw upon." Such words are what I see are the substance of the encouragement a person needs from me. However, not so seldom a person, on hearing such words, is skeptical, he or she has either never heard a word of praise before or questions whether I am just tossing off an impersonal and insincere compliment. That person might challenge me, "What qualities? What resources?" My answer is to cite just how I feel.

Almost everyone wants to see himself or herself as handsome or beautiful and in my opinion there are just such qualities in everyone. I might say, "I think you are beautiful [handsome], you have fine features, I like the way you dress." What I say varies greatly with what strikes me most: a person's intelligence, thoroughness, artistic sense, ability to act vigorously, imagina-tiveness — there is no end to such qualities. Such a word of honest praise from a person privy to another's most troubled inner life has almost always had a powerful impact.

Many people who have come to me want not only a way to get what they want in living and encouragement to do so but they also want to know just how they get in their own way. They might say something such as, "I want a girlfriend [a boyfriend, a good relationship with my boss, to make things great with my wife or husband] but everything I try turns sour. I don't know why. What do you think?" My answer to such questions comes from looking at what it is in that person which irritates me. I have found that the charac-teristics that irritate me almost always irritate others. We all have an unde-sirable side. I have come to see that those needing my help want my opinion about that so as to better see themselves and better deal with themselves. I feel it is highly important to wait until such a question is asked — and not to offer such an opinion until then no matter how well-meaning my intention. I always offer my opinion tentatively in such a statement such as, "It might be that you are so eager to talk about yourself that you don't listen to another person" *or* "It might be that you are so careful that you are afraid to take any risk of failing" *or* any more of the multitude of ways we get in our own way.

Criticism in any form is a highly sensitive matter. I have over the years found a good working definition of the difference between constructive criticism and destructive criticism. Such differentiation has nothing to do with the correctness of the thoughts expressed. It has to do solely with the subjective impact on the person hearing such words. If that person feels in-stinctively that such criticism is meant to help it is accepted in good spirit, even if it is not necessarily agreed upon. That is constructive criticism. If such criticism is felt as hurting, unjust or harming, it will block any further helping. That is destructive criticism. If I sense that there is any hint of the latter reaction, I must make clear my intention and my possibly mistaken judgment. The value of such a definition in my eyes is that it helps the helper avoid unintentionally hurting a person; it makes the helper exquisitely sensi-tive to how his or her words are perceived.

Many have an urgent need to talk about their parents, their early life, and their difficulties in growing up. It seems to me self-evident that they should be encouraged to do that. That goes with the helper's effort to put himself or herself in another person's shoes. It means that the first meeting ought to take a long time, as long as one can manage. For me, it is usually between 2 and 2½ hours. I see that there are two important considerations in dealing with matters about a person's past. The first is that one must make a clear connection between what has happened in the past to how one deals with one's life — for better or worse — in the daily life of one's present. I say something such as, "Alright, then, how do you think that what happened then has affected your difficulty in handling your life now?" I put this forward because sometimes people wanting help do not do that; they end up going over and over their past story as though stuck in a broken record.

The second is that too many youth and adults blame others — usually their parents — for their present difficulties. In such instances I say something such as, "Your parents probably did not do too well but they did the best they could. It does no good to you to go through your life blaming them; you are just looking for a convenient scapegoat. You are an adult now. You yourself now determine the course of your life, not them. The only way to better your situation, in my opinion, is to change yourself — and forget about changing them. If you can better the way you deal with them [such as, for example, to ignore their criticism instead of flaring up *or* to say your own mind instead of being docile *or* to do your own thing instead being dominated] you will have taken a giant step forward in your own life."

I treat the very first meeting with a person I would help as a critical turning point in their lives. I literally put that thought into words. Such people are stuck in their living and it invariably will take a determined effort to change the course of their living. It should have the character of a crisis, and if it doesn't, I try to bring that forth. One should come away from that first meeting with the impression that one has come upon a new and wonderful opportunity to turn one's life completely around with the help of a person who wants to help do just that. That first session must have a great impact. It ought to leave a person with new hope and new optimism. That is why I spend so much time on it. Later sessions are usually only 45 minutes long, once a week. I make clear, though, that I can always make room to see a person at any time in between. I also make clear that the person can call me at any time, day or night. I especially make that clear if there is a problem with taking narcotics, getting drunk or killing oneself. I say, "At least call me and talk things over first." Thus, I treat our first contact as an emergency situation. If the person I would help has difficulty seeing things this way, I explain my reasoning for it.

I set forth the above approach because I have heard repeatedly from people that that is what they did not get when they turned to other professionals. They felt that they were simply one more person in a very busy professional schedule. They did not like that.

The first meeting must *always* end with a course of action. With my help, the person must, in the end, come to a possible way of getting just what he or she wants out of his or her living, and a course of action must be tested out in the interval before our next meeting. We can then look at what worked or didn't work and why. The first meeting should never just tail off with the assumption, "discussion to be continued." I have heard that from many who were disappointed in their previous helping contacts. The translating of thought into action is what gives movement and progress to the entire course of the helping contact.

That matter of continual movement and progress is what should characterize the entire middle course of helping. I begin every new session with what is uppermost in a person's mind just then. That is usually what has happened since we talked last: What he or she has done and what happened, what new thoughts have arisen as a result of that action. At times completely new problems and questions arise which must be dealt with.

The need for a person to develop self-confidence is central to that middle course of helping. For one is trying to do something new and difficult with one's life in the face of great uncertainty; one is trying to turn it around from the worst to the best. It took me some time to come to what I see as central to gaining self confidence: the willingness to try repeatedly and to face failure. It seems to me that too many people are so geared to having to succeed that they cannot face the prospect of failing. Yet such failure is part and parcel of living, it is part of trying, it is part of finding new and better ways to deal effectively with one's living. One learns from one's mistakes and one's failures. Thus, I might say, "Give it a good try. Do your best — that's all you can ask of yourself. If it doesn't work, we can have a good laugh about that and find a new, better way." I see that that is just the kind of encouragement people need.

I encourage a person to think for himself or herself, to bring forth his or her wildest ideas of how to get what is wanted in living. We look at those ideas together. I encourage a person to try them out. I see it as important to never put down a person's ideas. For it seems to me that there are far too many in the worlds around us who do just that in the name of "being realistic." That is the prime source of people's fear of failing, of being ridiculed, of looking dumb. That should not come from me — quite the opposite. In this context of encouragement one of the most powerful things I can say is this, "There are ways for people to get almost everything they really want in living if they dare to try. We will together find a way for you. *If I could find a way to do so in my life so can you.*"

This way of looking at the middle course of helping almost always works. I have set forth above an idea of what I see that most people are looking for in the way of support. The ultimate test of the worth of such an idea is whether or not people respond well to it. And that is just what I have seen.

There, however, is a serious kind of difficulty which does occur at times and which blocks any action. In those instances a person, although seeing the logic of such action, cannot test out a course of action. When that person thinks of doing so he or she becomes paralyzed by overwhelming feelings of panic, of the threat of complete loss of control, of a possible eruption in rage or violence or of a premonition of abject failure. Encouragement is not enough. Neither is an understanding of the roots of such feelings in one's past. I see that those feelings are expressions of processes that lie deep inside all of us. They are central to what makes us tick, for both better or worse. I see that to deal effectively with them means understanding the basic elements of how we function as human beings. That is a subject I will deal with at length later on in the chapter "Where Creativity, Courage, Initiative, Dynamism, Achievement and Self-Fulfillment Come From." In that chapter I set forth a new explanation of such a process, an explanation I utilize to help people understand and deal with such paralyzing feelings.

The end of a helping contact, seen in the above perspective, becomes obvious: It is when one has gotten what one spelled out at the very beginning that one wants for oneself in one's living. I set forth that endpoint because very often people who have come to me have at the onset no clear idea of when to end. It is as though the helping contact can go on and on endlessly. That lack of clarity is revealed in questions that people have asked me during the course of a helping contact. "Am I getting better? Am I improving? Am I making progress?" It was as though they thought I had a special knowledge of what real progress was, an understanding beyond their own comprehension. My answer to such questions was that a person will know instinctively if there is such progress. For he or she will experience the unqualified success in getting what is wanted. There is no need for my judgment on that score. At the very end of a helping contact there is nothing left to talk about. One has gotten what one wanted. One feels great. It becomes self-evident to that person that it is time to stop.

There are three important elements which I have come to see ought to be part of the ending of a helping contact. The first is the idea that a similar problem is likely to arise in the future. In such situations one should recall what helped in the helping contact to deal with that problem, to remember what one learned about oneself. The second is the reassurance that one can always return to talk over any concern. Even those who seem totally confident on ending have let out a sigh of relief and have said, "I'm so glad you said that." I see that relief as understandable since one is now on one's own without the continuous support one previously had. However, despite such reassurance it is rare that a person has come back. The third is for me to ask the question, "What helped most in our contact?" I feel it is extremely important to know how a person I have helped experienced what helped. I have often been surprised at the answers I have received. They remembered a remark I had made which I had forgotten or they pointed to some trait of mine that impressed them or they pinpointed an incident in our contact that I did not attached great importance to. Such knowledge has greatly sharpened my own understanding of what people have needed from me.

How long does helping take?

Some professional helpers think it is possible to provide effective helping in a predetermined limited number of sessions such as, for example, six sessions. The underlying reason for such an approach is the need to save time and money for both those giving help and those receiving help. The idea is to focus on one or another problem which seems to be central to a person's difficulty and resolve that problem quickly.

For me, this approach and the reasoning underlying it are untenable. As I see it, the approach I have set forth moves as fast as one can and does limit a contact to the shortest possible duration. To set an arbitrary cut off point is to place an unreasonable pressure on both parties and to cripple helping. What then emerges is, in my opinion, at best only a superficial helping contact.

CAN EVERYONE BE HELPED TO TURN THEIR LIVING FROM THE WORST TO THE BEST?

Many might well wonder whether the approach I have set forth can, indeed, help all those with psychological or psychiatric difficulties who need help. Much as I would like to give a categorical "yes" answer to that question, I cannot. What I can do is give the answer I believe is right and make clear why I see it is important to hold such a belief until it is disproved.

I would like to believe that everyone might be helped to turn one's life completely around to get the best out of one's living. The importance of such a belief lies in the consequence of seeing things that way: Every person in need ought to have an opportunity to get such help and get it along on the lines I have set forth. In those instances where I have failed in my helping efforts I would like to believe that someone else could have done a better job.

I set forth that opinion because it seems to me that far too many professionals are not willing to exert themselves to such a great degree, that they are unwilling to invest so much of themselves in such a helping effort. It is, in such instances, easy to rationalize that some people, because of their nature or their kind of difficulty are beyond such a helping effort. Even more distressing for me is the approach of many of my psychiatric colleagues who set in medications on the basis of a particular diagnosis without any helping effort along the lines I have set forth. In both such situations I see that one gives up on a person without even giving that person a reasonable chance to turn his or her life completely around.

SHOULD MEDICINES BE USED IN SUCH AN APPROACH?

The use of medications in professional helping is both generally accepted and in wide use. Such medications — known as psychopharmaceuticals because of their effect on one's emotional state — are seen by many professional helpers as offering a distinctive advantage. It is felt that by relieving distress, such as severe tension, they greatly enhance the possibility of an effective helping dialogue. I strongly disagree with that point of view.

Such medications *are* usually effective in relieving distress but the price paid, in my eyes, is the undermining of the helping effort. For I see that such distress has a special, positive, value. It is a warning signal and an impetus to action. It is a warning signal in the sense that it tells a person that there is something distinctly wrong with how he or she has been living, something which ought to be faced, tackled and dealt with. It is an impetus to action because the need to relieve such distress provides the powerful force which drives us to significantly change our lives for the better. Taking away that distress by the use of psychopharmaceuticals also takes away the drive, impetus and determination needed to change our lives to get what we truly want out of our living.

It is clearly possible to effect a helping dialogue in the face of extremely distressing symptoms — if one does so in line with what I have described as the ABCs of Successful Helping. Such distress, greatly troubling as it is, can almost always be lived with if one has a clear idea that there is a good, workable, way of being rid of it.

When one utilizes medications, it is far too easy to end up in endless discussions without any significant change in a person's life for the better. The fact that such medications do provide relief confuses people. One imagines that the dialogue of helping goes hand-in-hand with such relief, a wrong assumption. There is the appearance of improvement without any substance; one remains still basically dissatisfied with one's life. It is an easy way out for both that person and that helper: It is as though one can turn one's living around with a minimum of emotional effort.

There are two situations where I would say that the use of psychopharmaceuticals is justifiable. The first is in an acute situation in which the distress is so completely overwhelming that any attempt at a dialogue fails. In such instances emergent relief is needed. However, I feel it should be time-limited to a few days at most. Otherwise there is a great risk that such medication will never be stopped. The second is when one has given up completely on any form of dialogue along the lines I have laid out. Unfortunately such instances do occur. Relief of symptoms in such instances does, at least, make life more bearable.

Medication should be only a last resort — and not a first resort as it far too often is. It seems to me that people in severe distress should have the chance to get the kind of help I have set forth without the use of medications. Far too often people are not offered such help. Instead they are put on medications at the very start and then find it almost impossible to stop with such medication out of fear that their distressing symptoms will return full-blown.

Is THERE ANY ADVANTAGE IN SEEKING HELP FROM A PSYCHIATRIST AS COMPARED TO OTHER PROFESSIONAL HELPERS?

It is assumed by some people that psychiatrists, because of their high status and their special training as physicians, ought to be better qualified to help people in distress than other professionals. I do not agree. I see that what makes for a good or bad good professional helper is independent of one's specialty background. It is solely dependent upon one's mastery of what I have already set forth as the ABCs of Successful Helping. I do see, however, both advantage and disadvantage in seeking help from a psychiatrist.

My medical training has given me two advantages. First, it has given me a detailed knowledge of somatic difficulties. That has been useful because psychological and somatic difficulties are often closely interwoven. In such instances it is important for me to decide whether those somatic difficulties are part of the psychological difficulty or an independent condition. Furthermore, people I have helped have often been troubled by somatic conditions. My medical background has helped me advise them as to whether or not the medical care or treatment they are getting is good or bad.

The second advantage is that psychiatrists in their training are required to work in psychiatric hospitals and to take responsibility for those with the most serious of difficulties. Other professionals often have had little or no such experience or responsibility. It is not uncommon that other professional helpers will not take on individuals who are diagnosed as suffering from a psychosis. It is common to refer such difficulties to psychiatrists. I find that approach unfortunate. I see that to understand and help individuals it is necessary to have worked with those who are most in need, those worst off. For, as I noted earlier, it is an understanding of how to help those in the worst of states be rid of their distress that is the key to knowing how to turn life around for people in general.

There is, to my eyes, one clear disadvantage in seeking help from a psychiatrist. The specialty as a whole has been moving increasingly away from a psychological orientation and increasingly towards a biological orientation. The risk is greater today that a psychiatrist will approach his work on the basis of making a diagnosis of mental illness and of utilizing psychopharmaceuticals — to the detriment of what I see are the basic principles of successful helping.

HOW DOES ONE HELP A PERSON WHO HAS NOT VOLUNTARILY SOUGHT HELP SUCH AS THOSE FORCED INTO A MENTAL HOSPITAL, CORRECTIONAL INSTITUTION OR PRISON AND THOSE COERCED INTO SEEKING HELP BY COURTS, SCHOOLS OR PROBATION AUTHORITIES?

There are three reasons for raising this question. The first is that there is a great deal of pessimism concerning the possibility of helping such individuals. Many see a self-evident need for help but feel that it is often almost impossible to make such helping work. The second is that it concerns a great many people. It concerns, in part, the parents of children and youth caught up in such situations, and, in part, the families of adults similarly caught up in such situations. Those parents and families are greatly worried about the future life of such children, youth and adults. The third is that it is difficult to recruit professional helpers for such work and those that are so engaged are often greatly frustrated in their helping efforts. For these three reasons I see that what is needed is a clear idea what is good and bad in such helping. I would thus like to share my own experience and my own optimism gained over many years of such work.

The basic problem is that almost everyone forced or coerced into such situations feels that he or she is being unjustly punished. That problem is usually ignored by potential helpers. They assume that if they are well-meaning and show a personal interest a person will respond to their efforts to offer help. Such efforts are usually rebuffed. Their questions are ignored or dismissed. If pushed that person will respond, "I don't need help. I don't have any problem." In such a situation it is easy for the helper to give up, to imagine that that person is beyond helping. What that helper does not realize is that he or she is seen as being part of a world outside that person which is oppressive and punitive.

Seen this way, the initial helping step should be to disassociate oneself from that world. My way of doing so is to say something such as this, "I know you don't want to be here, that you feel you are being punished unjustly. I want you to know that I have nothing to do with that. My aim is solely to get you out of that situation. I want to help you get the authorities off your back.

I am 100% on your side. If you don't believe me you can test me out. What we talk about is strictly between you and me; it does not go any farther."

In the context of force and coercion, it is important to keep in mind that a person feels greatly hurt by what has happened. He or she has lost command or control over his or her life. That is belittling. The helper is seen as part of a system that forcibly controls him or her. Without recognition of such a reaction, a helper's efforts to bring forth what is troubling that person are seen as condescending, as though coming from a person whose position of power makes that person superior. That is the reason why such efforts usually engender belligerence, anger and suspicion. The way I have found to deal with that problem is to assume that that person is in good part right in justifying his or her actions that led to being in a mental hospital, correctional institution or prison or being coerced into seeking help by the courts, schools or probation authorities.

It might seem strange to assume that such individuals might be right. Yet to me it is self-evident that they have their own reasons for their actions, reasons which make good sense to them. What I see is right is the motivation for what they have done, if not the means. People use narcotics because it effectively relieves the unbearable desperation in their living; some turn to prostitution because it is the only way to get the large sums needed to buy narcotics; people steal because it seems like, for the daring, the quickest way to get the money they want; kids truant because school is boring and other activities are exciting; others are boisterous and disturbing because they want attention and recognition; still others rape because it is a way to get sex and prove one's manliness; people have their own good reasons for extreme suspiciousness, feelings of being persecuted, for wild activity, for outburst of uncontrollable anger. Such a list could go on and on. Those forced into a mental hospital see themselves as being rightfully distressed about what has been happening in their lives — and not as being mentally ill and in need of treatment.

Such a perception about the rightness of a person's motives comes from being able to put oneself in the shoes of such persons. I ask myself why I would do such things. If I can do just that it is easy to find qualities in those persons which I can admire. It seems to me that most potential helpers do not see the need for putting oneself in those persons' shoes nor the need for liking and admiring such persons. That would seem particularly so when crime or craziness is concerned. But I see that perception is what is necessary as a precondition for helping. I see that it must be voiced. I say, "There are a lot of things I like about you [I name them]. I think you have your own good reasons for doing what you did. I would very much like to hear them."

Such an approach usually works. It opens the way for the special kind of friendship I see as essential for successful helping. Despite such a positive groundwork a person might find it difficult to put into words his or her reasons for what he or she did. In such a situation I try to pinpoint a good beginning by saying, "Tell me how you got into this mess." The person in question does recognize that he or she is in a mess, that he or she doesn't want to be in the present situation. That kind of opening leads to the question of how that person can avoid the same thing happening in the future. Such reasoning usually strikes a responsive chord — even with those who cannot see any reason for their being forced into their present situation. They can understand that all who act on the same motives as they have had don't end up being coerced. They can understand that somehow they have failed to convince others of the understandable motivation for what they have done. Those kinds of questions provide a good kick-off point for helping. If things get this far I see it as important to say right out, "I want you to know one thing. My only aim is to help you get what you want out of your living."

It is important to discriminate between that person's motives and means. A helper ought to question such means for they have been ineffective. That is what a person needs help with, that is what has gotten that person into his or her present situation. For those forced into a mental hospital that questioning means looking together at that person's ways of thinking or acting which others see as disturbing. That means helping a person get a new perspective on how others see his or her actions. It does not mean justifying the point of view of others.

For those referred because they are considered delinquent, pre-delinquent or criminal such questioning often means that the helper must be able to put himself or herself into an environment in which such behavior is often the rule and not the exception. That was often the case when I worked in Harlem. I often found myself in the position of trying to help a person be deviant — an exception — to how most others led their lives. It meant learning how life on the streets actually was.

An event long ago in my work life seems to me a good illustration of that last point. I worked part-time at the Manhattan Rehabilitation Center, one of several such Centers set up by the New York State Narcotics Addiction Control Commission. That particular Center was the only one for women. There were places for over 800 women. It had the character of a prison in that it was locked and had strict rules about permissions and visiting. But it had an array of rehabilitative activities and programs that made it less puni-tive than a prison. A person convicted of a narcotics-related crime, almost always involving heroin, could chose between being sent there or to prison. Most chose the Center. As the only psychiatrist there at that time I had to make an assessment of every new woman admitted. Otherwise I had free rein to develop a program after my own interests. One activity particularly interested me.

That was as co-leader of a therapeutic group which met once a week and had seven or eight participants. My co-leader was a man who had had a nar-cotics problem himself, was wise to the way of the streets, but had no special training in such helping work. He was liked and respected by the women in the group. The event that made an impression on me was when one young woman began to justify her innocence about being committed in a way that all the others knew immediately was false. My co-leader attacked that ex-cuse aggressively and all, including the woman concerned, recognized that he was right. I saw that I did not have the street knowledge to do the same; I saw that I had a good deal to learn on that score.

In the end, then, the problem of helping those forced or coerced into such situations boils down to helping them get what they themselves want in their loving friendship, learning, work, idealism and private life. It is clearly not possible to help all such persons. For many have either given up on that score or have found that the way of thinking and acting they have developed is enough for them. Nevertheless, I see that the approach I have set forth of-fers a different and promising way of helping those who do want such help.

WHAT IS PSYCHOTHERAPY?

Psychotherapy has become commonplace in everyday living. It is not at all remarkable to hear a person say "I'm in therapy" or "I'm seeing a therapist." People know without thinking that one is talking about psychotherapy.

What that means is that a person is getting help for oneself by seeing a specialist regularly for discussions. However, beyond such a sweeping generalization it is very hard to pin down just what psychotherapy is. For it covers almost every conceivable aspect of such discussion-based helping. Furthermore, it is even harder to pin down what is good or bad psychotherapy.

For me, the key to making that distinction is to make clear why I do not use the terms "psychotherapy" and "psychotherapist" but instead use "helping" and "professional helper." Psychotherapy as practiced today has usually been an obstacle to effective helping. Emphasizing the goal of "helping" does away with that obstacle.

Psychotherapy was once an invaluable pioneering concept. It summed up the idea that one could help another with serious psychiatric or psychological difficulties by a listening-to and talking-with approach. My own approach to helping stemmed from what I saw was of great value in different psychotherapeutic approaches. What happened after that fruitful beginning was a result of attempts to refine psychotherapy as a special and specialized discipline. The two parts of the term "psychotherapy" — "psycho" and "therapy" — came to literally mean the treatment of psychological conditions. That is what I see as the source of the problem with psychotherapy.

"Therapy" is a medical term meaning special treatment techniques to deal with pathological conditions. The "psycho" part of "psychotherapy" is extremely vague. It refers to any troubling condition considered to be psychological in nature. The result of such a way of looking at helping was that psychotherapy usually came to mean the use of complex techniques to treat conditions that were themselves so complex that understanding their nature required a highly specialized schooling. It was not uncommon to develop a special language for each different psychotherapeutic approach to explain such complexity. The result of such presumed complexity was that far too often psychotherapy in practice became a convoluted intellectual exercise distant from the basic elements of how to effectively help people in distress.

It was as though the psychotherapist had some profound knowledge of a person's complex psychological processes that could not easily be put into everyday words. An understanding of the severe difficulties of people and the means to deal with them was something beyond the comprehension of ordinary people. It was as though a person had to blindly trust that the psychotherapist's knowledge of such extremely complex factors would bring forth the self-understanding needed to relieve his or her distress. The result was that such self-understanding became a perpetual and unreachable goal. That, to my mind, is a major reason why psychotherapy so often could go on and on endlessly. I saw that to make helping work what people needed was a clear and commonsense idea of what was taking place.

For me, the term "helping" offered just such an idea. People could easily make sense of the idea that one person can help another in distress by listening sensitively to that person and by talking together about how to tackle that distress. It avoided any implication of mysteriousness or incomprehensibility or pathology. For me, it offered a concreteness and down-to-earthness which present-day psychotherapy usually does not offer. There was, however, a benefit to using "helping" which transcended even that great advantage.

In the previous chapter, "The ABCs of Successful Helping," I set forth my perception that there are three basic principles which underlie *all* effective helping between two individuals regardless of whether or not such helping is offered by a professional helper. Such situations would include what happens between a parent and child, a husband and wife, two friends, a teacher and a student, a work supervisor and a subordinate, a sports coach and an athlete. Seen this way, the word "helping" was just the right word to connect what I was doing as a specialist and what people in general do. It made clear my view that there is a common core in all effective helping. That point of view was the direct opposite of the idea that a professional helper's expertise lay in special treatment techniques which had nothing to do with how people in general help each other.

I saw that my own expertise was something people needed when their own efforts to help themselves or another were not good enough, when the helping problem seemed beyond them. If my helping was better than theirs was, it was because I had made it a full-time occupation, because I had refined it by constant trial and error, because I had exposed myself over and over to the many different facets of helping — and not because it was in essence different from what they did. The difference was between what an amateur and a professional does in any endeavor. Both use the same basic principles but the professional has refined a higher expertise by making that endeavor into a life's work. Seen this way, what the professional helper has is a refined knowledge of how people in general can help each other.

This way of thinking was central to making a connection between my work as a psychiatrist and the needs and living of people in general. It put into a new light the nature of my expertise.

CHAPTER 7. THE EXPERT IN LIVING

Why and how do people get trapped in the worst aspects of living? What underlies the different problems that a psychiatrist has to deal with? How can one explain the cause of such difficulties? It became increasingly clear to me that I had to have good answers to those questions if I were to know just what my expertise as a psychiatrist was.

For my job was to help people be rid of those difficulties. That is what was wanted from me as an expert. But to help people be rid of those difficulties I clearly had to have a good idea of what caused them. There could hardly be an elimination or a reversal of those difficulties without some idea of what led to them in the first place. Put more pointedly, I saw that the only criteria of the worth of any idea of causation was whether or not it served as the basis for the elimination or reversal of such difficulties. An idea of causation, seen this way, was clearly central to defining my expertise as a psychiatrist. However, coming up with such an idea left me facing a formidable problem.

For a psychiatrist's expertise was generally considered to be an ability to make psychiatric diagnoses — and there were hundreds of psychiatric diagnoses. It seemed to me that those psychiatric diagnoses included every conceivable difficulty of human beings, from the slightest to the severest. Modern psychiatry was not limited to its original concerns with the diagnoses of psychoses and neuroses. It now encompassed a great sweep of the distresses, handicaps, shortcomings and failings of people. Alcohol abuse, narcotics abuse, persistent stealing, starving oneself, overeating, every imaginable fear, problems in achieving an orgasm, sexual deviance, over-activity in children were just a few of the difficulties encompassed, each of which warranted a special psychiatric diagnosis.

The questions facing me were these: Did each diagnosis identify a discrete condition with a specific cause and specific approach? Or did each broad diagnostic category that comprised a number of diagnoses indicate a specific causation and a specific approach? Or were there a combination of causes and approaches underlying different diagnoses or diagnostic categories? If so, how did such causes and approaches combine? Without good answers to those questions it would be impossible to define what approach would eliminate or reverse such difficulties. The great problem I experienced in confronting those questions was that no diagnosis gave any idea of causation or reversal. They were all simply descriptive.

The criteria for making a psychiatric diagnosis were that there had to be several symptoms present in combination and a characteristic story of their development. It was assumed that such a composite picture represented a distinctive psychiatric condition. Originally those conditions, each bearing a psychiatric diagnosis, were called mental illnesses. It was assumed that one would eventually find, as with medical illnesses, a cause for each illness. Now such diagnoses are called mental disorders. That development only obscured for me any idea of causation. Mental disorder was, for me, a catch-all, nebulous term. It simply meant the opposite of a mentally ordered state — whatever that might be. Furthermore, it was of little help that psychiatric diagnoses were grouped together into broader categories with such designations as substance abuse disorders (alcohol, narcotics, tobacco etc), schizophrenic disorders, paranoid disorders, affective or mood disorders (such as depression), psychosexual disorders, anxiety disorders. For there was still no idea of any specific causation underlying those broader categories. It was as though a psychiatrist's expertise stopped at being able to place a given difficulty into a special descriptive category. All in all, I felt left up in the air.

To make matters worse, as previously noted, it was rarely possible to make an unequivocal psychiatric diagnosis. Symptom pictures widely overlapped. Indeed, many psychiatric diagnoses were combinations of several diagnoses. For example, the diagnosis "schizo-affective disorder." Thus, it was not surprising that experienced psychiatrists differed greatly in making diagnoses. My conclusion, then, was that psychiatric diagnoses were arbitrary and artificial categories. They did not identify discrete conditions. They gave no clear indication of causation and an approach to elimination or reversal. I came to see that the whole idea of psychiatric diagnoses was a dead end. In the end, then, I found myself having reached what seemed like an inevitable conclusion: Psychiatric diagnoses were of no use to me in defining my expertise as a psychiatrist.

I was left in a quandary as to what my expertise as a psychiatrist was. I was distinctly dissatisfied with the many different theories put forth about causation. The theories about biological-genetic causation were all speculative since they did not lead to any measures that eliminated or reversed any condition. Psychological theories to explain what underlay different diagnoses were invariably far too complicated for me to utilize in practice. Attempts to combine ideas of biological and psychological causation also did not lead to any approach that would eliminate or reverse a given difficulty; they seemed to me like well-intentioned but meaningless efforts to straddle an impossible divide. There was no teasing apart the biological from the psychological elements of causation. Finally, and most importantly, none of those theories fit with my idea of turning the worst of living into the best of living.

I found myself going in a different direction. I had worked with a wide range of the difficulties psychiatrists deal with. Since I saw that the helping principles I had arrived at were effective in reversing all of those difficulties, it seemed clear to me that there must be one common causative factor underlying all of them. Defining that factor would be essential to defining my expertise as a psychiatrist.

That causative factor was desperation in living. I saw that people came to psychiatrists or to psychiatry because they were at an extreme of desperation. That is precisely how they felt. That is what they needed help with. It was that sense of terrible desperation which disappeared when they received the help they wanted and needed. When that happened their different symptoms disappeared.

Such an idea of causation made good sense to me. For a sense of extreme desperation in living was what people revealed to me when they could confide in me. They did not seek help because they felt themselves mentally ill or sick or suffering from some kind of strange disorder. I saw that the word desperation best summed up the combination of frustration, anguish, futil-ity, distress and despair that one experiences when one's living seems com-pletely blocked, seems at a dead end.

The idea of desperation in living offered a great advantage when I tried to understand causation and reversibility. For it was self-evident, at least to my eyes, that desperation in living existed on a sliding scale. It could be mild, it could be intense, and it could move in degree in both directions. It was thus reversible. It arises when we feel thwarted in trying to get what we want out of our living — and there is always something more that we want for our-selves in the future which is difficult to attain. Such desperation disappears when we get what we want.

Seen this way, desperation is part and parcel of living. Everyone has ex-perienced it. It is not as though severe desperation is something confined to those who are supposedly abnormal, ill or disordered. I came to see that our ability to get the most out of our living depends upon how we have learned to deal with desperation.

I saw that desperation only became a psychiatric problem when people felt that they could not deal with it, when it became overwhelming. That was what underlay the worst states in living. At the extreme of despera-tion there is suicide. One gives up completely. Just short of that, though, is craziness. One retreats into a fantasy world of one's own making. One tries to wall oneself off from everything that hurts so painfully. Thus, I could see that my expertise as a psychiatrist began with knowing how to help those at the extremes of desperation, those nearest suicide and those walled off in craziness.

Before reaching such extremes, though, desperation reveals itself in dif-ferent ways, in tension, fears, depression, rage, abuse of alcohol, narcotics, tobacco and food, outbursts of violence. I could see that underlying the dif-ferent symptoms that bring people to psychiatrists was an attempt to deal in some way with a sense of one's desperation in living. Later on, in Chapter Nine, I will set forth my idea of why and how desperation takes different forms.

Looking at desperation this way brought clarity to what my expertise was. My job was to help people find the resources within themselves to deal with their desperation. It was to help people experience the great wonder in living. That was the key to reversing the severest difficulties of people. That was the key to turning the worst of living into the best of living. The very basic elements of our living were at issue.

I came to see that the expertise which I and other professional helpers shared was an expertise in the art of living.

It seemed to me that I had arrived at a good idea of both the cause under-lying the most serious problems in our living and the help which is needed to deal with those problems. Desperation in living was what we all have to deal with. The kind of help we need from another person is based upon three ba-sic principles of helping. People share a common problem in living and share a common need for helping. We need help from experts only when despera-tion becomes extreme and when the helping efforts of others have failed.

Seeing things this way gave simplicity and clarity to what I was doing. It was difficult enough helping another in extreme distress but at least I had a clear idea of what was needed in my efforts. That simplicity and clarity offered another advantage of immeasurable value. It served as the basis for my efforts to help others who, in turn, would help others. Thus, it gave me a good means of helping parents who would help their children. It also served as the basis for even more indirect helping.

With such clarity and simplicity in my teaching and supervisory efforts, psychiatrists and psychologists in training could easily grasp and utilize what I was saying. Much later on, after I had moved to Sweden, such clarity and simplicity was of great help to me in being able to reach people effec-tively despite my working in a new language. Finally, it was just that clarity and simplicity which was essential for my project in prevention. That was the means I had at hand to make my idea of helping understandable to and utilizable by personnel without any training in psychiatry or psychology.

I had clearly arrived at an important conclusion about the nature of my expertise: My way of helping others was an art form — not a science. Such expertise depended upon just who I was, what I had experienced in my life and how I communicated my ideas.

The good psychiatrist or professional helper was akin to the good parent and the good teacher. Success in helping, parenting and teaching depended upon just who was doing it. My guidelines for helping underlie success in all three endeavors. What is more, everyone has the capacity to be good at help-ing, parenting and teaching — if those general guidelines are followed.

That point of view is the direct opposite of a scientific approach. In a scientific approach, there are hard and fast rules to follow which would insure success. In that view, there are helping techniques or treatment measures that lead to success regardless of who utilizes those techniques or measures. That is not my view. There were no hard and fast rules to follow that will insure effective helping. What determines success is solely the personality of the helper.

Such a distinction is of paramount importance. There is a prominent, if not dominant, point of view not only within psychiatry but also within psychoanalysis and psychotherapy that those specialties are sciences, sciences that are evolving rules and techniques which would insure success if properly applied.

Telling examples of such blindness to the art of helping can be found in the numerous studies which have attempted to show — or prove — the effectiveness or lack of effectiveness of psychotherapy or psychoanalysis. Results for two groups of people with similar problems are compared, with only one group receiving the specified "help." Much attention has been given to developing scales measuring effectiveness and the statistical comparability of such groups. But almost none of the studies makes a distinction between good and bad helping, nor do they define what is good or bad in helping. The end result has been many studies that seem to show effectiveness and just as many studies which seem to show the opposite. One could believe whatever one wanted to believe.

For me it was self-evident that how each of us develops during our living depends upon the distinctive personalities of those who have helped us along the way, our parents, close relatives, friends, teachers, coaches, bosses. We would have gone in another direction if we had been influenced by different people. The very same applies to the psychiatrist, psychologist or other professional helper we might meet up with. I see that to deny the unique and determinative effect of the specific encounter between a professional and the person he or she would help is to deprive oneself of the expertise needed to help another person.

If there are basic guidelines underlying all successful helping, what, then, is special about the expertise of the professional helper? These are the attributes of such expertise:

- The professional helper can see a continuum between the worst and the best of living.

Because the professional works with those at the extreme of desperation he or she has a clear idea of what happens as that is reversed — and also a clear idea of causation, what moves desperation to an extreme state. He or she has the ability to see optimism when others see only pessimism.

- The professional helper can see that hidden behind the worst-appearing, most frightening, states of human beings there are fine qualities which can be mobilized and brought forth.

The professional is not put off, intimidated or repulsed by the features of extreme desperation but can see that within each is the kernel of a distinctive positive quality: within craziness is creativity, within rage is courage, within panic is initiative, within violence is dynamism, within hopelessness is achievement, within self-destruction is self-fulfillment. How those connections are made will be dealt with later, in Chapter Nine. Here, the point I would make is that the professional can see the hidden, fine, attributes a person has — the beauty each person had as a small child and still has — while others cannot. He or she can see the resources for success in living while others can only see the signs of failure.

- The professional helper can see the worst of states and the continuum between the worst and best within himself or herself.

Because the professional is confronted constantly with the need to look at the desperation inside himself or herself, he or she knows instinctively: how to show affection for a person who is desperate, how to put himself or herself in that person's shoes and how to bring a sense of equality to the give-and-take of the asking for help and the giving of help. Others are not confronted with the need to constantly look at how they handle their desperation. That is why helping those who are most desperate is difficult. The professional has sharpened an expertise by using himself or herself as the tool of helping.

How does one acquire those attributes? Where does the knowledge come from that makes a professional helper an expert?

When people have trusted me, they have let me into their innermost, private, world. They have shared with me — usually as with no one else — their feelings, thoughts, hopes, desires, ambitions, resolves, fears, frustrations, contradictory impulses. In this way I learned about the depth and breadth of the human experience.

It became clear to me that that inner world was where my prime focus as a psychiatrist was. For that was where our resources to deal with living lie. That is where our desperation is found. That is where we react to everything happening to us so that we move either towards the best or the worst of living. For those reasons I saw that knowledge of that inner world was basic to my expertise as a psychiatrist. It was that knowledge which led me to an answer to the question I raised at the start of this chapter: Why and how do people get trapped in the worst aspects of living?

I could see what it was that fed into our inner world that made for the worst or best of living. It was a matter of the ambitions, desires and hopes we have for ourselves. I could sum all that up in one word: the rewards we seek in living.

For it seemed to me that the idea of rewards in living best describes the goals or ends that move us, both in our day-to-day living and in our long-term living. The idea of rewards gives a concrete focus to what we want out of our living. It pins down just what the wonderful life we want is. And — as I came to see things — it was the *nature* of the rewards we seek in our living which made the difference between experiencing the worst of desperation or the great wonder in our living.

There are real and false rewards in living. What traps us in desperation is a futile pursuit of false, unfulfilling rewards in living. What gets us out of that trap and makes for the great wonder in living is the pursuit of the real rewards in living.

Chapter 8. The Real and the False Rewards

Living can be looked at in six fundamental spheres: loving, friendship, learning, work, idealism and a private life (a term I use to include leisure, recreation and times when one is alone).

Those spheres can overlap, for instance when one's work is of a clearly idealistic nature. Nevertheless, there are real and false rewards distinctive to each of those six spheres of living. When my helping efforts were successful, an idea of such real and false rewards became clear.

For when a person gets a clear idea of what one ought to be getting out of a given pursuit and goes about getting that, he or she becomes filled with a great new enthusiasm for that aspect of his or her living. One sees it as meaningful. One talks, for example, about meaningful work, meaningful studies, a meaningful marriage, a meaningful friendship. One knows exactly how that feels. Meaning conveys an idea of living that is rich, rewarding and wonderful. That kind of reward in any one of the six spheres of living could sustain a person throughout an entire lifetime. That reward is part and parcel of the best of living.

In contrast, it is not at all difficult to understand what a person means when he or she speaks about meaninglessness in such areas as work, studies, marriage or friendship. Meaninglessness conveys an idea of living that is empty, devoid of real reward and of any wonder. One's living is experienced as superficial. The rewards one gets out of those pursuits are at best only fleeting. That was the usual situation which individuals who came to me wanted help with.

My aim in this chapter is to make clear what I see are those real rewards which bring a sense of fulfillment to our living and to contrast that with what I see are the false rewards which undermine our living.

LOVING

Getting the best out of loving gave rise to a host of serious problems people needed help in dealing with: extreme jealousy, sex without loving, sex without pleasure, difficulty in finding a partner, infidelity, the need for prostitution, a relationship characterized by bitter fighting, an empty marriage, a threatened divorce.

It came as a jolt to me one day when I suddenly realized that underlying almost every psychiatric and psychological difficulty I have had to help adults with — including craziness, paralyzing tension, depression, narcotics abuse, psychosomatic difficulties, violence and obesity — was the problem of getting the best out of loving. Sometimes individuals suffering such difficulties did not bring forth that underlying problem until they felt they could trust me. At other times it was right out in the open. And in many other instances that was the reason why they sought help. It was a realization of the great extent of that problem which led me to see why it was both the most central element in our living and the most difficult one to deal with.

I could see why loving was so important in our living. Most people during early adult years look forward to a future life that will combine the best of sex, love and marriage. I see that the crucial element in that sex–love–marriage linkage is clearly loving. For when two people are deeply in love with each other they experience sex and marriage as indescribably wonderful. In contrast, when there are great problems in loving there are also great problems with both sex and marriage.

Sex, if it exists at all, becomes primarily self-gratification; marriage becomes primarily a formal contract that holds the two together. Given such a perception of the importance of loving in our lives, the next question I had to answer was why it seemed of such *central* importance in our living. For it became clear to me that the sex–love–marriage linkage must in some way be central to our living if it could underlay almost all of the severest distresses in our living.

The answer that made sense to me was that loving — more than any other aspect of our living — epitomizes what we see as adult about ourselves.

The masculine man is the epitome of the adult man. The feminine woman is the epitome of the adult woman. I saw that there is no separating adulthood and sexuality. To see that connection one need only look at youth and how at that time one tries so hard to find his or her own identity as a man or woman. Even if an idea of marriage comes later, sex and loving is matter number one for most at that time. For most that means the interplay between a young man and young woman. It usually takes a woman to make a man feel like a man and a man to make a woman feel like a woman. [Even in a same-sex relationship it seems to me that the basic problem of making one good whole of sex, loving and marriage is the same; that is, if one defines marriage as a long-time loving relationship with only one person.] Yes, one wants the pleasure of good sex. But one wants it most with a person one sees as attractive, a person one would like to share one's living with, a person one can love and will love back. One looks forward to a time when one will share the most intimate aspects of one's living with just one person. So one eventually gets married.

I've never yet seen a situation in which two people married tentatively, to try it out so to speak, with the idea of a possible divorce in the back of one's mind — even though some have claimed later on, after a divorce, that they did so. One marries with the expectation of staying married. Given such an expectation, why is it that marriage so often goes wrong? Why is it that all the problems concerning loving afflict the very rich and most successful just as much as everyone else? Why is it so difficult to make the sex–love–marriage linkage work well?

It is so difficult because there are no good rules to follow. Each person has to find his or her own way.

In contrast, there are pretty good rules to follow to get a good measure of gratification out of one's work, studies and recreation. What is involved in the sex–love–marriage linkage is the most private, most personal, most intimate aspect of our living. It is also the most sensitive, the most charged, the most difficult to deal with. Yet, it is also usually the most desired and rewarding aspect of our living.

Thus, when one succeeds in making the sex–love–marriage linkage work one's life is glorious — and when one fails one's life is a hell. When one succeeds it brings a profound sense of self-confidence as a man or woman; when one fails it brings a profound sense of inadequacy as a man or woman. It is the very nearness to just one other person which brings with it the possibility of being terribly hurt. One exposes oneself, warts and all. One opens oneself up for possible ridicule.

That, in sum, is why I see that the difficulty in making such a linkage lies at the root of most of our psychiatric and psychological problems.

That difficulty comes to a head in early adulthood. One would increasingly have not only sex but sex with a person one admires as an ideal of masculinity or femininity, as a person one sees as particularly handsome or beautiful. The problem in that regard is that such a person may easily be seen as someone almost beyond one's reach, one so desirable that one may well fail in arousing a corresponding admiration.

One would make a great impression. And the more one would impress the more one risks failing to do so. One faces embarrassment — and the more desirable the other person seems the more potential embarrassment one faces. Given the desire to impress that person, such a sense of embarrassment can easily be overwhelming in the area of sexual performance. In such a situation it is easy to see oneself as extremely awkward, incompetent and insecure.

It is at this time that it becomes important to know the difference between the real and false rewards in loving. The primary problem — the false reward — is seeing loving almost exclusively in terms of sex and sexuality. It is as though a partner ought to be the acme of the sexual man or sexual woman — and only that.

It is not hard to see where that image comes from. It is abundantly present in popular culture and epitomized on film screens directed specifically towards youth and young adults. The hero or heroine is often superman or superwoman. There is often a game of conquest to play out: to seduce or to be seduced, the man as seducer or the woman as seductress. The culmination is sex with each other. It is as though having wonderful sex with a person who appears as an ideal of beauty or handsomeness is an end in itself, the end of the game of conquest.

Such images came up repeatedly in my work with young adults. One felt oneself terribly insecure in the face of possibly failing in such a test of one's manhood or womanhood. It seemed to me that that there were two ways of dealing with such insecurity, both of which gave rise to serious problems later on when trying to link together sex, love and marriage. One way is to play super-tough, the all-knowing and supremely sexual man or woman just like the roles played out on the film screen. The other way is to withdraw from sex and sexuality, to withdraw from testing oneself out with another person.

One eventually gets married because that is for most people the ultimate confirmation of being adult, of being a man or woman. One may plunge into marriage or back into it. Unfortunately, one often brings those same tough or passive roles into one's marriage — and they then characterize the rest of one's married life. Both of those approaches lead to the same flawed perception undermining the possibility of a good marriage.

What I have seen repeatedly is that two people unfortunately see marriage as an end in itself, as a solution to putting sex, love and marriage together — instead of as a beginning. It is as though that aspect of one's life is taken care of, is out of the way. One has achieved a confirmation of one's manhood or womanhood. One can then get on with the other aspects of one's living: career, child raising, recreation, a social life with one's friends.

The sex–love–marriage linkage becomes simply another compartment of one's busy life — and not a matter of central concern. An individual with such a perception is not ready for those problems that will arise in every marriage. One fails to see that marriage is only the beginning of something new and must be worked on, deepened, developed.

People do not fit together like two pieces in a jigsaw puzzle. There are differences in backgrounds, interests, personalities, hopes, desires and ideas of how to best bring up children. That is why problems and conflicts are inevitable. That is why one is easily hurt when differences crop up. One is not ready to deal with the problems a marriage brings with it. To deal with such problems it is usual to follow a pattern — intentionally or unintentionally — set by one's parents, the marriage one knows best. Unfortunately, that is too often not a very good example.

When I say that marriage is only a beginning I mean that there is a need to change oneself on the part of both individuals. There is a need to compromise, a need for give and take, a need for tolerance, a need to give up some of one's own identity and the strong beliefs that identity is built upon. Above all, there is a need for tenderness towards one's partner.

That need is most necessary at those times when one feels hurt or wronged by one's partner. Easier said than done. It is far easier to see that need for tolerance and tenderness as a problem for one's partner rather than for oneself. It is far easier to be angry rather than to be tolerant and tender.

All of which can make the matter of living together every day of one's life, at the very least, a trial. So one may well back off from the marriage. One throws oneself into those other aspects of one's living noted above: one's career, raising one's children, managing the home, one's recreational interests, one's social life. The two then live mostly side by side — instead of together. Then comes the realization that there is something terribly important missing. Marriage has become hollow, it is a marriage mostly in name only. Even if one may still be fond of one's husband or wife, far too often such fondness rarely comes forth. It is taken for granted. There are arguments, usually voiced but sometimes unvoiced.

Sometimes a truce is made. More often the marriage is marked by open conflict. When one feels criticized and attacked, there is a strong impulse to answer in kind, to counter-attack. That makes things worse. For each knows very well the other's weak spots. So each hurts and feels hurt. Not so seldom, sex becomes an issue.

I have heard repeatedly from men that when they come home from a hard day's work they want sex as both relief and gratification; they feel that one's wife should understand that. On the other hand, I have heard repeatedly from women that one's husband's only interest is in sex, in pleasing himself; they feel that one's husband should understand how weary she herself is after struggling with her own jam-packed day. Often that kind of battling relationship is the only thing that holds the marriage together. It is as though even if one battles constantly that is better than the aloneness of not being married.

In such a situation it is not surprising that there is almost no linkage between sex, love and marriage. One may seek escape in extra-marital affairs, prostitution or pornography. It's not what people really want but it's seen as better than nothing. There is some momentary gratification. There is also some sense of confirmation that one is truly masculine or feminine. Most often the profound lack of fulfillment in one's loving saps one's energy in every other aspect of living: work, friendship, recreation. Often the dam breaks for one partner or the other and there is divorce.

What, then, is a better alternative? Such an alternative hinges on how one defines the real reward in loving.

As already noted, when there is good loving, sex and marriage take care of themselves. One doesn't need or desire sex with another person. One also knows that the marriage is solid. When there is good loving, the gratification far outweighs the compromise needed to make a marriage work. To make a marriage work well, then, it is necessary to have a good, clear idea of what is the best in loving. Granted that there is no perfect loving and no perfect marriage, if one at least has a good clear idea of what the ideal of loving is, that is half the battle won. At least one knows where one wants to go. I have my own idea of such an ideal. It came from two sources: first, from seeing marriages that did work well; more importantly, it came from my efforts to help people caught up in marital strife to get what they wanted.

The essence of loving at its best is the most intense, the most private and the most exquisite sharing of living that can take place between two individuals. There are three aspects of that sharing which make loving uniquely rewarding in our living. Those three aspects are sensual, psychological and social. Those three aspects define, as I see it, the real reward in loving.

Good loving is sensual: It is the joy of uninhibited sex in which the pleasure in giving surpasses even the pleasure in taking.

Such joy is found in the exquisite sexual pleasure which two people, drawn to each other as though by an intense magnetic attraction, can give each other. There is a mutual giving and taking between two individuals who see both themselves and their partner as beautiful, desirable and admirable. Each brings to such sex a pride in his or her own masculinity or femininity. They share an intense desire to please and be pleased by such another person, to arouse and be aroused. Each helps the other in doing just that.

Such sex lets one become, once again, a child. It lets two adults play together, experiment with each other. Such sex brings with it a special freedom: the height of spontaneity, of letting go. It is as close as one can come to a purely emotional experience. It is the opposite of being composed, in control, presentable, intellectual, achieving. When this aspect of loving works well each person reinforces the other's self-appraisal as being a beautiful, desirable and admirable man or woman.

Here are some of the hang-ups that prevent people from getting the most out of the sensual aspect of loving: They don't see themselves or their partner as a beautiful, desirable and admirable man or woman; They see sex as taking, pleasing oneself, rather than also giving, pleasing another; They don't see the need to help the other in sex; They see sex in terms of expert performance in which they fear failure, fear making a fool of oneself; They are unable to shed the mantle of being adult — being in control, competent, well-adjusted — and to go back to the playfulness of childhood and its experimenting, daring, abandon; They assume that, instead of sexual desire and enjoyment being mutual, a man must convince or compel a reluctant woman to have sex; They see sex in marriage as a duty or obligation connected only with having children and often imagine that loving can be fine without sex; They see sex as something dirty or lascivious, still heavily tainted by sex without loving — as in the utilization of women, prostitution, rape and pornography — and not something which fine, beautiful, people indulge in; They make no effort to appear sensual, sexually attractive, beautiful.

That last point needs amplification since I see that there is no separating the sensual aspect of loving from one's perception of beauty in another. Too many people imagine that beauty lies in one's facial features or body build, elements one is born with and which cannot be changed. Thus, it is easy to see oneself as irredeemably unattractive, not beautiful. One puts oneself down, feels inferior.

In contrast, I see that beauty stems from one's personality, how one sees and feels oneself as being masculine or feminine. It is reflected in how one carries oneself, speaks, smiles, looks, dresses, takes care of one's body, does one's hair. Those features, though seemingly superficial, are simply the outward reflection of how one sees oneself as a sexually attractive, beautiful, man or woman. That, to my mind, is why everyone has within oneself a special beauty and sexual attractiveness. Fortunately, different people have different ideas of what is beautiful. Also, fortunately, roughly half of the marriageable population is looking for a special, beautiful, partner in the other half.

Good loving is psychological: It is the strongest form of encouragement, understanding and good advice which two people can give each other in dealing with their respective lives.

Such encouragement, understanding and good advice comes from the trust, respect and admiration each has for the other. It is those three qualities which insure that one can open up completely about one's most sensitive, private and embarrassing self without fear of being ridiculed, condemned or belittled. One can, then, get the encouragement, understanding and advice one needs at those times when one is insecure, self-doubting or crushed by events. One can accept criticism from one's wife or husband because one knows instinctively that such criticism is meant solely to help, not to hurt. We need such criticism because we are all blind to the worst aspects of ourselves. We all need insight into that part of ourselves. Such criticism helps us to both bring out the best in ourselves and to deal better with the worst in ourselves.

What, at bottom, makes the psychological aspect of loving work well is that there is a sense of equality between the two, neither sees himself or herself as superior or inferior as a human being to the other. Each respects and admires the special qualities, wisdom and attributes of the other. When that respect characterizes loving, each person feels a great pride and pleasure in the accomplishments of the other. One knows that one has been a part of those accomplishments. There is in the psychological aspect of loving an interdependence which fosters the independence — the self-confidence — of each person in the rest of his or her living, in one's work, recreation and social life.

Here are some of the hang-ups that prevent people from getting the most out of the psychological aspect of loving: They don't see each other as equally admirable, rather one feels oneself superior or inferior to the other; They cannot trust each other completely and cannot open up about private, sensitive matters and get help with those matters; They are constantly on their guard against being hurt, ridiculed, put down; They see criticism from one's husband or wife as hurting rather than helping; They are unwilling to compromise on their convictions, instead there is constant battling on that score; They see themselves in constant competition as to who is best and are jealous, not pleased, at the successes of the other.

Good loving is social: It is that unique sense of solidarity which exists between two individuals when they know that they are side-by-side in facing the wider world outside them.

Such solidarity comes from an unquestioning loyalty between the two, one far exceeding other loyalties. It insures that they will stick by each other through thick and thin. We need that loyalty when we are confronted by all the different kinds of difficulties that can happen in our outer worlds of work life, contact with authorities, friends, extended family. There are pressures, confrontations, criticism, sometimes attacks. There is no over-evaluating the strength and comfort derived from knowing that one is facing such difficulties with the support of another who believes in one unquestioningly. Despite differences of opinion and even conflicts one knows that when important matters must be confronted in their outer world they can rely on each other completely. Loyalty to each other is paramount.

The need for such loyalty is particularly relevant in facing one insidious and highly harmful difficulty from that outside world. That difficulty is the well-meaning advice of family and friends who are critical of one's partner. When two people have a strong sense of comradeship they automatically reject such criticism, they defend one's partner. When there is such loyalty one does not bring one's private complaints and conflicts to the ears of such people. Those complaints and conflicts should be worked out in face-to-face dialogue. The social aspect of loving makes for a unique kind of friendship; one may have many friends and find different assets in each but this one friendship and its rewards are far beyond all the rest.

Here are some of the hang-ups that prevent people from getting the most out of the social aspect of loving: There is little sense between them of a loyalty which supersedes all other loyalties; They cannot count on each other in time of need, help is at best reluctant and given out of a sense of obligation; They are just as likely to take the side of an opponent or attacker assuming that what is called for is some presumed distance, impartiality and objectivity; They don't see any special friendship between themselves but seek that primarily from others outside the marriage; They complain bitterly to close friends and relatives about their marital conflicts, get support for their implied condemnation of their spouse and thereby perpetuate the undermining of the marriage; They turn to others for encouragement, understanding and advice, instead of to each other, thus breeding jealousy and mistrust.

If I were to sum up in a single word the heart of good loving in all its three aspects it would be: *fun.* That means fun in simply being together, talking together, doing things together, laughing together, sharing living together, having sex together. That simple word conveys the down-to-earth nature of what pleasure is and should be. It puts in a nutshell the great emotional reward of loving. A marriage should be fun. If it's not that it's simply empty responsibility.

The following three examples are meant to give an idea of how I have made use of the above idea of the sex–love–marriage linkage to help people.

A young man in his mid 30s came to me because he felt he had no social life at all, was tense and depressed about his social isolation and felt that with others he had to keep up a facade of false pleasantry. He had a responsible mid-level executive job and was actively engaged in sports and music. He had had one short-lived affair with a girlfriend. She had taken the initiative to it and then broke it off leaving him crushed. He felt that she was far more knowledgeable than he was about sex. He did want to meet someone but felt himself too unsure of himself to do that. He wanted advice on what to do.

It seemed to me that he, first of all, needed a word of honest praise from me. I said that it was clear to me that he was well-liked by others in his work, that he was very effective there, that he was highly accomplished in his different sports activities. I made a special point of noting that I thought that I saw him as handsome and attractive to women. On one occasion, at my suggestion, he brought in his musical instrument, played for me and was clearly pleased at the praise he got. We talked about women he might like to meet. There was one woman at his work he thought was very attractive. He was afraid to approach her, fearing rejection. I encouraged him. I said that in my opinion one must take chances in living, must risk failing, must test oneself out. We went over what he might say in approaching her. I said that it is not so important whether or not he succeeds. It is important that he dares and tries. If he does, he will eventually meet someone who likes him as much as he likes her. The most important thing is to realize that good loving between two people is not simply a matter of sex and sexuality but of sharing life and having fun together.

He did try. She was clearly flattered and said so. But she already had a steady boyfriend. He did not feel rejected. Rather he felt proud of himself and of the initiative he had shown. He approached other women. He began to have an active social life. His tension disappeared completely. He was pleased with his life. After we had stopped we happened to meet by chance on the street. He was with his fiancé. He was clearly both proud and pleased to introduce her to me. I heard later on that he had gotten married and was doing well.

I was contacted by a diplomat who was in the midst of a severe marital conflict. He and his wife battled continuously. He was in his 40s, she in her 30s. He wanted a divorce and his wife refused to consider that. Both had been married previously and her young son lived with them. They came to see me together and I saw them, first, separately.

It was clear that there was almost no affection left between the two of them. He had given up completely on the marriage but felt he wanted to avoid a bitter divorce proceeding. Her focus was solely on his not taking his responsibility as a husband. That is what they battled about. It seemed to me that she clung to him and to the prestige of his position as though marrying a person of such rank was a mark of her own accomplishment. She agreed that the marriage was now empty, that there was little left of it except each taking the social responsibility of husband or wife. She was clearly worn out by their fighting and did not know what to do. She wanted my opinion.

I said that I agreed with her, that the marriage was an empty one and I could understand how terrible she felt about that. Nevertheless, I could see a bright future for her. I considered her very attractive and said so. I said that she would have no trouble finding someone else if that was what she wanted. I said it was far better to look forward to a long-lasting marriage in which the core was a high degree of loving and sharing between two people than remaining stuck in a marriage where those elements were, and had been, so clearly missing.

She realized I wanted the best for her in her future life, that I was not taking sides with her husband in what I said. That was why she could accept what I had said. She seemed obviously pleased, encouraged and grateful. She then saw no point in either the fighting that wore her out or in the marriage itself. Her husband appeared greatly relieved. There was distinctly less antagonism between them. They both felt that they had gotten the help they wanted.

A couple came to me because they were constantly fighting and were afraid that they were near a divorce. They had two small children. There was no longer any sex life between them. She was decidedly more dominant and highly critical of him. He was more passive and evasive. It seemed that they both had backed into the marriage.

Initially I worked with both of them and then only with him. I tried to help her be more tolerant of him, to support him and to curb her criticism. I tried to help him take more initiative in his family and work life. Although we discussed different aspects of their lives, my main focus was on how they could start from scratch, enjoy life with each other and spend time alone together without the children. Over several months there was a marked improvement.

I still recall vividly a telephone call I received from him some time after we had stopped. He wanted my advice on a matter concerning his work. He spontaneously added that he was very thankful for was my insistence on their getting a babysitter. At first it had seemed to them that such insistence exaggerated what was essentially a trivial matter. They originally put up many roadblocks: it was so difficult to find a babysitter, it would cost a great deal, they were each so busy with other things that they would hardly have time to spend together in the evenings, let alone take a vacation together. Finally, I had to put it to them bluntly: If they did not have time to have fun together, I saw that there would be little chance of saving the marriage and helping them get what they wanted out of it. I was greatly pleased that that message did come home to them.

The idea that at the heart of a marriage is two people who have great fun together has been brought home to me repeatedly in my work in helping children.

What children need, first and foremost, is a sense that there is solidity and stability in the home. When that is present they grow up with the security which fosters self-confidence. And, to my mind, there is nothing more important to a sense of solidity and stability in a family than living with two parents who clearly have fun together, who enjoy each other, who laugh together.

I had long ago come to the conclusion that the single most important factor contributing to most of the psychiatric and psychological difficulties of children was a lack of such solidity and stability in the home. Children sensed a constant undercurrent of tension and dissent between their parents. There was nothing that took the edge off such tension and dissent. They did not experience that their parents enjoyed each other's company, that they had a great deal of fun in simply being together. Such a situation bred a lack of self-confidence. In contrast, when there was a large measure of obvious pleasure and fun between parents there was a decidedly more relaxed atmosphere in the family. There was give-and-take. That was what gave a family solidity and stability. That was what bred self-confidence.

When I have worked with parents I have tried to help them see the logic of such a perception. When they began again to have fun with each other the atmosphere in the family invariably changed dramatically for the better. For that spirit is catching. Their children pick it up. There would then be a great improvement in the well-being of their children. All of which raises the question: How does one help two married people who are terribly split apart, sometimes near to divorce, find such fun and love together? In my work I have had to face that question countless times.

The key is to help the two start all over again from the beginning. It is to rekindle the spark that once brought them together. I take it for granted that there was once such mutual attraction in almost every instance, that they did not choose each other at the start with a gun pointed at their heads, that they did not have to marry, that they did not have to marry just that person. Over the years, though, that initial spark is often covered over in mutual re-crimination and defensiveness. Each sees the marriage primarily in terms of fulfilling one's responsibilities as a husband, wife and parent.

I talk with each parent separately to bring forth that original remembrance — and then make clear that it ought to be worthwhile to give one last good try to see if one can blow new life into that original attraction. The best way to do that is to take a vacation together, without children or friends and without any of the responsibilities of one's usual daily life. Invariably the two have not taken a vacation alone in years — if they ever did so. It was as though getting married was the end of such sharing.

That idea of a vacation together might sound simple. It rarely is. At that point, one or the other or both usually point to those pressing, essential things that simply must be done in one's work or in one's social obligations or in one's parental duties which mean postponing — usually forever — such an attempt. It is as though both have grown so used to living at arm's length that they are afraid of any effort to upset that balance, hope might well turn into disillusion.

The only answer I have to such resistance is to make clear that making their marriage work has to be priority number one for both — or else they ought to forget about making anything better of it and of helping their children. If they accept that idea, I make it clear that there should be only one thought in each person's mind during such a vacation: to please the other one, to make one's husband or wife laugh. In short, to have fun together.

When that is so, there is no great trick to making the sex–love–marriage linkage work well.

When two people in love get tangled up in bitter dispute, they both ought to be able to suddenly step back, laugh at themselves and realize what great fun they could be having instead of fighting. After all these years I can still remember way back from my early psychiatric training at Harvard how that sage professor of mine, Elvin Semrad, put it so pithily: There is nothing quite so wonderful as making up with your wife after a terrible argument..

FRIENDSHIP

There were two ways in which problems about friendship came up in my work.

First, there were problems which individuals brought up themselves — invariably as a side issue to more urgent concerns around loving, learning and work. Such problems included: Feeling isolated, having no friends at all; Having only superficial friendships with no really close friend whom one could trust and confide in; Feeling inferior to others who seemingly were so popular that they had many good friends; Being ostracized from, or victim- ized by, the dominant youth group.

Second, there were the problems of children and youth who were referred for help by their parents, the schools, police or the courts because of a con- cern about friends who were considered a bad influence. That often meant being in a delinquent gang. What was seen as a bad influence was truanting, the use of drugs, fighting with other gangs and involvement in crime.

It was out of my efforts to help individuals deal with both those kinds of problems that I came to see what the real and the false rewards in friendship were. Central to that perception was an understanding of what happens dur- ing the time of transition between childhood and adulthood, what happens during one's youth years. For at that time of life friendship plays a pivotal role in determining every aspect of the character of one's future adult life.

At that time one is physically capable of living on one's own. What one needs is the confidence that one is ready to deal with living on one's own. It is just then that one needs most urgently a clear image of oneself as an inde- pendent individual capable of shaping one's own future life. I came to see that how one comes to see oneself during that transition time crystallizes to a major degree one's future orientation to loving, friendship, learning, work, idealism and a private life. One makes critical decisions at that time about one's future life in all those spheres of living.

That is a tall order. It is as though one is taking a giant step between the sheltered living of childhood and the complete independence of adulthood. One would break away, one would stand on one's own. One needs emotional distance from the intimacy of the family, an intimacy unavoidably imprinted with the superiority of one's experienced, mature parents and the inferiority of one's own self as being inexperienced, immature and a child. And because that is usually such a giant step for youth it requires a large measure of courage.

Friendship with those one's own age makes for such courage. It does so because such friends are keenly aware that they are in the same boat. They are keenly aware that they share the same challenges, ambitions, problems, frustrations and potential pleasures in the areas of learning, work, loving, free time and idealistic commitment. What gives friendship such power at that time of life is that it is usually much easier to deal with all those matters together with same-age comrades rather than alone.

Such comradeship is built upon having fun together. There are a whole raft of activities and interests that make for such shared fun. In addition, no small measure of that shared fun is the pride and pleasure one derives from identifying with those elements of the youth culture special to each new generation: its clothing, music, entertainment, dancing styles, recreational pursuits, food preferences. Those elements set one apart from one's parents. It is just such a bedrock of shared fun and shared identity which makes it possible for same-age friends to support each other in facing common problems. I think that is the source of their courage.

If friendship makes for such courage, that courage is reinforced many times over in a gang of friends [I use the term "gang" without any negative implication; it was the best term I could find to convey a sense of the strong bonding among a group of youth; in contrast, "youth peer group" seemed to me too intellectual and too pale a term].

Being a part of such a gang adds to friendship that heightened sense of strength which comes from sharing a solidarity with a number of fast friends. There is an even stronger sense of a common identity. There is often a special group identity characterized by a unique name and distinctiveness in dress, hair style and language. What one would find difficult doing alone or with one or two friend becomes far easier with a gang of fast friends. Thus, there are group exploits, adventures, pranks, feats of daring. There are contests and sports competitions. There is the pleasure of enjoying together concerts and films. In all that there is a bonding within the friendship gang which gives it a great power to influence the lives of its members.

I saw that the friendship of one's youth years determines in large part how one sees oneself as an adult and how one, later on, relates to other adults.

One's perception of oneself as an adult is inseparable from how one sees oneself as a man or woman, one's perception of sex and sexuality. To appreciate the importance of friendship I see that it is necessary to look again at the central role and singular difficulty of sex and sexuality during the youth years.

That matter is the single most important issue at that time. One strives to appear, and to be, masculine or feminine. One does one's best to learn the unwritten rules of how to behave, to make headway, to consummate sex. For youth, sex is invariably the most exciting, the most challenging and the most difficult aspect of one's life. It holds out the promise of great pleasure but is surrounded by the strictest of taboos. In approaching sex and sexuality it helps enormously to have the support of one's friends of the same sex. That is a major reason why one's closest friends and gang members are usually of the same sex. One goes out together to dances, parties and on dates. There is in such friendship a sense of shared brotherhood or sisterhood. I saw that out of that experience emerges an image of what is masculine or feminine.

That image plays a distinctive role in determining the character of one's future behavior as an adult man or woman. Because of the great power of friendship in the life of youth such an image can markedly reinforce, alter or displace the image of masculinity or femininity set by one's parents. It is just such an image which determines in large part how one later on deals with loving and marriage.

Of equal importance is the influence of youth friendship in determining the character of one's relationship with others later on in one's adult years. How one learns to make and be friends as a youth provides the basis for both one's future adult friendships and for one's future way of cooperating with others in group endeavors.

Such group endeavors are an integral part of one's educational life, work life, recreational life, social life and, if one is politically or religiously engaged, one's idealistic life. In those different group endeavors there is invariably a need for teamwork. Such teamwork depends upon how individuals feel towards each other. It was clear for me that a sense of friendship and comradeship plays a major role in the effectiveness of such group endeavors and the gratification one derives from such effectiveness.

The friendship one experiences as a youth sets a basic frame of reference for one's participation in adult group endeavors in the following ways:

- It sets the criteria for being an insider, on the fringe, or an outsider of the group
- It sets the character of leadership and decision-making
- It sets an attitude towards working together with those of the opposite sex
- It sets the limits of what is tolerated and what is not tolerated in thinking and behavior
- It sets the means for resolving conflicts.

Friendship during youth clearly is a central factor in defining adult maturity and adult interrelationships — for better or worse. It was essential to know what one should be getting out of friendship, its real reward, that which makes for the best of one's living. I saw it as equally essential to know how one's perception of friendship can be self-defeating, the way in which a false idea of what is important in friendship leads to meaninglessness in living.

The same prizing of toughness that underlies meaninglessness in loving also underlies meaninglessness in friendship. One admires and strives to appear strong, powerful, willful. Those features come together in an exaggerated image of masculinity or femininity, an image of superman or superwoman. That such an image should also characterize friendship during youth years is not surprising since, as I see it, the need to crystallize one's sexual identity is central to both loving and friendship at that time.

I see that there is nothing wrong in wanting to be strong, powerful and willful. Those attributes are necessary to face and deal with the difficult and critical decisions in the transition from childhood to adulthood. The problem arises when those attributes so dominate friendship that it becomes, in essence, one-dimensional. Those who appear toughest are most admired, most desired as friends. One looks up to those who seem toughest. One would emulate such toughness. It is as though all other personality attributes pale in comparison. It is as though the main reward from friendship is a confirmation that one is super-tough. When that happens one finds oneself living up to a pretense.

For such toughness is far over-exaggerated, it is a caricature of courage and confidence. It is bravado. It is as though one has to continually play a role of being super-tough, a role which denies that one has any doubts, weaknesses, difficulties, insecurities. There is an emptiness in such role-playing for both those who play it and those who are impressed by it. For when I have worked with those who seem so super-tough they say that it is mostly an act, that others expect it of them, that even if they get admiration from others there is another troubling, insecure, side of themselves which they must not and cannot reveal. And those who would emulate such a super-tough role do not see the emptiness behind it. They see that their only difficulty is a lack of toughness. They see that their own doubts, weaknesses, difficulties and insecurities are marks of gross inadequacy as a human being.

To understand the harmful effect of such toughness it is necessary to understand how toughness can permeate the youth friendship gang.

It would seem to be a universal phenomenon that youth form friendship gangs. At the nucleus of such friendship gangs are those who are most popular, most admired. Being a member of such a gang usually brings with it the recognition and status of popularity. Such membership may foster the best of friendship — or it may foster the worst of friendship. That worst of friendship stems from friendship gangs that are built upon a hierarchy of toughness.

Leaders are those who appear toughest, strongest, most manly or womanly. There is then a descending order down to those at the bottom who are weakest — except for those who are so weak as to be excluded. The base of the gang is power. There is a pecking order from those at the top who are most powerful and have the ability to dominate others down to those at the bottom who are subservient. There is an authoritarian structure with little tolerance for deviance. What that structure does is solidify a wrong idea of what is desirable in friendship.

Toughness is equated with superiority. Lack of toughness is equated with inferiority. There is no sense of being coequals. There is a fear of showing weakness and sensitivity or a need for help from others. One keeps one's inner self to oneself. There is no room for dissension, for free discussion. The prime focus is on feats of daring.

In such a friendship gang one derives gratification from identifying with strength and power. But there is no feedback from such friendship that can help one with one's insecurity, particularly one's insecurity about sex and sexuality. Questions concerning learning, work and idealism usually have lowest priority. One thus gets little help on those important issues.

Such gang membership fosters two paradoxes: One gains solidarity with others but is left isolated: One is a hero when with the gang but a coward without it. Such solidarity and heroism leave the individual friendship gang members poorly equipped to stand on their own and to act independently.

That combination of solidarity and heroism often need to be continually reinforced by acts of aggression or violence. Such acts are needed to prove that the gang is just as tough and superior as it imagines itself to be. Thus, there may be mobbing of those who appear weak, inferior, alone, different or dissenting. There may be thefts, vandalism, gang fights and gang rape. It is as though for some youth the confirmation of being truly super-tough is gang violence and, especially, gang violence combined with sexual assault.

Even those outside such youth friendship gangs are often greatly influenced by its image of toughness. For in many schools and neighborhoods such friendship gangs consist of those who are seen as most popular; it is a mark of prestige to be a member. Even if one is not accepted as a gang member one can, nevertheless, emulate such toughness.

The serious consequences for one's adult life of such an image of toughness is an emptiness in three areas: in one's self-perception of maturity, in one's friendships, in one's relationship to others in group endeavors.

One's adult self-perception is that of being super-strong and super-competent, a person without weaknesses. One lacks self-criticism, difficulties are the faults of others. Since one cannot accept one's possible inadequacies, one cannot face or deal with them; one lives with a constant sense of unexplainable frustration. Sensitivity and tenderness are marks of weakness and inadequacy.

Such a self-perception is particularly harmful when it comes to making one good whole of sex, loving and marriage. For, as I see it, making that good whole is built upon just such sensitivity and tenderness. What happens instead is that one separates sex from love and marriage. The result is that there is no gratification in loving and marriage. Instead, intentionally or not, men use women and women use men. For the tough man, a woman is primarily a source of sexual pleasure. For the tough woman, seduction of a man is the path to wealth, status or security. There then follows for both the persistent undercurrent of bitterness and disillusion already described in the section on loving.

A self-perception of being super-strong, super-competent and without weaknesses carries over to one's adult friendships — with the same negative effect. One seeks friends with the same self-perception. Just as in youth years one cannot open up about one's private life and get help from others. One's friendships are superficial. One is forced to maintain a facade of cheerfulness, conviviality, small talk and "everything going well," even when there is little feeling for any of that. One cannot really trust others, cannot let down one's guard. One may have many acquaintances but no truly close friends.

Friendship groups are often hierarchies of power based upon popularity with a descending list from high to low status. Often such friendship is seen as something to be manipulated, the underlying thought being, "What can he (or she) do for me?" Or there is suspicion: "What is it he (or she) wants from me? What is behind his (or her) friendliness?" Missing from such friendship is a sense of the affection and the admiration one wants from others. One does derive a sense of solidarity — but little else. Worse still, such solidarity often adds to one's difficulty in loving or in marriage. For one often seeks companionship with others of the same sex as an escape from such difficulty instead of confronting and dealing with it.

Experience of the super-tough youth friendship gang seriously undermines one's participation in adult group endeavors.

- If one has been rejected by the dominant youth gang, one perceives oneself as an outsider even later on, as being alone and not acceptable; one does not easily fit into group endeavors.

- If toughness has been combined with a disparagement of the opposite sex — such as in exaggerated machismo or feminism — there will be an undercurrent of severe conflict in mixed groups; such an undercurrent will make cooperation impossible, will undermine the effectiveness of the group and will thus bring to one's participation in such groups a profound sense of frustration instead of gratification.

- If one has been part of an hierarchical, authoritarian, youth gang built on toughness, one is used to dominating or being dominated. One then has no tolerance for dissenting opinions or for dialogue as the means of resolving conflicts. Such a situation quashes individuality and the individualistic contribution that each individual can bring to a group endeavor. There is no development of one's self-confidence. There is no effective teamwork and the gratification that comes from experiencing oneself as an important member of one well-integrated team.

Why is it that an exaggerated toughness is often so highly prized in youth friendship?

It seems to me that being tough, dominant and aggressive is often highly prized in society itself. Youth pick up such an image from their parents, teachers, recreational leaders, police and, through the media, from political, industrial and military leaders.

Of particular importance is the teacher and recreational leader. Both deal with children and youth in a group. Those groups are natural settings for developing childhood and youth friendships. The teacher and recreational leader set the ground rules for group participation. Whether or not they chose to be, they are the adult leaders of these groups. And, if they have strong personalities, they are usually looked up to and their perception of what is desirable in a person is absorbed.

They are often looked up to as a counterbalance to what is experienced with one's parents. The closeness within the family exposes the child or youth not only to the finer qualities of one's parents but also to the other side, the side with warts on, the side that makes for temper outbursts, irrational demands, indecisiveness, distance and all the other less desirable aspects of a person. It is often that children and youth imagine that adults outside the family don't suffer from such flaws. For what an adult reveals within the intimacy of the family is usually not what he or she exposes to others. The end result is that the strong teacher or recreational leader, seemingly flawless, is not only looked up to but has a profound influence on how those in the friendship group see each other.

What those adults communicate, intentionally or otherwise, are qualities in children and youth that they prize most. Unfortunately there are such adults who favor those who seem strongest. In this way their attitude fosters a preferential group hierarchy of toughness in the classroom and recreational setting.

That attitude reflects a widespread prizing in society of those who seem powerful and tough. There is often a tacit disdain in public life for those who appear weak, flawed, dissenting or sensitive. It is usually difficult for youth to see that such an image of power and toughness is often a pretense, that behind that pretense is insecurity and emptiness. Such an image is particularly attractive if there is little real reward in other aspects of one's living, in one's learning, work, family life, recreational life. That is so whether or not one is well-off. But that lack of real reward is often overwhelming in poverty ghettos and particularly black poverty ghettos.

During my years of working in Harlem it became clear to me that youth friendship there was often built upon shared acts of violence, thefts, destruction of property and the use of heroin. There was a thrill and instant gratification in those activities. Part and parcel of that thrill was the idea that what one was doing was daring, a test of courage, a disdain for danger, a mark of super-toughness.

However, even if such violence, thefts, destruction of property and use of heroin were less prevalent among those who were more well-off I saw that the underlying problem of chasing after a false reward in friendship — the confirmation of one's toughness — was the same. The difference was only superficial. In my working with youth who were more well-off I found among many the same need to appear super-tough with the same deleterious consequences for one's self-perception of maturity, one's adult friendships and one's participation in group endeavors.

The superficial difference could be traced back to the social conditions of growing up in Harlem: Work opportunities for other than menial jobs were scarce; Educational incentives were poor and instruction was usually characterized by deadening rote; Recreational facilities and instruction were inadequate so that pick-up sports — usually basketball — were the prime recreational outlet with the strongest and toughest players being most popular. In sum, there was in Harlem far less of a socially acceptable outlet for one's energy and a far greater need to turn to violence, thefts, destruction of property and the use of heroin as a confirmation of one's toughness, of one's masculinity or femininity.

That situation led to a problem in my work that I had not anticipated, a problem that made me acutely aware of the power of the youth friendship gang.

Many boys and some girls were referred to the center where I worked because they were disruptive in class and insolent towards teachers. Very often I could help those students deal with the classroom situation and with their teachers so that those problems completely disappeared. The student, his or her parents and the teacher were then greatly pleased with that result. But I was not.

The problem was that I knew that that student was not studying and not learning anything in school. The majority of boys went through school in that way and were given a diploma for simply attending school. Far more girls did study, did pass tests and did graduate with a legitimate diploma. It seemed to me that the main reason for that difference was that there were far more good jobs available for black women than for black men. Thus, the incentive for studying and getting a diploma was greater. However, long after my work in Harlem I came to a better understanding of why I had failed, an understanding that had to do with youth friendship.

I came to see that to get a student involved in learning I had to help him become a deviant from most other boys his age. He had to go against the dominant attitude towards studying and face possible rejection, derision and mobbing. Studying did not go with toughness. I usually failed in that effort. I saw that situation as testimony to the great power youth friendship wields. In almost all instances a boy's parents wanted him engaged in his studies but their influence was usually not strong enough to counteract that power.

I saw that that power was just as strong with youth who were more well-off — even though less apparent. It was less apparent because for most such youth attractive work opportunities were within reach, education facilities were better and organized recreational activities were available. That made it easier to channel one's energy into such socially acceptable pursuits. Nevertheless, such opportunity did not sure insure that there would be a great enthusiasm for studying, work or recreation, that those pursuits would bring a meaningful engagement, that youth would not bond with one's friends in an image of super-toughness. What I found in my work was that there often was an emptiness in one's learning, work and recreation and that, as with those who were poor, one turned to friendship and its super-tough image of masculinity and femininity to escape from that emptiness. The problem I faced in helping — how to get the best out of friendship — was the same.

Toughness as the basis for friendship is a distinctly greater problem with boys and men than with girls and women. Toughness fits better with the male image of machismo. It is more tempered in the female image, which usually has a greater emphasis on softness and warmth. That might be because women traditionally have been far more involved in child rearing. It also seems to me that, as a result of that difference, it is easier for women to find close friends whereas men are more isolated. Despite such a possible difference, girls do sometimes form friendship gangs that are built upon a hierarchy of toughness. Even if there is usually less violence than with boy's gangs, there can be mobbing, fighting, thefts, excessive drinking, the use of narcotics and the making of quick money through prostitution.

It took me years to appreciate the great importance of friendship in our lives and to gain an insight into how it works for better or worse. In part that was because problems with friendship were rarely the reason why individuals sought help. In part that was because friendship as a cause of severe difficulties was rarely a major focus in psychological and psychiatric texts. Thus, it took me years to understand that I must bring up that matter during a first meeting with someone needing help. And it took me years to arrive at an idea of what one should be getting out of friendship to experience how wonderful it can be. The practical test of such an idea was whether it worked, whether one got what one wanted and could thereby discard what didn't work. That, then, was the basis for my perception of the real reward in friendship.

To define that real reward, I had to differentiate first between loving and friendship.

Loving and friendship are two overlapping aspects of affection, though there usually is a clear distinction between loving and friendship.

A friend who becomes a lover invariably crosses over a definite, unequivocal, dividing line — that of having sex together. More importantly, in loving at its best one's lover can be seen as one single friend whose friendship lies on a plane far above all other friendships. It is so far above that it becomes unique. There is in loving at its best an intimacy and intensity of affection which other friendships cannot approach. It became clear to me that that difference in intimacy and intensity brought different kinds of rewards to loving and friendship. Such a lessened intimacy and intensity brought to friendship three special advantages.

First, loving at its best is possible only between two individuals. Friendship is possible with many. Loving gives great depth to affection; friendship gives it breadth. In friendship one can derive great pleasure and benefit from the distinctive attributes of a number of different individuals in a circle of friends. Friendship can enrich one's life by an intimacy with those of differing national, cultural, religious and economic backgrounds.

Second, the greater intimacy and intensity of loving invariably results in severer conflicts when things go poorly. One can easily become severely entangled in such conflicts over long periods of time. It is easy to lose one's sense of perspective about such conflicts. In friendship it is easier to back off from conflicts when they arise. When one has several friends it is easier to vary the intensity of one's friendships. One can thus derive the great benefit of affection from one friend even when things go poorly at times with another friend.

Third, friendship during youth years usually serves as an essential introduction to adult loving. Friends at that time of life are faced with the same acute need. They need to know what to do when they have a powerful attraction to another person. When facing that need, it is of incalculable help if one has the encouragement of friends one trusts. It helps enormously to be able to open up and get feedback from a friend or friends grappling with the same problem. One can compare experiences. With such encouragement one dares to risk failing. And, as I see it, risking failure is the essential pathway to eventual success, the endpoint being what one would get out of loving.

What is it, then, that underlies those three advantages of friendship? What makes friendship work well so as to enrich one's life? What is, in sum, the real reward that one should expect from a good friendship?

Among truly good friends there is a sense of mutual acceptance, tolerance and esteem based upon a taken for granted assumption that they are coequals.

That, as I see it, is the real reward of friendship. That is what one should get out of friendship. If one doesn't get that there is, to my eyes, no real friendship. In such good friendship one both gives and gets such acceptance, tolerance and esteem. And doing so is of inestimable importance for one's sense of self-confidence and self-esteem.

Self-confidence and self-esteem comes from the special message conveyed by such friendship: *Acceptance* says that one is a desirable person in the eyes of others one's own age; *tolerance* gives one the leeway and encouragement to test out one's thoughts and actions; *esteem* says that one is prized for one's own special attributes.

That kind of friendship can sustain a person through a lifetime — even when there is little or no satisfaction in the rest of one's life.

Being a member of a youth friendship gang characterized by mutual acceptance, tolerance and esteem among co-equals adds immeasurably in developing a sense of self-confidence and self-esteem.

In such a friendship gang each individual has a special and valued role to play in making for group solidarity. Such roles may be that of leader, conciliator, activist, idea person, comedian, protector. One can liken the effect of those different roles to the emotional meshing that makes a sports team work well together. Each person then feels he or she is valued as a special individual. In such a friendship gang there is a confidence that one will not be ridiculed if one needs help or tries in a personal endeavor and fails. Instead, one will get understanding and encouragement. One gets commiseration at one's setbacks and praise for one's successes. One thus gets the leeway to develop one's own individualistic way of dealing with living. It is in that way that the solidarity of the friendship gang is translated into a self-confidence of each of its individual members. In such a friendship gang there is no need to constantly prove one's toughness by aggression and violence.

That kind of group experience is of incalculable advantage later on in adult years. It prepares one for working well in group endeavors in work, studies and recreation. It provides the sense of underlying comradeship which makes those groups work well. There is effective cooperation. One has learned that effective leadership does not mean dominating or steering others. There is a clear gratification in being a part of such a group endeavor.

My helping efforts were the source of the above perception of the real and false rewards of friendship. Those efforts forced me to make clear in my own mind three things: First, why individuals did not get what they wanted out of friendship; Second, what they ought to be getting out of friendship; Third, how they could go about getting just that. The test of the rightness or wrongness of the answers I eventually came up with to those three questions was whether they worked in helping individuals get what they wanted.

There were those who had no good friends. They imagined that they were exceptional, that others had many good friends, that they were inferior to those who appeared so popular. What they needed from me was a word of praise for their special qualities and the encouragement to try and make friends. They had to hear that those who appeared so popular often had no real friends. In practical terms such helping came down to discussing just whom they might like to be friends with and then daring to approach that person and not being afraid of being rejected. It was a matter of realizing that everyone needs a truly good friend and that everyone has something fine to offer another in such friendship.

There were those who felt their friendships were largely empty because they were dominated by another. It was as though they resented that domination but went along with it because it was better to have some companionship than none at all. What they had to hear from me was that they had a right to being treated as an equal, that it was a matter of respect and self-respect, that if that situation could not be changed by standing up for oneself it was far better to look elsewhere for what they wanted from a friend. They, then, needed the encouragement to do just that.

There were those who felt they had to maintain an attitude of super-toughness but had no real friend whom they could open up to and confide in. What they had to hear from me was that they had fine qualities which spoke for themselves, that there was no need to be tough to have good friends. I had to spell out what I admired in them. I had to make clear my opinion that such toughness got in the way of what they really wanted. It prevented them from getting to know another person really well. It gave them no leeway, no right to fail or make mistakes. And, if they were leaders, they had to hear from me that a good leader is one who can bring forth the best in others — not dominate others.

My helping efforts brought to my awareness a completely different aspect of the rewards of friendship. I came to see that the same rewards of friendship were basic to what happens between a mentor and a person he or she would help.

In chapter five, "The ABCs of Successful Helping," I set forth my perception of the fundamental importance of affection in the giving and receiving of help. That importance was reflected in the often expressed view of those whom I had helped that they saw me as a special friend, one whom they liked and trusted but was outside their regular life. I also saw them as a special friend. I liked them and found pleasure in the affection we shared.

To my mind such friendship was characterized by a sense of co-equality. Those I would help set the goals of helping, I offered a way to such goals; they decided whether such a way made sense or not to them. In such a give-and-take there was no talking down to a person, no condescension, no implied sense that "I am the expert and you ought to heed and respect my word because of that." I could see that such a special friendship was characterized by mutual acceptance, tolerance and esteem. I accepted them as they were, I showed a tolerance for their right to live and develop their lives as they would, I showed them esteem through my words of honest praise. They accepted me into their lives, they tolerated my, at times, poor or clumsy advice, they gave me the esteem I needed when they listened to my words of helping and utilized them.

I could see that my role in helping was that of a mentor — and that the friendship we shared was the foundation of good mentorship.

I could see, then, that between a good mentor and the person he or she would help is the same sense of co-equality and the same mutual acceptance, tolerance and esteem. The good mentor sets an example of those characteristics. That example is easy to emulate since it is what individuals want from a mentor. It was just such an example which I saw was characteristic of the good teacher, professor, recreational leader or work supervisor as mentor. That was similarly the basis of good friendship between any older and younger person.

It did not seem at all far-fetched for me to see that there is in that friendship between an older and younger person a central significance of wide-reaching significance. I could see that that was how the best of qualities of individuals are handed down from one generation to another.

LEARNING

There were two kinds of learning problems I was faced with in my work — one was right out in the open, the other was hidden.

The first kind concerned those children and youth who were doing extremely poorly in school. Some were near to dropping out or had done so. They were referred by the school, their parents or the truancy and delinquency authorities. The second, hidden, kind concerned those who were doing well in their studies. Learning difficulty was not the reason for my seeing them. The reason for their coming to me was usually a symptom which was hard to pin down: an apathy or undefined frustration in their living, a sense of constant tension, a feeling of being somewhat depressed, a physical symptom, such as stomach distress, for which no somatic cause could be found.

Only later on in our discussions did it become apparent that a problem in learning underlay those difficulties.

I came to see that those two kinds of learning problems were only superficially different. I saw that there was a common factor underlying both of them: Learning was boring. In the first instance students just quit, opted out, did, instead, what was fun. In the second instance students did what was expected of them and did that well but without any enthusiasm, they felt that they were wasting their time, that they weren't getting much out of their school work, that it was meaningless.

It was my need to help those children and youth which brought with it an idea of what one should be getting out of learning, its real reward. That was the key to turning boredom into enthusiasm. To get at that real reward, though, I first had to understand what underlay such boredom — or, as I came to see things, how a pursuit after a false reward resulted in a futility in learning.

To define that false reward it necessary to begin with how learning is usually perceived by teachers, professors and students. It is usually seen as the acquisition of knowledge. One acquires knowledge to prepare oneself for an occupation, to understand the basic elements of living and nature and to participate in society. To that end one studies mathematics, language, history, the sciences.

Teachers and professors see that their job is to present a body of knowledge as clearly and thoroughly as possible. They invariably have a course outline of subjects to be covered over the course of a term. Their aim is to get students to effectively comprehend and assimilate such knowledge. The way to such comprehension and assimilation is for students to go over the notes they have taken in class and the material found in text books until such matter is committed to memory. The measure of how well students comprehend and assimilate such knowledge is their performance on tests and examinations.

Students invariably see that the reward in learning is doing well on such tests and examinations. That is what they work towards. There is a clear measure of pride in getting high marks; there is, likewise, a clear measure of disappointment in not doing so. The reward of learning becomes, in actuality, doing well on tests and examinations. And that is what I see as the false reward in learning.

Learning seen this way *is* boring. Memorization does pay off — but it is invariably a rote process. There is little fun or excitement in doing so. There is very little enthusiasm for learning. Indeed, learning for many is often stressful in the extreme.

I saw it as unusual to find among students any burning enthusiasm to go to school. Most went as a matter of course. That was what was expected of them. They did their homework, but it was usually a chore. They looked forward to going to school primarily because it was there one met one's friends again almost every day. Learning, though obviously important for one's future work life, was secondary.

I found that the same lack of enthusiasm even characterized many university students. In a way it was even more severe. Tests, examinations and written assignments were far more difficult. Not only was the knowledge to be acquired more complicated but such acquisition was bound together with the rewards of greater future income and higher prestige. It was thus harder to quit or change course. Such a situation easily fed into a private sense of frustration that persisted even after one's studies. It was as though the reward of one's career lay mainly in income and prestige — and not in any deeply rooted enthusiasm for the substance of one's work.

A burning enthusiasm is precisely what students ought to have for learning. They ought to look forward eagerly to their studies. What, then, is the way to that end? How does one tackle that problem of a lack of enthusiasm for learning? Where does one start?

The answer to those questions came from looking at how most teachers and professors see their work and, more importantly, how they do not see their work.

As noted above, they see their work as presenting a body of knowledge as clearly and thoroughly as possible. They do not see their job as arousing a burning enthusiasm for the subjects they are teaching.

Since they do not see their role in that way they invariably do not communicate or instill any great enthusiasm for what is being taught. Indeed, they themselves often have no such burning enthusiasm for what they are teaching. That is not a requirement for their work. That is not what they experienced in younger years from their own teachers or, later on, from those who trained them as teachers or professors. If some students show a total lack of enthusiasm for or interest in learning, those students are seen as having a serious problem with their motivation. That is a problem for psychologists and psychiatrists. To my eyes, those students are simply showing right out in the open what many other students feel inwardly. They are the tip of the iceberg.

Where did that perception come from? There were three sources. *First*, it came from what students, even very successful students, told me: School was boring, sometimes horrible; teachers and professors were alright but not great. *Second*, it came from what I and my friends had experienced: There were at best only a handful of teachers or professors who made a strong and lasting impression, who instilled such enthusiasm. *Third*, it came from what teachers themselves told me during my project in prevention during which I worked with groups of teachers.

In my own experience, learning sometimes had the character of an ordeal. I remember well one particular course which, even though an exaggeration, epitomized the character of that ordeal. It was a college course in organic chemistry, a required premedical course. We learned in the very first lesson what we had to do. The instructor came in a half-hour early and began writing, in a very fine hand, chemical equations on an extremely wide blackboard. He started in the upper left hand corner and progressed until the entire blackboard was covered. We learned that we also had to come in a half hour early and try to keep up with him. When the class officially began, at 8 A.M., we all were busily copying what he had already written. And after he had finished writing we kept on writing furiously while trying to listen, at the same time, to what he was lecturing on. That experience took all the fun out of what should have been an extremely fascinating subject. And such ordeals seemed to get worse the higher I went in my education. In medical school we were at times required to learn a hundred pages or more of a textbook from one day to the next. Such experiences were intimidating, daunting, sometimes crushing. They took the excitement out of learning.

I saw that many children, youth and young adults had the same experience. That experience often instilled an aversion to learning instead of a sense of confidence. In sum, learning was made to appear an extremely difficult and daunting undertaking.

The helping problem confronting me, then, was how to instill an enthusiasm for learning when little on none was present. To do that I had to make clear in my own mind just what the real reward in learning was.

The real reward of learning is the thrill of discovery.

One searches for answers and one finds them. Underlying such searching is the core of curiosity we are all born with, that core of curiosity that is so wondrously exposed in very small children and that ought to be central to every aspect of our living during the entire course of our lives.

The reward of learning is experienced as the acme of surprise, excitement and revelation — the ah-hah! sensation — that comes with a new-found understanding which transforms incomprehensibility into know-how, ignorance into intelligence, confusion into clarity and darkness into light. For me, that sensation ought to pervade learning from the very earliest years.

Seen this way learning is easy and fun. For it should be fun to discover new knowledge, to find out what makes things tick, to learn how earlier discoverers found their own way to new knowledge. Seen this way, learning is a very private thing. It isn't an ordeal. One gets a thrill out of knowing for the first time what one did not know before. I came to see that it was the teacher's primary task to make learning easy and fun.

There is no environment comparable to the classroom for spreading out before the student the whole panorama of knowledge, all that mankind has learned up to now and what remains to be learned. What should be instilled in the classroom from the very beginning is a seductive fascination for finding out about everything imaginable. One's curiosity should be constantly stimulated — instead of dulled.

Classroom learning ought to lead one up to that point where our knowledge borders on the unknown. It should lure one into a search to discover new knowledge. It should raise questions for which there are no obvious answers.

Seen in such a light it is the task of teachers and professors not simply to communicate what is known but, more importantly, what remains to be discovered, what is still unknown. To do that one must communicate how our present knowledge came to be. For that knowledge came about as the result of the efforts of earlier discoverers, those who used their imagination to see things in a new and clearer and truer light. One ought to learn how explorers in every field of endeavor found their way to new discoveries. In that way one can also imagine oneself as such an explorer.

The above perception of the reward of learning is an ideal. It is an ideal one ought to try and make a daily reality — even if doing so is difficult. I set

it forth because learning is rarely seen in this light and thus there is little attempt to make it a reality. Indeed, it seems to me that many teachers and professors would criticize this view of the real reward in learning as being naive
idealism. Such criticism can be boiled down to these fours questions: Can
one expect most teachers and professors to enthuse students in the above
way? Or is it only the exceptional ones who can do so? Do most students
have the capacity to learn in the above way? Or is it only the exceptional
ones who can do so?

I would answer those questions about teachers and professors by asking
and answering two other questions: Why do teachers and professors teach?
What is the fun in teaching? It is not enough to say that there is no particular
fun in teaching, that it is simply a job to be done or that the reward is seeing
that one's students do well on tests. What one should get out of teaching —
the fun of it — is seeing the glint of discovery in the eyes of one's students. I
see it perfectly reasonable to expect that most teachers and professors can
bring forth that glint — if they are ready to reveal their own enthusiasm.
That doesn't strike me as a superhuman task.

What is the basis for my assuming that most children and youth can and
will respond to teaching when it is offered in this way? It came, in part, from
what I experienced in my personal life and, in part, from my work with children and youth.

I remember back when I was a youth that there were a few teachers who
obviously got such a kick out of what they were teaching that they could
enthuse an entire class. After all these years I can still remember vividly from
my high school days an event in our English class. We all filed in as usual,
took our seats and waited. After the usual bustling there came several minutes of complete silence. Miss Browder, a large imposing woman, looked
piercingly at us and then, in a high-pitched penetrating, weird screech, burst
out: "When shall we three meet again?.......Fair is foul and foul and foul is
fair, hover through the fog and filthy air." All of us were shook up. It was the
witches' preamble to Macbeth. We sat entranced for the rest of the lesson.
I also remember my college course in calculus. I can still see Mr. Breakwell,
our calculus professor, at the blackboard, building up little itty-bitty squares
into columns of different heights in sequence to explain how the area under
a given curve can be determined by a formula. He was so wrapped up in what
he was doing — almost mindless of the class — that I became wrapped up in

that too, as I think most of us were. Those and a few similar experiences led me to think that a good teacher could get an entire class of students excited about what he or she was teaching. It wasn't a matter of just reaching those who were exceptional students.

There was another personal experience that reinforced my assumption that almost everyone has the capacity to experience the excitement and challenge of learning. Over the years I came in contact with many craftsmen, such as carpenters, plumbers and other repairmen, who might be considered ordinary people since they had little higher education. I was struck by the ingenuity some of them showed in tackling problems whose solutions were far from self-evident. I was also struck by the obvious gratification they got out of discovering a new, highly personal, way of solving those problems.

Finally, I saw the enormous curiosity of my own children, when they were small, to get answers to an endless number of questions which were difficult for me to answer: What is energy? What is God? How does it feel to be dead? I had to come up with answers that made simple, clear common sense. Furthermore, I saw how they could sit for hours trying to solve a puzzle, totally engrossed in the challenge of doing that. It seems to me that most parents have also seen those characteristics in their own children. For me, such great curiosity spoke for a clear potential of children in general to experience the great wonder in learning, discovering things for oneself.

Those personal experiences laid the groundwork for my efforts to help those children and youth with problems in learning.

I came to see that my job was to try as best I could to be that kind of ideal teacher who could enthuse students. To do that I had to ask myself what was the great fascination in mathematics, history, languages, psychology, chemistry, physics, biology and the rest of what is taught in schools and universities. I did not have to know the details of those subjects but I had to communicate what I saw was the thrill of discovery in each of them.

When I reflected on those different subjects and used my imagination, I came up with what I, personally, saw was fascinating in each of them. I saw that the way to stimulate the enthusiasm of children and youth was to tie those subjects to matters they could easily grasp: the mathematics needed to build bridges and roads, the language needed to write or speak so as to convince others about the importance and value of one's ideas, the biology and chemistry needed to discover new medicines, the physics needed to make motorcycles, cars, boats and planes that work, the psychology needed to help oneself or another person when one is deeply troubled, the history needed to understand why wars were fought so as to prevent wars in the future. What all those questions had in common was the word "how." They tied learning to the practicalities of how we live our lives and how we might live them even better. They stimulated the curiosity that children and youth have about how to make good sense of things in their everyday world.

What I tried to imbue in students was the idea that learning was a very private matter. It was a finding out for oneself. It was a personal challenge to make good sense of things. One did one's best to that end. That was what mattered. One ought to get rid of the idea that learning was a competition with other students to see who did best on tests.

Such a perception was often difficult for students to accept. Their experience had told them that if they were unsuccessful in such competition they would not get good jobs, would not get into the best universities, would not have a promising career. That perception had been instilled in them by their parents, their teachers, and their fellow students. Despite that concern they could see that there might be something extremely fascinating in each of the subjects they studied. They could, in that light, see that learning might be something highly personal, that when one dug into whatever subject which interested one, one's life could be enormously enriched by such new-found knowledge.

The question that often troubled students was how to deal with the tension they felt about taking tests and examinations. To answer that question I tried to convey the rather unusual idea that the true competition we face in learning is not with others but with ourselves. It is simply to do the best one can in any given learning situation. If one is convinced that one has done the best one could do, one should not flay oneself with the idea that one failed to do better. Most students could see that such an approach was far better than getting uptight about possibly failing, about cramming at the last minute for exams, about feeling crushed if others got better marks.

I likened that idea of competition with oneself to running a race. If one felt that one had run a great race, the very best one could, there would be a great gratification in that — whether or not one won that race. On the other hand, if one won a race after a half-hearted effort such victory was a hollow one. Seen this way, winning is certainly nice but secondary.

It was gratifying for me to see that my approach to learning often worked well. When that happened it freed a student from the fear that his or her best might not be good enough. It made it much easier to do one's best. It stimulated an enthusiasm for learning. Students could see classroom learning in a different way. If they had poor teachers, such teachers, instead of being a source of anger or frustration, could be disregarded. One could find stimulation in the material being covered. If one were older one could search for knowledge in books.

My need to help those with difficulty in learning in school led me to see classroom learning in a new light. I could see a direct connection between what happens in the classroom and the most private and personal aspect of living. I could see that it was just such a direct connection that made for how each of us can experience the great wonder in our living.

How we go about getting the best out of our living — in its every aspect — depends upon how we learn from experience. Each of us must find things out for oneself. When faced with what we don't know how to deal with in the different aspects of our living we have to discover new ways to do just that. That is the private and personal character of learning. Seen this way, learning is basic to our living. And, how we go about such basic learning can be profoundly influenced for better or worse by what happens in the classroom.

As ought to be clear at this point, what classroom learning can do — and should do above all else — is to stimulate our curiosity. For it is our curiosity which impels us to find out things, to learn for ourselves. I, furthermore, saw the classroom as the setting *par excellence* to bring forth our curiosity.

For in the classroom one can be exposed to the exciting stories of how a driving curiosity on the part of individuals resulted in all the knowledge we possess today. One can see how those individuals were driven in a highly personal way by a need to find out, how they saw such finding out as adventure.

At the heart of such adventure is the challenge of moving into a new, uncharted, territory with an expectation of excitement, discovery and mastery. That, to my mind, was how our present knowledge of every subject under the sun came to be and how our future knowledge will come to be. Such a spirit of adventure was precisely what moved discoverers of new knowledge. That spirit is what should be vividly brought forth in the classroom. When that is done, I could see that it was only a short step further to see that such a spirit of adventure could characterize not only classroom learning but one's personal learning about living in all its aspects.

For such classroom learning can imprint in the student's mind that what is important in living is the adventure of finding things out for oneself, of asking difficult questions and pursuing hard-to-find answers, of letting oneself be driven by one's curiosity.

Such a spirit of adventure can act like a giant magnet in our living. That magnet can draw us irresistibly and progressively into all the pursuits of our living. Learning then becomes a compelling personal challenge to make new and better sense of all the unknown, puzzling, frustrating, taken for granted, conflict-laden or seemingly impossible things in our loving, friendship, work life, idealism, recreation, leisure life. Problems in living become personal challenges to learn how to deal with them.

The essence of learning — of finding out — is what brings forth our ingenuity to deal with every aspect of our living. I see that the great wonder in our living is realizing that, indeed, we do have within us the ingenuity to make the very best out of our living.

Work

People rarely sought my help because of a problem in their work life. Nevertheless, a serious work problem often came to the fore during the course of our discussions. Over time I came to see that how we deal with our work life plays a major role in the causation, reversal and prevention of psychiatric and psychological difficulties.

The problem that came to the fore was that people found their work meaningless. They went to work day after day but did so without any enthusiasm. Such meaninglessness could characterize one's work regardless of whether such work was of high or low social status. The importance of such meaninglessness was often not apparent because people had learned to live with it.

One might grumble about such meaninglessness but one accepted it as an unfortunate part of one's living, something one could not do anything about. In such a situation it was easy to think that one worked solely to secure one's livelihood.

That perception was in marked contrast with problems in loving. Problems in loving were usually far too painful to live with. Such problems hurt just too much. In contrast, in one's work one could function robot-like, something which was almost impossible to do in one's love life. I saw that that was a major reason why people readily sought help for problems in their love life but rarely did so for problems in their work life. I saw that that was also a major reason why it was easy to overlook the great significance which work has for every other aspect of our living.

It took me some time to realize what should have been self-evident: Given that we spend by far the major part of our adult life in our work, meaninglessness in our work life cannot but have a profound effect on our living in general.

It seemed to me that many people imagine that they can compartmentalize their living, that they can block out the effect of meaninglessness in work from the rest of their living. I saw that as an impossibility. I saw that a great and persistent dissatisfaction in one's work life would inevitably take its toll. It became clear to me that if I would help a person I would have to, in every instance, go into the details of that person's work life. When such meaninglessness was present I would have to help that person deal with it.

To do so forced me to think about the role work plays in our lives. I had to make good sense of what we ought to be getting out of work — out of every possible kind of work. I also had to make good sense of what undermines our best efforts to do so.

My point of departure had to be an understanding of the problem facing me, namely, the meaninglessness people experience in their work lives. I came to see that underlying such meaninglessness was a futile pursuit after a false reward in one's work.

That false reward is the idea that fulfillment in work comes from acquiring a greatly refined skill, proficiency or adeptness. It is the idea that such skill, proficiency or adeptness is the essence of expertise in work. One pursues such an end by great persistence, by keeping one's nose to the grindstone, by learning by heart a body of complex, complicated, ideas or techniques or routines. Expertise becomes synonymous with the mastery of complicated work tasks until such performance becomes exceedingly efficient, almost automatic, almost error-free.

The reason why such an approach is a pursuit after a false reward is because its attainment doesn't insure meaningfulness in one's work. On the contrary its attainment often leads to meaninglessness. To understand what underlies such meaninglessness — and the falseness in such a pursuit — I saw it necessary to look at how people usually make a direct connection between the social status of work and its presumed meaningfulness.

There is a commonly-held perception that those occupations or positions which have highest social status and highest prestige — those with high specialization, high pay or high power — are more meaningful than lesser occupations or positions. Typical of that perception is the assumption that what appears to be a highly complex work performance — such as that in the sciences and professions — brings with it more meaning than other pursuits which appear less complex. There is an assumption that different kinds of work are meaningful or meaningless because of the inherent nature of the work itself.

Making such a direct connection between the complexity of work and its meaningfulness results in dividing occupations into broad categories of social status: Work which is most complex is for *experts*, it has high meaning and high social status; Work which is moderately complex is for *skilled workers*, it has a modicum of meaning and moderate social status; Work of the simplest complexity is for *unskilled workers*, it is meaningless and has lowest social status. In that last category are assembly line workers, temporary workers and manual workers. The end result of such a division, though, is often meaninglessness in all three categories.

Such meaninglessness stems from the commonly-held perception of what expertise is. For how expertise is usually seen epitomizes the idea that work of the greatest complexity is the most rewarding and brings with it the most meaning. Or, more to the point, how expertise is usually seen epitomizes the false reward which underlies meaninglessness in every kind of work.

Expertise usually brings forth an image of those who have mastered either a lightning-like technique or a dazzling competence or an exhaustive knowledge of one's field. One expects that such mastery will bring with it meaningfulness. What one is not ready for is that such mastery often makes it so easy to deal with most problems that one's daily work can easily fall into a deadening routine. The end result is that, after one has acquired such mastery, there often comes with it the boredom of routine. One could almost do such work in one's sleep. There is, then, little enthusiasm for ones' daily work, little meaning in it, little reward. That difficulty is compounded by those problems for which one's mastery has no ready answers. Such problems add to the boredom of routine the frustration of inadequacy.

That frustration arises because, as one acquires an increasingly higher degree of specialized knowledge and skill, one reaches that cutoff point separating what is known from what isn't known, separating what one can deal with effectively from what one cannot deal with effectively. That situation can be particularly frustrating for the expert. For one has spent a great deal of time and effort in acquiring an advanced expertise. The realization that such expertise doesn't work after that cutoff point can be extremely disheartening.

In the face of such difficulty it is easy to back off from such problems. One does what one can do easily, almost automatically, and simply accepts without question the limitations on one's expertise. One assumes that the very difficult problems in one's work are simply beyond what experts possess of advanced technique, competence and knowledge. The unfortunate end result of that backing-off is that one finds oneself with a refined expertise but gets little pleasure out of it.

To make matters worse, there is a special difficulty which further complicates the work of experts: For those in such high status occupations it is particularly easy to become caught up in a rat race, the fierce competition to be best, to get to the top and to stay there.

Reward and success in that rat race is usually measured by the acclaim one gets from others. Such acclaim often makes for an even worsened situation. For the pride one experiences in one's work then comes from a sense of superiority over those who have not reached such heights — and not from a gratification from the work itself. Such a sense of superiority does not make up for the emptiness one experiences in one's daily work, rather it intensifies such emptiness. It greatly widens the gap between how others see one's work and how one knows it to be. Others assume that one's work is highly meaningful yet one knows that that is not so. The end result is that one feels that there is something basically wrong in one's work life, that something essential is terribly missing. What makes matters worse is that the higher the status of one's work, the harder it is to leave it, to hop off, to quit. For, then, one would not even have left the pride of having come that far. The emptiness would be even worse.

My perception of the meaninglessness in expert work came from two sources: my helping efforts and my personal experiences. In the helping situation people could reveal the emptiness they experienced in their work. In my personal experience I saw how colleagues and friends in academia and applied specialties often went about their work with a complete absence of enthusiasm.

What often makes the situation of those in expert work extremely discouraging is that such meaninglessness doesn't seem to make any sense at all. On the face of it, it would seem that after having come so high and having mastered such expertise one ought to find one's work highly gratifying, one should not find a distressing emptiness in one's work. One doesn't know why one has become trapped in such meaninglessness nor how to get out of it. One cannot see that such meaninglessness stems directly from the idea that acquiring a highly refined skill, proficiency or adeptness is the basic reward of one's work. One has acquired such facility but it doesn't bring meaningfulness in one's work.

It is just such a flawed idea of what expertise is which underlies not only meaninglessness in expert work but meaninglessness in every kind of work.

Those in skilled or unskilled work usually do not see the meaninglessness which those in expert, high status, occupations can experience. They wrongfully assume that those in such occupations are getting the meaning that they do not find in their own work.

Those in *skilled* work assume that the boredom or frustration they experience stems from the lesser nature of their work. Those in *unskilled* work assume that the boredom or frustration they experience lies in the absence of any great need for skill, proficiency or adeptness. However, in contrast to those in high status occupations, both those in skilled and unskilled work have a convenient explanation for meaninglessness in their work.

They assume that the reason for the boredom or frustration they experience is that their work is inherently far less meaningful than high status occupations. They do not see that those in high status occupations can suffer the same boring routine and frustration that they experience. The end result is that they can end up just as stuck in the meaninglessness of their work.

They too don't look forward with any great enthusiasm to their coming work day. One work day is just like another.

For many people in all three categories — expert, skilled and unskilled work — the incentive for working is solely to insure economic security and to provide the many different pleasures which money can buy. Work is seen as solely a means to those ends. One lives for the hours away from work.

One bears one's work because that is the only way to secure the income needed for living. As one grows older, one increasingly looks forward to retirement and being rid of work. One becomes increasingly burnt out.

In all that, what ought to be the secondary goal in one's work — what one earns — becomes the primary goal. Such a lack of enthusiasm for one's work takes a great toll on people. For people *do* want their work to be meaningful and they are invariably deeply troubled when it is not.

In the face of that conclusion, the practical question was this: How could I help individuals in all three categories find the meaning in their work that they want?

To answer that question I first had to find good answers to a number of other questions: Why do so many people think that the highest status work is the most meaningful and that the lowest status work is meaningless — and then find disillusion, frustration and boring routine over the whole range from high to low? Why do so many people mistakenly imagine that meaning in their work will come only after they have acquired a refined skill, proficiency or adeptness? Why is it that the pursuit of such a false reward in work is so deeply imbedded in the minds of many people?

That faulty perception of work comes about as the result of the way most teachers teach and the way most work supervisors supervise. It is the result of what many people experience during their student years and during their early years of work. That, as I came to see it, is the direct cause of the problem of widespread meaninglessness in work.

The groundwork for work is laid in school years. Learning — in its most directly utilizable sense — is preparation for work. The problem in such preparation is that the pursuit of a false reward in learning carries over to the pursuit of a false reward in work. The pursuit of error-free performance on tests carries over to the pursuit of error-free performance in work — with the same resultant boredom or stress in one's day-to-day activity. The lack of enthusiasm for learning carries over to a lack of enthusiasm for work. What most teachers fail to convey in learning is carried over to what most work supervisors fail to convey in work.

Such work supervision usually lays great emphasis on proficiency and efficiency. Work supervision means overseeing that work is done without mistakes. One is trained to perfect certain techniques or to acquire a specialized knowledge of a given field. The communication of a great enthusiasm for the work at hand is missing in such work supervision — just as in teaching.

Where does such enthusiasm for one's work come from? What should one be getting out of one's work regardless of its social status or stage of development? What is that special wonder which meaning in all work ought to bring to one's living? In short, what perception of the real reward in work could help me help others?

The real reward in work is the unparalleled pride in oneself that comes from turning one's own special creativity, courage and initiative into a unique expertise.

Let's start off by looking at small children. It is just at that stage of life when the source of our creativity, courage and initiative is most readily apparent.

When I look at small children I am struck by their imagination, daring and curiosity. I see those characteristics in their wild, uninhibited, fantasies, their lack of fear, their endless eagerness to explore. To my mind, it is just such imagination that is the source of our creativity, such daring which is the source of our courage and such curiosity which is the source of our initiative. I, furthermore, see those three characteristics as fundamental to getting the best for ourselves out of both learning and work.

For learning, in its broadest and best sense, can be seen as a continuous process of confronting and tackling all the different aspects of our living and, in doing so, trying to turn our imagination into creativity, our daring into courage and our curiosity into initiative. And work, seen from such a perspective, is simply learning which is specialized, focused and concentrated to its uttermost.

Work gives us an opportunity to dig deeper and deeper into all the mysteries, perplexities and problems of one specific area of our interest. I see that every area of work has, at bottom, such mysteries, perplexities and problems. To get the most out of work means seeing such mysteries, perplexities and problems as a personal challenge to one's ingenuity. The challenge in work, then, is coming up with our own original answers to those aspects of our work. As we do so and as we find our own good answers, we experience an inordinate pride in ourselves. We see developing in us an increasing expertise. I see such expertise as unique in the sense that it stems from the personal challenge each individual experiences and is expressed in each individual's special way of dealing with the problems in his or her work.

It is only in our work that we have the opportunity, the time and the duration to develop such a unique expertise. It is the only area of our living in which we can claim to be an expert at something. That is why I see that the real reward in work is a pride in ourselves which is far beyond comparison to that pride we derive from succeeding in any other area of our endeavor.

That definition of the real reward of work applies to all work, even to the most unskilled of work. I see that it is one's perception of expertise that can make work at every level uniquely rewarding.

The difficulty in understanding why and how that is so arises, to my mind, because of a confusion between what is skill and what is expertise. I see a clear and definite distinction between skill and expertise. Such a distinction, however, is rarely made.

It is usually assumed that expertise is skill developed to a high degree of refinement. *Skill* is usually perceived as adeptness in one's work which comes as the result of meticulous attention to and conscientious persistence in learning a body of complex ideas, techniques or routines. *Expertise* is usually perceived as the mastery of such skill until one's work performance becomes exceedingly efficient, almost error-free. The problem with such a perception of expertise is that the appearance of expertise is mistakenly assumed to be its true reward. Such a perception misses what really goes on inside the true expert.

The true expert finds a personal challenge in his or her work — the challenge to solve the mysteries, perplexities and problems of one's work by means of one's own special creativity, courage and initiative. Expertise comes with the enthusiasm to dig into all the unknown aspects of one's work and make new and good sense of that. Expertise brings the excitement of discovering one's own unique way to success in one's work.

Seen this way, the development of skill and the development of expertise may or may not go together. The sense of personal challenge that is basic to expertise may or may not underlie the development of skill. When it does, the result is a drive to develop one's skill to an ever-higher level and an unceasing enthusiasm for one's work. When it does not, one develops a refined skill but without any great enthusiasm for one's daily work and without reaching that much higher level of skill one could have achieved.

I would sum up my idea of expertise in the following way: Expertise is a characteristic unique to the individual. Expertise is how different individuals tackle thorny problems in one's work life and come up with new, different, original ways to effectively do so. It is the application of skill in one's own individualistic way. That is where I see that the true reward in work lies.

Why look at expertise in this way? My answer is that it offers a way of helping individuals who have no enthusiasm for their work and see no meaning in it turn that situation completely around. It offers a way of finding a new enthusiasm for and a new meaning in every kind of work. That is where one finds the great wonder to be derived from one's work life.

Looking at expertise this way explains for me the meaninglessness which many presumed experts experience. The skill, proficiency and adeptness one has acquired is a carbon copy of what other presumed experts have acquired. Acquiring such carbon-copy expertise, instead of being an exciting personal adventure, becomes either a monotonous routine of applying one's skill or a hopeless frustration in realizing that one's skill cannot be effectively applied.

It is the inner aspect of the individual that differentiates the true expert from the seeming expert. The true expert can solve thorny problems that appear unsolvable. He or she can do so precisely because such problems are seen as a personal challenge.

When I look at experts in different fields of endeavor it seems to me that such a contrast between the true and the false expert is striking.

There are *physicians* who have an uncanny ability to get to the root of difficult medical conditions and thereby bring a marked hope and optimism to their highly troubled patients; in contrast, there are physicians who rely almost exclusively on tests and routine procedures to make a diagnosis and, when such means do not reveal unequivocal causation, leave their patients with the pessimistic conclusion that there is no effective treatment available.

There are *lawyers* who are so resourceful that they can find effective ways of overcoming intimidating legal or bureaucratic obstacles and thereby offer their clients the justice they seek and need; in contrast, there are lawyers who are able to deal with routine matters adequately but who far too readily deem it impossible to overcome intimidating legal or bureaucratic obstacles and thus offer only pessimism and futility to many who seek their help.

There are *professors* whose lectures are so inspiring that they kindle in their students a great desire to delve as deeply as possible into that specialized field; in contrast, there are professors whose lectures are so complex, stilted and pontifical that they leave their students with a dismaying sense that that field is understandable only to those few who are of genius caliber.

There are *researchers* whose original, radically different way of looking at phenomena results in the remarkable discoveries which greatly advance the well-being of mankind; in contrast, there are researchers who churn out enormous quantities of journal articles that are simply an elaboration and rehashing of old ideas, techniques and approaches that lead nowhere.

There are *executives*, usually the hands-on kind, whose receptive and unconventional style can enthuse those in an entire organization and thereby ensure that that organization works exceedingly well; in contrast, there are executives, usually the hands-off kind, whose impersonal and authoritative style leaves people disgruntled and the organization itself, despite repeated restructurings, in a state of debilitating stagnation.

There are those *political leaders* whose inspiring vision of a far better nation can unite people behind efforts to achieve such an end; in contrast, there are those political leaders whose words sound like hackneyed clichés and whose stereotyped, narrowly partisan, approach only mires the nation ever deeper into a quagmire of divisiveness and hopelessness.

This contrast between true and false expertise is meant to make clear that most of those in expert positions are not true experts. They rely on carbon-copy skills. They do not see their work as a personal challenge. Consequently, for people to think that expertise is the province only of the experts — as is common — blocks their efforts to get the best out of their work. They are prevented from seeing that personal challenge — the *sine quo non* of expertise — can be found in all work.

That conclusion led me to look at the distinction between skilled and expert occupations.

It is common to make such a distinction. Each category encompasses a wide swath of occupations. Among skilled workers one might include crafts-men, technicians, repairmen, nurses, social workers, police and personnel in such areas as banking, transportation, communication, penal systems and care facilities. Among experts one might include scientists, professors, doc-tors, lawyers, engineers, top-level executives, industrial, military and po-litical leaders. The trouble I ran into in trying to pin down the distinction between skilled work and expert work was that the harder I tried the more difficult it became. I found three reasons for that difficulty.

- The *first* reason was that there were some occupations that are eas-ily seen as both skilled and expert work. That includes the work of artists, actors, writers, entertainers and athletes.

- The *second* reason was the impossibility of pinning down a definite transition point in any line of work between those who are still not experts, but on their way, and those who are at the top of their spe-cialty. It is as though there is a sliding scale of increasing compe-tence so that official certification of expertise at any given point is both rough and arbitrary.

- The *third* and most important reason was that such a distinction did not hold up when I looked at different kinds of work. I saw that those in supposedly skilled occupations could easily be regarded as experts at their work and that those in supposedly expert occupa-tions could easily be regarded as simply possessing a high level of skill.

It became clear to me that a division between skilled and expert occupa-tions was artificial and untenable. That perception led me to see that there was a continuum of increasing skill in every kind of work, from the unskilled to the highest skilled. Seeing work this way was the basis for my conclusion that there is expertise — and the element of personal challenge — in every kind of work.

Let me begin with unskilled and low-skilled work. For such work is commonly seen as the epitome of meaninglessness. Because such work is usually seen this way it throws into sharpest focus the problem of how to find personal challenge in every kind of work.

I would pinpoint the question at issue in this way: How can one find personal challenge in the seemingly most routine work, that work which could be done with a minimum of prior training? How does one find such personal challenge in such jobs as working at a checkout counter, working on a garbage collection truck, working on a road repair gang, working as a filing clerk, working on an assembly line?

To answer that question, I would start by looking at how young adults often see unskilled and low-skilled work. It is usually at that time of life, right at the beginning of one's career, when the problem of a lack of enthusiasm for work is most troublesome. It is usually at that time of life that it is most pressing to see that doing unskilled work can carry its own reward of meaning and enthusiasm. It is at the start of one's work life, when one often takes on such work out of economic necessity, that one needs a good idea of what all work can and should offer.

Young adults are often greatly troubled by the idea that such jobs are inherently meaningless. Their co-workers are often older adults who have worked at such jobs for years, who perform them mechanically and with obvious boredom and who see such work as a dead end. It is easy to think that only more complex and more responsible jobs are meaningful. In such a situation one is highly likely to perform such work without any enthusiasm and to feel one is wasting one's time.

What is needed is to stimulate the curiosity which most young adults still have about every aspect of their living. It is to get them to look beyond the rudimentary skill required to do such unskilled work effectively. For I see that personal challenge can be found in every kind of work — that is, if one is curious enough to dig into it and ask oneself questions about its why and wherefore. When one does so one might come up with questions such as these:

- Could this job offer a singular opportunity for exposure to and insight into the larger field of work that it is a small part of?
- In what way is this apparently simple work an essential element needed to make the larger enterprise it is a part of work well?
- How might such work be done better so as to improve the overall effectiveness of the larger operation?
- Is it necessary for a human being to do this work or could it be done by a machine or computer or eliminated altogether? What kind of machine? What kind of computer operation? How could it be eliminated?
- Could this job be broadened to include other tasks and, thereby, make it more varied and more stimulating?
- In what way might this job be an essential first step towards more complex, more responsible and more challenging work?

- Might this work offer a fine opportunity to learn about the human element in a field of endeavor? Such as: What makes for good teamwork in a special line of work? Or: How might one better deal with customers or clients so as to give them that best possible service or help they want?

To try to answer such questions involves just such digging into one's work. I see that such an incentive to dig into one's work brings meaning to and enthusiasm for one's work even if such work is at the lowest rung. Seen this way the meaningfulness work offers has nothing to do with its social status, pay or power. For some individuals certain work, irrespective of such factors, offers the most exciting engagement imaginable while for others the same work would be the epitome of boredom.

It seems to me that there are countless examples of individuals who have started from low-skill work at the beginning of their career and developed from it a new insight with far-reaching consequences. The example which comes immediately to mind is that of Sam Walton who started very small and went on to develop Wal-Mart, currently the largest chain of retail stores in the United States. What such individuals brought to their work, as I see it, was not greater skill or greater talent but a different way of perceiving what they were doing — and the will and energy to follow up on such an individualistic perception.

Such will and energy does not have to be on the magnitude of a Sam Walton. When I look back on those whom I have met, two individuals come readily to mind. They made something quite special out of their work and got a special meaning out of it just because they saw it in a different way than what is usual.

- I think of Cecil, an older man who operated for many years the manual elevator in the building of the Northside Center where I worked in Harlem. On first meeting he seemed to me proud, distant and sullen. Over the years, as I got to know him better, he would ask me many questions about my work. I was greatly impressed by him and by his utilization of what was on the surface a simple job to delve into and satisfy his curiosity about a field of work far removed from his own.

- Earlier, when I was a resident at Harvard's Boston Psychopathic Hospital, I was similarly impressed by the Hospital's telephone operator. She had been there many years and would angrily scold everyone she talked to, including all the professors and chiefs of services, when they did not let her know where they were. We learned to accept such scolding because it seemed obvious that she was indispensable. She seemed to know where everyone was at any given time. In a communication sense she held the hospital together. She clearly saw her job in an unusual, highly challenging, way.

Young adults beginning in any field of work have one great advantage in finding meaning in their work: They are in a singularly fine position to ask searching questions about the why and wherefore of what they are doing. They are not expected to know much about that work. Since they are starting fresh and without firmly-rooted ideas, they can ask the most naive and the most basic of questions. They haven't been conditioned to accept the idea that established ways of thinking or doing things are necessarily true, best or right.

Their questions about why things are done in a particular way may well be easy to answer — but they may just as well be difficult to answer. Often things are done in a particular way just because they have become routine — even though doing things that way is no longer very effective, efficient or logical. Those who have been doing such work a longer time may well have become stuck in meaninglessness just because they accept unthinkingly and unquestioningly the ineffectiveness, inefficiency or illogic in their daily work. A beginner can have a better chance of not being stuck in such meaninglessness.

What beginners need is encouragement from their supervisors to ask such challenging questions. Asking questions is the best way of learning. Asking questions brings to the fore a person's curiosity and motivation. When the answers one gets makes good sense, those answers are much more readily absorbed and remembered — much more so than when one is simply instructed to do something in a given way. In the former situation one is an active participant in learning, in the latter a passive recipient. The former approach has a much higher chance of arousing enthusiasm for the work at hand. Thus, if beginners get encouragement from their supervisors to ask questions they are well on their way to getting the meaning they want out of their work.

Unfortunately, far too many do not get such encouragement. Their supervisors may well resent such questions feeling that beginners are in no position to question well-established routines and doing so is a waste of time that impedes effective work. Even more importantly, such questions may be resented because they are not easy to answer and awaken in the supervisor a deep-lying frustration in his or her work. Since such supervisors see no personal challenge in their work, they dismiss hard-to-answer questions as irrelevant to the work at hand. In doing so they stifle that sense of personal challenge that should be at the heart of one's work.

It is not easy to welcome challenging, even provocative, questions from beginners. I thus consider it important to spell out in more detail what makes for a good supervisor.

What makes for a good supervisor, to my mind, is best captured in the term *mentor*. That term adds to work supervision a highly personal interaction between two individuals. It calls forth an image of an experienced counselor who, with patience, understanding and kindness, attempts to guide another who is less experienced in his or her search for expertise and meaning in work.

The good mentor takes a special delight in working with beginners. Such a mentor sees his or her primary task as stimulating enthusiasm for the work at hand. To do that he or she welcomes every possible question.

The questions beginners raise, if asked in earnestness, invariably touch upon basic assumptions; they concern why things are done in a particular way and whether or not there is a better way of doing them. To come up with good answers the good mentor must be constantly re-examining his or her own perception of such basic assumptions. Such questions act as a continuing stimulus to the mentor's own efforts to make better sense of the work in question. The great reward for the mentor is seeing that those he or she would reach latch on to his or her ideas directly and do so with self-evident understanding and enthusiasm. The challenge for the mentor, then, is to be able to come up with answers which convey one's own enthusiasm for — and expertise in — one's work and to do so in clear, simple, easily understandable language.

Seen this way, mentorship is not simply a one-way street in which the mentor passes down information, skills and experience. It is a two-way street in which the mentor has just as much to gain as the person he or she would help. Seen this way, good mentorship should come from those who are most experienced and should not be delegated to others who are only a step or two above beginner level.

Since a person's work is that sphere of living which offers the opportunity to explore in greatest depth one specific area of interest, what takes place in mentorship is a sharing of the most exciting adventure conceivable.

What then does one do about those who do not see their work as an exciting adventure but rather see it as boring, a chore, a meaningless routine. How does one reach them?

That problem is just what I had to deal with in my own helping efforts. I could see a direct parallel between my idea of the three basic elements in helping and good mentorship.

The good mentor can easily voice a word of honest praise. He or she can create an atmosphere of mutual affection even with those who are very guarded, indifferent or dismissive about their work.

The good mentor is intimately in touch with his own early frustration in work and can readily put himself or herself in the shoes of the beginner. That experience is the source of his or her knowledge of what is needed to overcome such guardedness, indifference or dismissal and replace such reactions with enthusiasm.

The good mentor is prepared to answer the most challenging and most basic of questions and, thus is good at bringing forth such questions from those who are most guarded, indifferent or dismissive. Being able to do that gives the mentor the means for effectively communicating his or her own enthusiasm for the work they share.

In sum, then, a good mentor is a good helper.

Likewise, a good helper is a good mentor.

In my helping efforts I had to take on the role of the good mentor. I had to somehow bring forth an enthusiasm for a person's work. Even if I lacked a detailed knowledge of the particular work situation I found that, when I used my imagination, I could see what was challenging in different kinds of work. To do that I had to draw forth the details of such work from those I would help. In doing so I saw my own life enriched in a very special way: I learned a great deal about a wide variety of occupations.

In the following examples, my help was not sought because of a problem in one's work life. Nevertheless, such a problem became clear early on. The help these individuals got concerning their work situation was an important factor in making their living markedly better.

- There was an executive in a large concern. He felt frustrated in his work, he felt that there was a routine to it that was stifling. He was also troubled by the poor work of some of his colleagues when they worked together but he kept silent about that. He felt he could not take the risk of discussing his frustration with his immediate superior. He felt completely blocked. He wanted to quit and try some other work. I encouraged him to look into the alternatives he had in mind. After doing so he came to the conclusion that his present work offered the best future for him. With encouragement, he took the bull by the horns, spoke to his boss, received a promotion with greater responsibilities and found a new and markedly greater satisfaction in his work.

- There was a businessman who owned a number of apartment houses. Despite a high income he was bored by his work. He had had a dream of becoming a doctor but felt his age — being in the mid 40s — eliminated that possibility. I encouraged him to look into that possibility and cited the example of a colleague who had begun in medicine at his age. He did look into it and came to the conclusion that that was not what he really wanted. I then suggested that he might get more out of his present work if instead of simply making sure that routine matters were seen to — collecting rents, making repairs, attending to complaints, paying taxes, advertising vacancies — he took a personal interest in his tenants, got to know them as persons instead of simply rent-payers. He had plenty of opportunities to do so. He began on that new tack and it seemed to me that his work life significantly improved.

- There was a young woman who had a degree in economics but was unemployed and had been receiving unemployment payments for some time. She read employment notices in the press and was listed at employment agencies. It seemed to me that she was far too passive in looking for work and did not realize the importance of work in her life. I strongly encouraged her to be more active in her searching, to contact personnel departments, to ask for an interview. She did so. She finally did get a job. She was amazed that when she did so her symptoms of extreme tiredness and tightness in her chest disappeared completely. She said "Could it be that simple, just getting a job?" The work situation was not the only problem — or even the main problem — we talked about but, even so, it seemed clear that resolving that problem was of enormous benefit to her.

- There was a young lawyer who had been employed on a temporary basis in different agencies. She was extremely dissatisfied with her supervisors and with the work she was doing. It was exhausting to go to work. She told me that a legal education was only her third choice of an occupation; she was not accepted into the university programs of her first and second choices. She wasn't sure whether she wanted to continue in law. We talked a great deal about the details of the work she was doing and how it might be possible to get more reward out of that work. We came to the conclusion that she would give her present work a last, one-hundred-percent effort. She did that and I was greatly impressed with her effort and the success she achieved in her work. However, she felt no particular pleasure in the actual work she was doing. She realized then that what kept her from changing her work to something else was the prestige attached to being a lawyer. She thought that her parents would be upset if she quit. I felt that that she was giving up far too much of her life for such prestige and said so. She quit her job — and experienced a wonderful sense of relief.

The more I reflected on the role of work in our lives the clearer I could see the way in which finding meaning in our work has a profound effect on every other aspect of our living.

It bears repeating that work, more than any other aspect of our living, gives us a chance to excel at one particular endeavor. There is no other area of our living in which excellence is so well-defined, so directly a measure of how well we have developed the special gifts of creativity, courage and initiative which we are born with. It is our work that gives us the opportunity to target, channel and refine those resources to their uttermost.

All of us need to feel that we can, indeed, excel at something. I see that we all have within ourselves a reservoir of energy that cries out for release in such a pursuit of excellence. It is because work gives us the best opportunity to excel, in ever-increasing degree, that it also gives us the sense of self-pride, self-confidence, self-mastery and self-importance we need to succeed in any other endeavor of our living. It is just such a sense of self-pride, self-confidence, self-mastery and self-importance that we need to tackle the severer problems in our love life, friendship life and leisure life.

Just as with learning, the excellence that matters is a very private measure of ourselves — and not a competition to win out over others. What that "private measure" means is a striving to do our best and to continually extend such best. It is a lively competition we carry on with ourselves. When we feel we are doing our best — regardless of whether or not such best is better or worse than what others might be doing — we bask in a sense of our own excellence.

I see that the sense of self-pride, self-confidence, self-mastery and self-importance stemming from meaningful work can sustain us in our living — and make for a wonderful life — even when everything else appears to be caving in.

IDEALISM

There are two aspects of idealism in our everyday living, religious and political beliefs. People never came to me for help because they were troubled about those beliefs. Indeed, this section differs from those dealing with the five other spheres of our living in that religion and politics were almost never discussed at any length in my helping efforts. Nevertheless, it became clear to me that I would have to deal with them here for it seemed self-evident that strongly-held religious and political beliefs — those which become convictions — have a profound influence on how we live our lives. I could see that such an influence could be either negative or positive.

Some people's idealistic beliefs left them filled with an overwhelming bitterness or hatred directed at those who did not share their own religious or political convictions; such bitterness or hatred affected every other aspect of their living and left them constantly sapped of energy. In contrast, there were others whose idealistic beliefs left them with a sense of compassion and caring for others regardless of differing religious or political convictions; such compassion and caring left them with an uplifting sense of well-being that coursed through every other aspect of their living.

Given the importance that such beliefs can hold for our living I saw that I had to look at how they work inside ourselves. I had to make sense of how such beliefs act to either help us or harm us. In doing so I, first of all, had to look inside myself. I then had to look at the lives of those whom I would help and those whom I knew personally. I also had to reflect on the living of people in general from my own special perspective as a psychiatrist. And, in the end, I had to set forth my idea of how the matter of idealism affected my helping efforts.

I see it important to make clear that my aim in this section is not to discuss specific religious or political beliefs. Its focus is solely on how people utilize idealistic beliefs in their daily living for better or worse.

Religion and politics are commonly seen as two different matters, religion dealing with spiritual factors in people's lives and politics dealing with factors involved in the governing of people. However, my concern here is where religion and politics overlap. More particularly, my concern is where they overlap as they influence the thoughts and feelings and actions of individuals in their daily living. Most important in that regard is that they both serve to bond individuals together into a single people.

I came to see that the great bonding power of religious and political beliefs stems from their inherent idealism. They set forth an ideal way of living. That ideal way of living provides the principles governing everyday living and the ultimate goals to be striven after in people's collective living. Those principles and goals concern what is considered right, just, good, desirable, moral and honorable — both for the individual and for a whole people who share such a conviction. It is idealism, above all other factors, which makes for the solidarity of a given people.

Why do people share an idealistic conviction? Where does the powerful bonding of idealism come from?

Most people have a need to join with others in a common cause which they see possesses all those admirable principles and goals. Such common cause has taken many forms: realizing God's will; peace on earth; preparation for the hereafter; nirvana; universal freedom from fear and want; from each according to his ability, to each according to his need; the classless society; government of the people, by the people and for the people; the realization of the special destiny of the nation or culture.

Such ideas have gripped, and do grip, us both as individuals and as whole peoples. Those ideas have possessed, and still possess, the enormous power to bring a grandiose, ideal, abstract vision into something essential for the daily living of each separate individual. They have brought, and bring, a message that there are idealistic goals in each person's living which are of such transcendental value that they can override what we seek in our loving, friendship, learning, work and private life.

Those latter aims appear, at times, either unreliable or narrow. They can swing up or down as the circumstances of one's living change. Or they can seem egotistically focused upon only one's own personal needs. And, in the worst of times, they may appear totally empty, totally devoid of meaning. In contrast, one's idealism is the ultimate of constancy. It can provide a rock-hard foundation for living when one's life seems to be floundering on every other score.

At those times, when it seems as though everything one does is going wrong, it is easy to imagine living in general as being dominated by hopelessness, pettiness, materialism or destructiveness. Thus, there can be great comfort and security in the conviction of a greater rightness in the world, a rightness which gives hope and a rightness which one is a part of in one's own small way. It is as though such rightness acts like a righting power, like a giant gyroscope of living that will keep one's life in balance when everything else goes amuck.

The great power of idealism lies, as I see it, in the deeply rooted sense of security that comes from bonding with a large number of like-minded individuals. However, such security can be two edged: It can serve as either a bedrock for getting the best out of one's living or it can undermine the whole of one's living.

Such undermining occurs when one sees one's own conviction as infallible. One sees that there is only one right religion or only one right political way of thinking. Other religious or political convictions are seen as inferior, wrong, bad, evil or corrupt. Thinking this way makes people feel superior to other people. The tangible advantage of such a sense of superiority is that it greatly bolsters one's self-esteem, self-pride and perception of self-rightness. Such a conviction, however, has a grave, though insidious, effect. One often, unthinkingly, crosses a critical boundary line.

One moves from a difference in belief to a difference separating people in almost every aspect of living. One imagines, "They (those holding different beliefs) are basically different from us; they don't think, act, behave like we do; they don't have the same moral standards that we do." The issue is no longer a matter of conviction versus conviction. The issue becomes a seemingly irreconcilable divisiveness between people. Religious and political differences then become a convenient summation of far deeper hatreds and enmities that separate people — seemingly irrevocably — on the basis of nationality, color, appearance or culture. Individuals, then, easily become enmeshed in the bitter hatreds and enmities that pit people against people. People on each side imagine they have a monopoly on rightness.

It would seem obvious that neither side in such conflicts can have a monopoly on the rightness of their convictions — even though many people would like to imagine just that. In such situations something fundamental has gone askew in the thinking of individuals so as to enmesh them in such life-and-death hatreds.

The question that needs answering, then, is why have things gone wrong in people's thinking?

Things go wrong when solidarity is built upon blind faith. Conviction often stems from dogma. One accepts without questioning that one's belief is true, that that belief is the only possible way to perceive what is right, just, good, desirable, moral and honorable in living. Such a perception then leads to a vicious circle that bolsters one's blind faith. It does so by breeding hatred and enmity.

Individuals are not ready to accept the superiority of another's belief, particularly if they see their own belief as superior and infallible. The result, then, is dogma versus dogma. The serious problem with such enmity is that it greatly intensifies the dogmatism of one's own belief. One sees that one must defend one's belief at all cost against those who are a threat to it, those with differing beliefs. In such a situation solidarity with like-minded is built just as much upon enmity as it is upon a shared idealistic belief. The greater the perceived threat, the greater the need for absolute belief. It is as though the presence of enemies confirms the rightness of one's own belief.

One clings to hatred and enmity because of the great security offered in knowing that one is right and that others are wrong. That, to my mind, is the reason why so many individuals are consumed by the life-and-death hatreds pitting people against people.

Why do people think this way? Where does it come from?

It was not so long ago, as measured in generations, that most people believed in the divine right of kings, emperors, popes, patriarchs and prophets. They were deemed infallible. There usually was a hierarchical order of nobility with a descending line of royal or ecclesiastical titles. Each higher rank had authority over lower ranks. Peoples were ruled from above. Those at the top were nearest to God. They ruled with absolute authority. They defined what people should believe in. They defined idealism. They defined who were enemies of the people. They declared war. Most people obeyed. They did so because they assumed that idealism as defined from above was the basis for making their own people one powerful and righteous whole. Faith was complete, unquestioning — and blind.

Blind faith was utilized to mobilize a whole people to subjugate another whole people. The idea of a people's superior belief was used as a rationale, a justification and an excuse for such subjugation. In earliest years religion and politics were joined in justifying the waging of holy wars and conquests. In this way hatred and enmity were just as much a part of such blind faith as was idealism.

Much as one would like to think that that state of affairs is far behind us, I see that it is not. One can find in modern societies the same hierarchies of power that were characteristic of times past, even if today's modern societies are less rigid. And even though much has changed in religion and politics since then, there exists to a significant degree the same element of blind faith in many people's idealism.

There is just as great a need for the bonding of a people. That bonding comes in high degree from trusting those in religious and political leadership. The problem in that trust is that such leadership too often reiterates and reinforces the conviction that one's own people's religious or political belief is infallible. Many people still see a great need to protect themselves and their beliefs against real or potential enemies. Often ancient histories of injustices still dominate in the hatreds and enmities which persist in the here and now.

Warring is still a widespread phenomenon. One need only look at Bosnia, Kosovo, the Basque region, Sri Lanka, Rwanda, Kashmir, Algeria and the Middle East. It wasn't so long ago that the most powerful nations in the world seemed irrevocably divided between those that were communist and those that were non-communist — and were ready to go to whole-scale war on that score. The Viet Nam war was justified on the basis of fighting communism and its spread to other nations via the domino theory. In many countries the only factor that holds a nation together is military might and the security police. Nuclear warfare, despite its terrifying nature, is an increasing possibility today given the confrontation between Pakistan and India, the increasing world-wide power of fundamentalist Islam and the spread of nuclear weapons to smaller countries.

In all those conflicts vast numbers of individuals have been completely convinced of the infallibility — the sacredness — of their own convictions and were willing to kill and risk being killed for such convictions. The problem for the individual in all this is that old hatreds built upon blind faith are irreconcilable with living in today's world.

In today's world people holding different religious and political beliefs must be able to live and work closely and harmoniously together. That necessity is the result of two factors: the increased migration of peoples and the increased interdependence of peoples.

The vast migration of peoples in modern times has resulted in nations that are an intimate inter-mixture of peoples. That migration has swelled because it has become much easier for individuals to flee from poor and warring countries to wealthy and more stable countries.

In today's societies the increasingly complex interdependence of living means that in every area of living — work, services, education, housing and leisure activities — people from different backgrounds must deal intimately with each other. It is progressively less and less possible for peoples to live in enclaves isolated from each other.

Those two factors lead to an inevitable conclusion: Individuals must accept the idea that others with differing beliefs have a right to think differently, that no one belief has a monopoly on rightness. The overriding demand is the need for compromise. The alternative — thinking that one's own belief will ultimately prevail over those of others and dominate in a society or nation — is, to my mind, a clear impossibility. Those individuals who believe in the infallibility of their own religious or political belief believe in something that can never be realized.

Such unrealizable belief can be lived with when one finds a good measure of real reward in the rest of one's living. However, when such reward is missing one clings to one's unrealizable conviction as though it were a last desperate life buoy. Since there can never be a sense of fulfillment in one's idealism, one is locked into a state of bitterness, cynicism, prejudice and hatred.

Believing in the infallibility of one's own convictions leaves no room for live and let live, no flexibility in one's living, no tolerance for others. Instead, there is rigidity. One's sense of self-rightness becomes self-righteousness. One loses the perspective that one might be wrong. There is, then, no room for human error, for fallibility, for compromise with others who think differently. One gets security from one's idealism but the price one pays for such security is high. One is left exhausted, in a state of perpetual tension, deeply disillusioned and, often, obsessed by violent thoughts or acts. In the worst of states one imagines oneself persecuted by imaginary enemies. One clings to one's conviction solely because it offers security in a living that has nothing else.

That is why I see that the false reward in idealism is imagining that one's particular religious or political conviction is infallible.

The real reward in idealism is the sense of nobility which comes from seeing that one is doing one's bit, however small, to make a better community or a better society or a better world. Such a contribution imbues one's life with a sense of higher purpose, a higher purpose that transcends the more self-centered rewards in loving, friendship, learning, work and a private life. Such idealism can provide a solid foundation for all the other aspects of one's living.

The clearest example of such idealism is participation in organizations concerned with such aims as helping the poor, working for world peace, bringing medical aid to the needy, protecting the environment, fighting for fairness, justice and equality, fighting against injustice, exploitation and tyranny. I have met such individuals and am impressed by the enthusiasm that such participation imbues in them. There is, however, another aspect of such idealism that is not so obvious.

One can see the connection between idealism and "doing one's bit" most clearly in youth, at that transitional time when one is trying to determine the course of one's future life. That connection is reflected in the often-heard statement: I want to do something meaningful with my life. Doing something meaningful usually means a choice of work that carries with it an idealistic purpose beyond that of acquiring expertise or of gaining wealth. There is, to my mind, an aspect of idealism underlying all occupations.

- Underlying medicine, law, social work, religion, psychology and teaching is the desire to help others.
- Underlying the sciences is the goal of making discoveries that will improve the lot of mankind.
- Underlying work in industry is the making of products for people's good.
- Underlying sanitation, road building, park maintenance and police work is the desire to make the community a good place in which to live.
- Underlying entertainment, recreation and leisure activities is the aim of bringing pleasure to people.

- Underlying the arts is the ambition to bring to people beauty and enlightenment.
- Underlying politics is the goal of making a community or society work well.

The idealism underlying one's work is of immeasurable importance for the everyday living of individuals. And the more I thought about that importance, the more I was drawn to seeing idealism in a highly unusual way.

Idealism is a perception of how we would envision the ideal society and the ideal individual who lives in that ideal society.

- *The ideal society* can be described as one which is a composite of such ideals as justice, harmony, dynamism, prosperity, indestructibility and the stimulation of inventiveness; it is free of such plagues as oppression, exploitation, corruption, want and illness.
- *The ideal individual* can be described as one who is a composite of such ideals as honesty, loyalty, fairness, tolerance, and compassion; that individual is free from such vices as hatred, brutality, greed and deceit.

We know immediately what those ideals are. We can immediately recognize the compelling force they play — or could play — in our lives. I see that most people would want to live up to that image of the ideal individual. I also see that a great many people would willingly sacrifice personal rewards if they saw that such sacrifice would contribute to the making of such an ideal society. Seeing things this way gave me what I saw was the practical coupling between individual and society which made for the best of both.

That practical coupling, in a nutshell, is this: The awareness that one has an essential role in making one's society a more perfect — ideal — one acts as a powerful force for living up to such an image of the ideal individual. Such awareness can act to markedly diminish the hatred, brutality, greed and deceit among individuals.

Such a point of view about idealism is unusual.

We usually don't think very much about the making of the ideal society even though we can easily recognize its desirability. That goal usually seems distant, abstract and unreal, like pie in the sky. It doesn't seem a particularly important part of our everyday living. Yet, if we look more closely at what the idea of society is it ought to become clear just why the coupling between the ideal society and the ideal individual possesses such immense gyroscopic power in our living.

Society is best seen as that collective living which includes all those who share a common legal system and common social institutions of education, industry, recreation, health, welfare and enforcement. That legal system sets the ground conditions for the living of everyone in the society. Those social institutions provide the means for the betterment of everyone in the society.

Laws and social institutions are, however, only the structure of society. They may work well or poorly. They may either bring people together into one whole or divide people. Whether they work well or poorly depends upon one single element: A shared idealism. That, as I see it, is the real cement of society. It is that shared idealism which makes the life of each individual a part of the lives of all.

For it is we who obey or disobey those laws. And it is we who man those social institutions and make them approach their ideal functioning or, on the contrary, subvert that ideal. Either we obey those laws because we see the wisdom and justice in them or we obey them only because we fear punishment. Either we are motivated by the idealistic challenge in our work in education, industry, recreation, health, welfare and enforcement or we see our work as simply a technical job to be done as efficiently as possible.

What we do, for better or worse, depends upon our idealistic commitment to the society we live in. That commitment can only be one thing: the making of the ideal society. That is what unites everyone in common purpose. That is what makes for tolerance among people.

That goal is what underlies our willingness to sacrifice for the common good. That goal is what transcends the rewards of personal pleasure. And that goal of making the ideal society means, above all else to my eyes, the making of the well-integrated society. For, that idea of the well-integrated society provides the practical means that makes for both the ideal society and the ideal individual living in that ideal society.

It does so by giving each person an essential, clearly, defined role to play. That role is found in one's work. It is the sum total of everyone's work meshing well together which makes the giant wheels of society go round. Seen this way, our work is an inextricable part of everyone else's work. I see that the most important idealism for most people is an awareness that one's work is essential to making the whole societal machinery go round as perfectly as possible. Seen in such a light there is a sense of nobility in every kind of work.

One rarely thinks of one's work in such idealistic terms. Yet, if one reflects on that idea I think that such an awareness will become clear. The pride we take in our work is not only that we have done a good job. It is in equal measure that we are doing something of value, that our work is prized by others as giving pleasure or service or help or security or essential wisdom. Seen this way, the pride one takes in one's work can easily be seen in the larger context of doing one's bit, however small, to making one's society into one ideal, well-integrated, whole. Work is the best coupling between the life of the individual and the lives of all others in the society.

The idealism embedded in our work is the most powerful idealism in our lives because it is active, tangible and realizable. We can readily see that what we do in our work and how we do it can be of help to others in our society. We can readily see that an improvement in how we work and how we work together could greatly improve the lot of everyone. In contrast, religious or political idealism easily lends itself to a passive compliance. It is enough to follow the prescribed religious rituals of prayer or church-going or holiday observance. It is enough to vote for one's party in elections. That is why idealism coupled to one's work yields a practical every day meaning to our living.

It is the power of the idealism embedded in our work that makes our society work well. For when such idealism is dominant it allows people to work and live harmoniously together despite differences in political and religious convictions. I see that the making of the best possible society can be the source of the greatest source of pride we take in ourselves.

That pride in oneself is part and parcel of the special pride we take in being a member of our society. That pride in our society is clearly apparent in how we applaud and identify with the achievements of those members of our society who are outstanding in sports, science and the arts. Such applause and identification lets us see even ourselves in a heroic light. It is not only that those who are outstanding are heroes of our particular society. It is that we can easily imagine that we are an essential part of that society which gave rise to those heroes. Each of us would be a hero in one's own eyes, in the eyes of those nearest us and, if we are fortunate, even in the eyes of many others. Such a perception of one's own heroism is one of the most powerful of motivations in our living. It is just such a sense of heroism, which links together idealism, achievement in our work, and a sense of nobility in our living.

I see no way of separating the idealism each of us holds from the idealism that serves as the foundation for the society we live in. I see that our idealism more than any other aspect of our living is dependent upon the society in which we live. It is society that makes clear what is admired, what is permitted and what is forbidden in our collective living. That perception, however, raises two troublesome questions.

The first question is: What if the conditions for an idealistic engagement are lacking? What if there is no possibility of working in an idealistic organization? What if many people have no work? What if the prevailing sentiment is that one's work is simply routine labor and unessential to the welfare of the society as a whole?

The second question is: What if the prevailing perception among people is that the society one lives in is permeated by corruption, injustice, the abuse of power and the manipulation of idealistic beliefs?

Granted that all societies are in flux and far from perfection it seems clear to me that such a general perception of the ideal society is where we must be headed in our collective living. That is what people must believe. There must be constant movement towards full employment. And the overriding principle must be that the making of one just society must be paramount over the different religious and political beliefs it contains. The alternative is disintegration of the society and alienation of individuals.

When there is no such commonly-held belief, when most people see that the society one lives in is permeated by corruption, injustice, the abuse of power and the manipulation of idealistic beliefs, one may seek security in the false reward of idealism which often pit dogma against dogma. Such a situation makes for deep divisiveness and enmities within a society. Or one may disavow idealism considering it as unrealistic and naïve; one then lives by the principle of getting the most one can of wealth or power by whatever means possible. In both such situations there is little check on corruption, high and low level crime and violence.

This discussion of idealism has, of necessity, dealt with the issue of how a whole society functions. It has led me to the question of what goes into the making of such a just society. That matter, though, is beyond the scope of this particular section; it is something I shall deal with elsewhere. My sole focus here is on how different idealistic perceptions make for the best or worst of living of individuals.

It was in that context that I became aware of how the matter of idealism entered into my helping efforts.

Idealism entered into the helping situation primarily as it concerned my own beliefs. The fact that I had to help people from different backgrounds and those often holding different beliefs than mine forced me to look at my own idealism. It seemed self-evident to me that those whom I would help had a right to believe as they would. It was also self-evident to me that those beliefs were usually beneficial.

It was my many years of work in Harlem that crystallized what I saw as the great need for individuals to see themselves and their work as an essential part of society. For in Harlem great numbers were without work. Many others held menial jobs. And, most importantly, there was at that time, in the 60s, little prospect for better opportunities opening up. There was then little sense that those in Harlem were essential to the society. It was self-evident for me that prejudice and powerlessness was responsible for that situation. For many it was taken for granted that there was hypocrisy in the political idealism dominant in the rest of society. And that conclusion had a marked effect on the helping situation. For if one suspected that the professional helper did not share that same idealistic indignation there would be no common ground for helping.

There was yet another aspect of idealism in the helping situation that I came to see as having far-reaching significance.

When I reflected on the needs of people it became clear to me that — despite differences in religious and political convictions — almost all shared the identical needs and desires in the areas of loving, friendship, learning, work and a private life. Most people sought the identical real rewards that make for the best in living in those areas. I could help others with problems in those areas irrespective of our religious and political differences. It was that experience that led me to see that what I was dealing with in my work were basic and universal factors in the living of human beings. Such basic and universal factors meant for me that we can all live and work in harmony with each other, that we can all share the same idealistic aim of making the best possible society, that what each of us needs most in idealism is the conviction that one is an essential part of one's society.

A PRIVATE LIFE

There is a sphere of our living that, more than any other, is private, our very own. We do not have to share it with anyone else. That private life, as I call it, has two parts.

- One part is our *leisure time*. That is when we can give freest rein to our most self-centered pleasures. That part is private in the sense that we are free to do exactly what we want independent of the wishes, will, acceptance or cooperation of anyone else.

- The other part is what I call our *aloneness in living*. It consists of our innermost thoughts and feelings. Those thoughts and feelings are private in the sense that they are uniquely our own; we may or may not want to share them with someone else. Such private thoughts and feelings may come to the fore at any time but do so most commonly during our times of rest, falling asleep and dreaming. It is particularly at those time that we are acutely aware that, for better or worse, we are alone in our living.

I had to deal with both those parts in my helping efforts. There was, however, a marked difference in how they came up.

Many who sought help were painfully aware of their aloneness in living. It was just that sense of aloneness — of being unable to deal by themselves with their troubling innermost thoughts and feelings — which brought them to me. On the other hand, how one spent one's leisure time was rarely a cause of concern. It was usually I who had to bring that up and make clear why that aspect of living ought to be of central importance. It became clear to me that many people had serious difficulty with their living because they had a faulty perception of those two parts of their private life. I came to see that how one perceives those two parts makes for either enthusiasm in living or futility in living.

Far too many people see their leisure as a luxury and not a necessity. It is, in a sense, leftover time. It is that time which may be left over after one has done all the things one sees that one must do. It is spare time, superfluous time. There are two serious consequences of that perception.

The first is that one makes no time for leisure but, instead, fills one's days with such obligations as work, family responsibilities and social engagements. One is then worn out, exhausted, at the end of one's day. The second is that one fills one's leisure with various forms of entertainment. A typical picture of such entertainment is the person who comes home tired after a day's work, has a large meal and then sits watching television out of habit and not because what one looks at is particularly rewarding. One's leisure then takes on the character of deadening routine. It took me some time to understand what should be central in our leisure and why.

I came to see that what should be central is recreation. Recreation can take many forms: playing music, painting, dance, carpentry, chess, raising a pet, playing sports, collecting stamps — the list is endless. Recreation is a necessity in our living because it offers a release of energy in activity that offers pure pleasure. Recreation is active. We feel reinvigorated afterwards. The reason we feel reinvigorated is precisely because we are pleased with ourselves, because we did something in our own special way, purely for fun, and got a great kick out of doing that.

In all the other spheres of our living we must accommodate the wishes of others. When those aspects of our living go well, there is no problem. But when they don't go well there is a problem. We are left frustrated, we are left with a great deal of pent-up energy. And that pent-up energy cries out for release.

Recreation, in short, serves as an essential safety valve in our living. That, to my mind, is the real reward in our leisure. Indeed, I see that an engrossing recreational pursuit can, by itself, sustain an individual throughout a lifetime. In contrast, the false reward in leisure is seeing it in terms of time for entertainment.

It is not that entertainment cannot be rewarding. It is an important part of relaxation. We ought to make time for reading books, seeing films, listening to music, going to the theater, watching sports events, enjoying a great meal. The problem arises when those pursuits are dominant in one's leisure time. There is a passivity in such activities. There is no self-expression as there is in recreation. Instead of the ability to please oneself, it is a time to be pleased. The result is that there is no real safety valve in living. One does not get rid of one's pent-up energy. In contrast to recreation, one is not particularly pleased with oneself afterwards nor does one see those activities as a necessity in one's living.

Aloneness, in the eyes of many people, is seen as something completely negative, something associated with loneliness and isolation. It is not seen as having a positive side.

Seen that way, one does all one can to avoid any sense of being alone. One has a need for constant companionship, at times to the extent of an excessive dependency on others. Or one keeps busy, one fills up one's time with constant activity in good part to avoid the troubling, most private, thoughts and feelings that come up when one has nothing special to do. It is as though one could block out those thoughts and feelings. One often has great trouble falling asleep and sleeping just because those troubling thoughts and feelings come forth at such times. The result is that one never comes to grips with those innermost, troubling, thoughts and feelings. One finds oneself stuck in the same kind of difficulties time and again and cannot understand why. One's life takes on the character of an endless, unrewarding, treadmill.

It took me a long time to realize that being adult means, at root, being alone — and to perceive the great advantage of looking at living that way.

Our moments of aloneness give us time for reflection. It is then when we can get a better perspective on ourselves, when we can see ourselves from a distance. Most of our living is usually too intense, too up-close, for that. We are preoccupied with the action and doing of loving, friendship, learning, working and recreation. All well and good — but we also need time to back off from all that. Those moments of aloneness give us time to reflect on where we've been, where we are, where we're going, where we want to go and how to get there.

It is then that we look at our innermost thoughts and feelings. Doing so makes us acutely aware that we are, in the end, alone in deciding the course of our living. Seen this way the aloneness we experience is the key to self-determination in our living. That is its real reward.

It is in our moments of aloneness that we decide just what we want in all the other spheres of living, in our loving, friendship, learning, work and idealism. It is also then that we come to grips with the difficulties that stand in our way. One may well get help from others on that score but in the end where one goes in one's living and how one goes there is solely one's own decision. Seeing things that way means that one must take time to talk with oneself, to look at oneself, to make important decisions before one is forced to do so. What we get out of seeing aloneness in this way is an invaluable insight into ourselves.

The ultimate state of aloneness is sleep. As such, sleep ought to be a prime source of insight. To understand how that happens it is necessary to look, first, at what takes place as we fall asleep and, second, at what takes place during sleep.

When we go to bed we want to relax completely, we want to get away from the intensity of our awake life, we want to put the day to rest. Yet, as we lie there, it is as though another part of ourselves begins to take over our awareness. It is as though things spring into our awareness without our having control over what is going on.

What is taking place is that those thoughts and feelings which are most charged for us emerge just then. At that border time between being fully awake and fully asleep, our feelings take over from our deliberate thinking. It is as though there is a mechanism inside ourselves, one beyond our conscious control, which precipitates out from the day what is most important for us. In that precipitate we find the most satisfying of our successes and the most painful of our failures.

The best way to fall asleep — and the trick to making the most of that falling asleep time — is to let those spontaneous thoughts and feelings just come up as they will. When we do that we get a valuable insight into ourselves, into what is really most important for us. And that insight comes particularly from what comes up which is unexpected, that which surprises us, that which we had forgotten or thought was trivial.

Those things have a way of fastening themselves into our awareness at just that time of day. What is happening is that our feelings are telling us: "This neglected matter is important, it demands attention and reflection." If we listen to that message and wonder why that matter could be important we usually do come up with an answer, an answer which not only surprises us but which also hits the nail on the head. We get a new slant on the problems we would deal with. We get a new slant on how to tackle things the following day. That is what I think is so fascinating about falling asleep.

And that process of self-revelation is even more evident during sleep.

For it is there, in our dream world, where we find our most private secrets, hopes, fears, forbidden pleasures, conflicts, moments of glory, moments of panic. It is then when that most private part of us — our fantasy life — takes over.

We have good dreams and bad dreams. And, very often, perplexing dreams. Sometimes the message — the self-revelation — is strikingly clear, both in the dreams that gratify us and the dreams that torment us. But often it isn't. Which raises the question: Why?

It was Freud who came to the conclusion that there is a mechanism that protects us from being hurt by what is hard for us to accept about ourselves — even in our sleep. Such a mechanism disguises what is hard to accept. That makes good sense. For, after all, it is we who are doing the dreaming, it is we who are putting our dreams into disguises.

To understand why we disguise things from ourselves it is necessary to see that it is the very same protective mechanism that works both day and night. Even in daytime, we would avoid looking squarely at wishes that seem hopelessly beyond our reach and explanations that seem embarrassing or terrifying. That same avoidance is what puts our dreams into disguises.

The difference in dreaming is that we loosen the controls on ourselves. We let our fantasy out. But we don't throw away those controls. They're still there. Thus, for example, if things get really bad in our dreaming we can make ourselves wake up. Yet, it is because we loosen those controls that we let the elements of our fantasy life sneak out, even if in disguise.

So how does one make sense of those disguised dreams?

It was also Freud who gave us a means to get at the messages in our dreams, to get out the self-revelation. He called it free association. When we think of a dream or any of its parts and let ourselves say the very first thought that pops into our mind, what we get is an interpretation which is often right on the mark. There is nothing very mystical about that. It is the same process at work that makes it difficult to remember something when we deliberately try to do so but, later on, that memory suddenly pops into our mind.

However, such free association to our dreams is not as easy as it sounds. For, after we are awake, we would put our troubling and perplexing dreams out of mind. We usually have no inclination to look deeper into the dis-guised hopelessness, embarrassment or fear. We usually forget those dreams quickly. It often takes an act of will to recall them. Yet, such free associa-tion often does work. That is what I have seen when people have brought their puzzling dreams into the helping situation. In such a situation I say something like this: "We are going to try a little experiment in which I am going to ask you a question and you will say the first thing that pops into your mind." I then ask, "What does that dream (or part of a dream) mean?"

The first, spontaneous thought invariably brings a surprising, immediately recognizable, clarity.

Free association may be best described as a spontaneous, instinctive coming to the fore of thoughts and feelings we experienced earlier in our lives. The current task or problem we are facing in our living acts as a stimulus to bring into awareness those particular thoughts and feelings. It is as though we are searching inside ourselves for answers to the difficulties we are facing.

Such instinctive reactions can occur at anytime. We suddenly see what we are experiencing in a different light. It is important to trust one's instincts. That, to my mind, is the source of instinctive insight. That is how we find answers to any puzzling personal question. That is how we decide what we want for ourselves, how to get that and how to deal with difficulties that arise. Seen this way, it is the realization that we are alone in our living that makes us self-reliant. That is how we take control over the course of our lives.

What one should be getting out of one's private life is a wonderful sense of independence that comes as the result of combining the safety valve of recreation and the self-determination of aloneness.

In contrast, when one sees one's leisure solely in terms of entertainment and one's aloneness as something solely oppressive, one ends up with a life of insecurity and frustration. One's living seems directionless. One expends far too much energy in suppressing one's troublesome inner thoughts and feelings. There is no good safety valve in one's living. One has little insight into what is going on in one's life. That perception stemmed directly from my work in helping people.

I often saw that people had no safety valve in their living, no real spontaneous fun, no good release of energy. Yet I usually had a good deal of difficulty in getting people to see the necessity of recreation in their lives.

One would think that it would be easy for people to accept the idea that recreation is desirable. After all, recreation is a chance to enjoy the pure pleasure of any activity one chooses. Yet, there usually was a great resistance to seeing recreation that way. Typical responses were "But I'm not interested in anything" or "I'm not good at anything."

The difficulty underlying such responses is that people do not come for help for problems of how to spend their free time. There is much less motivation to change their way of doing things in that area than there is in loving, friendship, learning and work. That lack of motivation is reflected in the response "It would be nice to do something like that but I simply don't have the time." That matter of making time in our lives for something is a direct reflection of the priority we attach to such activity. Thus, such a response means that time for recreation has lowest priority.

The problem of making time for recreation is that one would then have to take time away from something else. Doing so often meant a significant rearrangement in one's life. Usually it is difficult to break a habit of working hard, taking care of one's responsibilities and filling one's leisure with enter-tainment. That problem is compounded by the idea many adults hold that they must be good at whatever recreational pursuit they choose. Children can be beginners, but not adults. One imagines it to be demeaning to start off as a beginner. One is ashamed to plunge into something and risk looking like a fool.

What I have tried to do in such instances is make clear the great need for a safety valve in our living. I make clear my opinion that they can choose whatever recreational activity they want — but choose they must. There is no alternative.

That helping effort was not as successful as I would have liked. It is just too easy to become fixated on the more pressing problems at hand. But when it does work the effect is gratifying. It is as though recreation takes the edge off everything else. It is as though one can begin to take the rest of one's life easier, with a grain of salt. There is a splendid sense of renewal.

There were instance in my helping efforts when I was successful. I have already, in chapter 2, given examples of the importance of recreation for two individuals. One, in "Detective Work," concerned the importance of playing the guitar; the other, in "What Worked," concerned the importance of sing-ing opera. Then there was a young man, constantly tense, who walked in one day beaming and completely relaxed; he was extremely pleased with himself because he had finally bought a motorcycle, something he had long thought about doing. Another example was of a middle-aged man who enjoyed play-ing golf regularly but felt guilty that it took away time from his family; he needed a word of encouragement to see his golf as an essential part of his life.

It seemed clear to me that many people lacked any engagement in recreation and, consequently, had no good safety valve. When I looked for the reason why that was so I began to see leisure time in a far wider perspective.

I could see two prime factors behind such a lack of recreational engagement: the enormous commercialization of entertainment and a widespread, seriously flawed, perception of recreation.

The development of large entertainment industries has fed into a passive leisure. Such industries concern sports, film and music. Great sums of money are spent to popularize such passive leisure. The success of such popularization has made it easy for people to fill their leisure in that way. Such a passive leisure is abetted by a common perception that recreation — typically sports — is something only for those who are best, those most gifted.

Such a perception usually starts early in life. Many recreational leaders who deal with children and youth consider that their competence lies in imparting technical proficiency — instead of in stimulating a general enthusiasm for a recreational engagement. That faulty perception stems in large part from a failure by those in education, psychology and psychiatry to recognize the essential nature of recreation in our living. Leisure time, by default, becomes something peripheral in living, something that is solely each individual's private concern. The unfortunate result of that failure is that too many people seek a safety valve in their living in such activities as over-eating, over-drinking, excessive gambling and spending sprees.

Of all the rewards we seek in our living, the most important one is the self-determination that stems from our aloneness in living. For how one deals with one's aloneness is the key to getting the real rewards we seek in every other sphere of living. It is in that aloneness — in our innermost thoughts and feelings — that we make the most important decisions in our living. At the core of my work was the task of helping people deal with those innermost thoughts and feelings that made their living unbearable.

It seemed clear to me that people could turn their living around completely, from the very worst to the very best. I have already set forth, in Chapter 7, "The Expert in Living," some of my ideas about what is involved in that turning around. It is time now to come back to those ideas, for they raise several questions about how to make that turning-around happen.

Underlying all psychiatric conditions, as I noted, I see a sense of desperation in living, and at the extreme of such desperation is suicide. I also wrote that a good professional helper can see that within craziness is creativity, within rage is courage, within panic is initiative, within violence is dynamism, within hopelessness is achievement and within self-destruction is self-fulfillment.

Seeing things that way raised the following questions:

- How does one making a connection between the worst of psychiatric states and the most admirable of qualities: between craziness and creativity, rage and courage, panic and initiative, violence and dynamism, hopelessness and achievement, self-destruction and self-fulfillment?

- What are the resources all of us have within ourselves to turn our living around?

- How does one make optimistic commonsense of all the severe difficulties that psychiatrists deal with, about their development and reversal?

In the next chapter I set forth my answers to those questions.

CHAPTER 9. CREATIVITY, COURAGE, INITIATIVE, DYNAMISM, ACHIEVEMENT AND SELF-FULFILLMENT

At thirty-one, he was extremely tall, extremely awkward and extremely shy with women. He became hopelessly entangled in a rocky love affair. She was small, pretty, sophisticated, vivacious — and broke things off when he couldn't make up his mind. He was devastated. There seemed to be no bottom to his despair. He could not work, stayed in bed, became emaciated, seemed in complete turmoil and was clearly and hopelessly sunk in a deep depression. His best friends, fearing he might kill himself, took away his razor, knives and other potentially dangerous weapons. Some very close to him considered him crazy. Over the following months, though, and with the help of his friends, he gradually began to pull himself out of that despair. He regained his previous great enthusiasm for living. Most particularly, he regained his previous great enthusiasm for learning about everything imaginable, about ideas, people and living. That enthusiasm struck many as rather remarkable for a man who had had very little schooling as a child and grew up in near poverty. But there was, indeed, something special about him. People were struck by his vitality, his zest for living.

Such vitality was the hallmark of his life. Out of it radiated all the best of himself: his humor, ingenuity, native wisdom, decency, honesty, sensitivity to the needs of others, gentleness, resoluteness. Out of it also came something even more important: the ability to, time after time, rebound from the despair of repeated defeats. That quality of vitality in him was catching. Others felt moved in his presence. Others saw not the physical appearance of an ugly man, they saw a man of surpassing beauty, they saw a man they could identify with and respond to. In later decades he became a symbol for all that was the very best of his nation, he became the personification of its idealism, its spirit of all men being equal, of all having the freedom to speak their mind, of all being part of the same oneness. He also became its leader during the worst period in that nation's history. His name is Lincoln.[1]

My reason for telling this story about Abraham Lincoln is to give a striking example of how one can move from the worst of states to the best of states.

That story raises this question: Where do the most admirable qualities in our living — creativity, courage, initiative, dynamism, achievement and self-fulfillment — come from?

My answer to that question came out of an understanding of what happened when people whom I helped went from the worst of living to the best of living.

I had come to the conclusion that my work as a psychiatrist meant helping people deal with crazy thoughts, feelings of rage, violence, panic and hopelessness and actions that were self-destructive. I saw that underlying all those elements was a sense of extreme desperation in living. I had also come to the conclusion that what they — and all of us — want most for ourselves are the admirable qualities of creativity, courage, initiative, dynamism, achievement and self-fulfillment.

One single word summed up all of those admirable qualities: *vitality*. That word put in a nutshell what I set forth in Chapter One, *Getting a Kick Out of Living*. Vitality was the opposite state from desperation.

To understand where those most admirable qualities come from I saw that I had to make a logical connection between the desperation that brought people to me and the vitality I would help them get for themselves. I had to make sense of what happens inside ourselves as we go from the worst of living to the best. It seemed clear to me that there must be a linkage that connected those two extremes in living.

---

1   I have adapted this passage about Lincoln's early life from David Herbert Donald's *Lincoln*, New York: Simon and Schuster, 1995, pages 84–90.

I found a way to make a commonsense connection between the extremes of desperation and vitality. These are the six linkages I arrived at:

- craziness–eccentricity–originality–creativity
- rage–defiance–boldness–courage
- panic–tension–readiness–initiative
- violence–aggression–striving–dynamism
- hopelessness–despair–aspiration–achievement
- self-destructiveness–indulgence–pleasure–self-fulfillment.

The two middle elements in each linkage make sense of what we experience in daily living, depending upon whether we are doing well or poorly in our efforts to get what we want most. There seemed an obvious connection between eccentricity and originality, defiance and boldness, tension and readiness, aggression and striving, despair and aspiration, indulgence and pleasure. It was as though one had to accept the negative aspect so as to get the positive aspect.

It was as though one had to test out one's ideas that might appear eccentric to arrive at originality. One had to muster up a sense of defiance to acquire boldness. One had to accept tension as essential to readiness to action. One had to realize that there is no separating the aggression inside oneself from the effort involved in striving to get what one wants. One had to see that aspiring towards an end also means facing setbacks and despair. One had to recognize that there is no clear line between pleasure and indulgence.

What I had come up with was a figurative sliding scale that I saw one swung through depending upon how one's living was going. At the very best there is vitality; at the very worst, desperation. It is just such a sliding scale that connects the worst within us with the best within us.

Everyone goes through such ups and downs in living, though rarely to either extreme. This sliding scale is most readily apparent when we look at young people. During those usually turbulent years when one is trying to find one's adult identity, it is common to see dramatic swings between the worst and best of states.

Such a perception of a sliding scale with six linkages raised three questions in my mind: What connects the different elements of each linkage together? Is there some factor underlying those linkages which explains why we move in one or the other direction? What are our resources for turning our living around?

I came to see that underlying each of the six linkages is a special resource we have for dealing with our living.

- Underlying the creativity–craziness linkage is *imagination*
- Underlying the courage–rage linkage is *power*
- Underlying the initiative–panic linkage is *self-mobilization*
- Underlying the dynamism–violence linkage is *self-assertion*
- Underlying the achievement–hopelessness linkage is *ambition*
- Underlying the self-fulfillment–self-destructiveness linkage is *self-gratification*

In our everyday living we try to make the most of these six resources — and all at the same time. When we can do that, they mesh together into one splendid whole of vitality. They mesh together because each resource fills a specific function in our pursuit of what we want most in our living:

- Imagination is the *source* we have within ourselves out of which we draw forth our own special way of dealing with living,
- The sensing of our own power is the *energy* with which we charge our imaginative ideas so that we dare to test them out,
- Self-mobilization is the ability we have to *focus* our energy at a particular time and place immediately prior to action,
- Self-assertion is our capacity for releasing that energy into the *action* needed to literally get what we want,
- Ambition gives us the *goals* that both spur us to action and are the targets for such action,
- Self-gratification is the *reward* we give ourselves for our attainments and that enables us to renew ourselves.
- Getting what we want most in living is the stimulus that moves us to seek new challenges, thus setting off this chain of functions once again.

All these elements make up one whole in the process of living. I call this the *Vital Process*.

I found it easier to visualize that whole process if I put the elements together into in one comprehensive picture: our resources for living, the functions they serve, and the sliding scales of vitality and desperation. That picture looks like this:

THE VITAL PROCESS

The Resources for Living, the Functions They Serve, and the Sliding Scale of Desperation and Vitality

THE VITAL PROCESS					
Function	Resource	The Sliding Scale			
		Vitality	Half-ups	Half-downs	Desperation
Source	Imagination	Creativity	Originality	Eccentricity	Craziness
Energy	Power	Courage	Boldness	Defiance	Rage
Focus	Self-mobilization	Initiative	Readiness	Tension	Panic
Action	Self-assertion	Dynamism	Striving	Aggression	Violence
Goal	Ambition	Achievement	Aspiration	Despair	Hopelessness
Reward	Self-gratification	Self-fulfillment	Pleasure	Indulgence	Self-destructiveness

Why look at living this way? Because it makes commonsense of what we experience in living.

Such a perception brings optimism to how we see our living. It makes clear that there is a way to turn the worst of living into the best. It identifies the resources we can draw on to do that. Our everyday living is a testing out of how to mobilize those resources.

- When we succeed magnificently we turn our imagination into creativity, our power into courage, our self-mobilization into initiative, our self-assertion into dynamism, our ambition into achievement and our self-gratification into self-fulfillment.

- When we fail miserably our imagination is turned into craziness, our power into rage, our self-mobilization into panic, our self-assertion into violence, our ambition into hopelessness and our self-gratification into self-destructiveness.

We usually don't succeed magnificently or fail miserably. Those are extremes. It is the middle range that we usually experience, depending upon whether we are doing better or worse in our living at a given time.

Looking at things this way pinpoints a problem all of us have in our living: the difficulty of dealing with the desperation we experience when our efforts are going poorly. One must come up with new ideas and test out those new ideas.

There is simply no way of avoiding desperation in living. We are bound to fail at times. Such failing is the impetus we need to find new, better, ways to get what we want. Seen this way, we need our desperation, strange as that may sound. We *need* to experience desperation in our living. It is our desperation that spurs us to bring forth the best of ourselves. We need to face the worst within ourselves in order to make the best of our potential.

I had, in that way, found an answer for myself as to where creativity, courage, initiative, dynamism, achievement and self-fulfillment come from. They come from our coming to grips with the elements of desperation inside ourselves.

The basic challenge in living is to learn from one's mistakes and from the desperation that comes with them. Failure, seen this way, is the path we must travel to arrive at success. We will fail, often many times at the same endeavor. We must draw from our failures new ideas of how to get what we want, then go back and try again repeatedly, and finally end up with just what we want.

The most important challenge for each of us is ourselves — our attempts to make something unique out of the stuff that we are. The worlds we live in will always be laden with problems, from the minute to the enormous. All of us have special resources to help us face and deal with the sense of desperation those difficulties arouse.

Looking at living this way was of decided practical utility in my helping efforts.

This perception helped me in my work in three ways:

- It helped me see that concealed behind the worst appearing of psychiatric difficulties were the most admirable of qualities

- It gave me a way of discarding psychiatric diagnoses and replacing them with an optimistic, commonsense, alternative

- It helped me dispel the fear people have of the worst states of desperation.

It helped me see that concealed behind the worst appearing of psychiatric difficulties were the most admirable of qualities.

The main problem in helping those who are at the end point of desperation is that the extremes of craziness, rage, violence, panic, hopelessness or self-destructiveness appear to make them unreachable. It is as though those features characterize the whole of the person. It is as though there are no admirable qualities to bring forth and build upon. A potential helper may easily feel that dialogue is futile. It is far easier to turn to medications.

To help a person it is necessary to see that those negative features conceal distinctive, positive, resources for turning one's living around. What I have set forth in *The Vital Process* offered me a way of seeing the best of assets hidden behind the worst appearing of states.

It gave me a way of discarding psychiatric diagnoses and replacing them with an optimistic, commonsense, alternative.

I found that in practice it was invariably impossible to make a clear-cut psychiatric diagnosis. There was a great overlapping of symptoms. That was so even when such diagnoses concerned the seemingly distinctive diagnoses of schizophrenia and manic-depression. There were invariably elements of rage, panic, violence, hopelessness and self-destructiveness together with craziness. The same applied to all other diagnosis. Psychiatric diagnoses, to my mind, represented a futile attempt to make a scientific classification based solely on descriptive features. The most prominent feature became the diagnosis. Psychiatric diagnoses offered no help in effecting a helping dialogue. What they did, in effect, was to confirm that a person was suffering from a mental illness for which there was, as yet, no cure. I saw that as a fiction. I found that there wasn't a single psychiatric diagnosis that evoked optimism in the general public. It seemed clear to me that psychiatry's diagnostic classification had to be discarded and replaced with something far more optimistic.

That is what I have tried to do with my idea of *The Vital Process*. I saw that people in need of help were troubled by a mixture of the elements of desperation, even though one element often appeared dominant. Looking at such difficulties this way gave a better understanding of what underlies the tension of neuroses, the craziness of psychoses, the hopelessness of depression and the self-destructiveness of substance abuse. My perception of a sliding scale between vitality and desperation offered, to my eyes, a far more optimistic idea of how such conditions arise and can be reversed.

It helped me dispel the fear people have of the worst states of desperation.

People who came to me for help were invariably fearful of the different elements of their desperation. The onset of crazy thoughts, feelings of rage, violence, panic and hopelessness and actions that were self-destructive evoked a fear that they might be losing a grip on themselves, that they might be suffering from a mental illness. The idea of mental illness invariably meant being a psychiatric case, being abnormal and being basically incurable. That fear paralyzed people. They were unable to deal with their desperation. I saw such a reaction as a direct result of the pessimism built into psychiatry's classification of mental illness.

After our first talk people would sometimes ask me, with obvious apprehension, what diagnosis I had arrived at. My reply was that I did not use psychiatric diagnoses because I had found them untenable and fear-provoking. I would go on to say what I thought that person had of positive resources to be rid of his or her troubling situation and to get what he or she wanted out of living. It was my idea of *The Vital Process* that enabled me find such words of encouragement,

The Vital Process is my attempt to put into everyday words an understanding of what happens inside ourselves during the course of our living. That understanding is, to my eyes, what we need to know about ourselves to get the great wonder out of our living. It provided the conceptual framework for my efforts to help people turn their living around from the worst to the best. It was, of necessity, a picture drawn with the broadest of brushstrokes.

What I saw that I had to do next was to spell out how to utilize such an understanding. That meant making clear what I saw was of central importance in our ability to get the best out of our living.

It was that need which led me to see that at the crux of our living is the ability to turn craziness into creativity.

CHAPTER 10. THE CRUX OF LIVING: TURNING CRAZINESS INTO
CREATIVITY

Why is the ability to turn craziness into creativity the crux of our living?
How does one actually go about doing that?

My answers to those questions came from seeing craziness and creativity
in a way markedly different from what is usual. It came, first of all, from seeing both a bad and good side of craziness.

What is usually taken to be craziness, the pictures we see of severe psychiatric disability, is to my eyes the surface expression of something lying
deep inside a person. It is as though there is a kernel of craziness deep inside that is not in evidence except when circumstances of extreme distress
bring it forth. In those circumstances that kernel of craziness bursts forth
and dominates the life of the individual. That is what we see as the bad side
of craziness. The good side is that it is precisely in that deep-lying kernel of
craziness that we find the linkage to creativity.

- The kernel of craziness I am talking about is what we have inside
  ourselves that is bizarre, eccentric, fantastic and wild. That kernel is the outer limit of our imagination. It is the freest part of our
  imagination, the most unrestrained, the most unbridled, the most
  uninhibited part.

- The creativity I am talking about is the imaginativeness we bring to
  bear on whatever we undertake that makes our accomplishments
  an expression of what is special and unique about ourselves.

I see that such a linkage between an internal kernel of craziness and cre-ativity is most apparent in works of music and art.

The examples that come first to my mind are the works of Stravinsky and Picasso, works in which the seeming madness in their creation is what is so spellbinding, the very hallmark of their creativity. That linkage is only slightly less apparent in thought and writing. I think there first of Einstein and Freud whose ideas, when they first saw the light of day, seemed to come from another planet.

It is important to make clear that I am not calling Stravinsky, Picasso, Einstein and Freud crazy, at least no more crazy than any of the rest of us. They appeared to be fairly well in control of their personal lives and rational in their living. It was only their works, when first brought forth, that struck people as being bizarre, as out of this world, as completely at odds with what was generally accepted. Today it is easy to forget the initial reaction to such works.

It is easy to forget:

- that when Stravinsky's "Le Sacre du Printemps" was first performed, most of the audience booed, stamped their feet, and walked out of the hall;

- that when Picasso first showed his pictures of two-faced heads, bod-ies put together seemingly any old way, and parts of rooms scattered around in a mish-mash, most people thought such weird pictures were so far-out that they had no connection with art and certainly not great art;

- that when Einstein proposed such things as light rays bending to the shape of the earth; that, in addition to length, width, and depth there was a fourth dimension, time; and that matter was totally con-vertible to energy and vice versa by a simple formula, $e=mc^2$ — his views seemed the result of an other-worldly imagination and were diametrically opposite to how people saw things,

- that Freud's ideas about sexual development in children were wide-ly dismissed for decades as the wild fantasies of a sex-fixated dirty old man.

It seems clear to me that one doesn't have to appear psychiatrically crazy to have a kernel of craziness somewhere inside oneself. It also seems clear to me that it is just that kernel of craziness that is the spark of one's creativity, that those whom we now deem as truly creative had the capacity to some-how turn that kernel of craziness into creativity. They had the courage to test out their craziest ideas, those ideas that went against the grain of how most people saw things. They did not fear the bizarreness, eccentricity, fantasticness and wildness within themselves but were willing to test it out.

All of which brings me to the question of how to make good sense of the linkage between craziness and creativity in the lives of everyone.

I chose the examples of Stravinsky, Picasso, Einstein and Freud because it seemed to me that one could easily see in their work a connection between an inner kernel of craziness and creativity. Those examples, however, might lead one to draw two wrong conclusions.

The first wrong conclusion is that one has to be exceptional — a born genius — to be creative. Not as I see things. We are all born with imagination, including its extreme forms of bizarreness, eccentricity, fantasticness and wildness. We all are born with the capacity to utilize our imagination to its fullest.

The second wrong conclusion is that creativity is only applicable to one's work. Even though creativity is most apparent in one's work, I see that we need to utilize our imagination in tackling the problems confronting us in every sphere of our living.

I see that we all have within ourselves an inner kernel of craziness, that we all have the imaginative capacity to turn that kernel into creative accomplishments, that we all, when we feel totally blocked in our living, can develop the severest of psychiatric disabilities. It is in that kernel of craziness that we find the source that either paralyzes our living or enriches it.

To understand how one turns craziness into creativity it is important to look at creativity in its smallest possible dimension — not its largest, most intimidating, dimension.

One can see that smallness most clearly in the uninhibited efforts of small children — in their drawings, ideas and fantasies. In those efforts we see the inextricable mixture of creativity and craziness. There is there a bizarreness, eccentricity, fantasticness and wildness that is captivating. Reality and fantasy are intimately intertwined at that time of life.

What makes for that mix of creativity and craziness? It is a direct result of what a child is experiencing at any given moment. It is a result of the all-absorbing curiosity and fascination small children have for everything that happens within themselves and outside themselves. That same curiosity and fascination ought to be at the center of our living throughout the course of our lives.

What happens during the course of living is that one's experiences over time constantly feed into that kernel of craziness. To see how that feeding-in works it is necessary to see how our imagination works.

Everything we have experienced can be best seen as a vast storehouse of our imagination. In that storehouse exists an immense accumulation of free-floating thoughts, ideas and images. They are free-floating in the sense that they are the bits and pieces of everything we have experienced during each moment of our living. What is important about those elements of our imagination is that they are not neutral. They are charged with every possible emotion, feeling and sensation.

That is why they are important to us. That is why they have remained with us. That is why they return to us so vividly. And they do return — in our spontaneous associations or emotional reactions to people and happenings, in our sudden sense of intuition or foreboding, in our impulses, in those thoughts that intrude into our awareness at times and in our dreams. All those bits and pieces of our imagination make up the bottomless memory bank of our fantasy life. We draw on that memory bank when we are faced with difficult problems in our daily living.

Such a problem acts as a stimulus to our imagination. It ignites a reaction in the memory bank of our fantasy life. That stimulus calls up into our awareness those different thoughts and feelings that might have some bearing on the problem facing us. It is as though down deep in our inner reaches there were billions of unconnected feelings, sensations, thoughts, fantasies and experiences which, at that very instant and under that very particular stimulus, become linked together. A new thought springs forth.

When the problem we are facing is difficult, the different thoughts that are evoked may seem at first like fantastically wild ideas. That is why, when we tackle something hard and suddenly get a great inspiration, we may cry out, openly or to ourselves, "Wow, I just got a really crazy idea of how to solve this problem!"

To get the most out of our living — its real rewards — what we must do is to bring our imaginative powers to bear on the problems we face in every sphere of our living.

When a problem facing us seems incredibly difficult we must call forth ideas from the freest, most unfettered part of our imagination, from our kernel of craziness. What we have to do then is see whether or not such wild, crazy, ideas work in reality. Whether or not a crazy idea turns out to be a creative one depends upon our readiness to test it out, upon how we go about that testing-out and upon the result that testing-out yields.

Such testing-out, as I have come to see things, is both the most difficult part of our living and the most important part of our living.

It is most difficult because the severest tasks we face in our living call forth from that kernel of craziness not just resources but also fear, helplessness and the possibility of failure. It can be frightening to look at the bizarreness, eccentricity and wildness inside ourselves. What makes things worse is that the more important the tasks we face are the more difficult and intimidating they also appear.

That is why far too many people avoid tackling the most important problems in their living. Such avoidance leaves one with a persistent sense of futility in living. For one's important problems don't vanish by avoiding them. The longer those important problems persist the more the likelihood that one's desperation in living will intensify.

In the previous chapter I set forth my idea that such desperation, at its worst, is a mixture of craziness, rage, panic, violence, hopelessness and self-destructiveness in various degrees. Of all those six features I have come to see that it is craziness which is the most frightening and most incapacitating — even when such craziness is not at all apparent to others.

For part and parcel of severe desperation — and all of the severe psychiatric and psychological difficulties in living — is the fear that one may be losing a grip on oneself, that one's life may be out of control, that one is trapped in helplessness, that one may be on one's way to becoming a psychiatric case, suicidal, — or, in a nutshell, crazy. Such a fear of craziness is the most terrifying aspect of one's desperation. That deeper fear is what I have become aware of when people whom I have helped could open up about what they had experienced.

Because I came to see things that way I have come to the conclusion that basic to the expertise of the professional helper is knowing how to help people deal with craziness. By that I mean dealing with both the fear of craziness inside ourselves that no one else sees and with out-and-out psychiatric craziness.

Later on, Chapter Twelve ("Coming to Grips with the Scariest Part of Ourselves"), sets forth an idea of how to understand psychiatric craziness and why such an understanding is important for the living of all of us. We must face that fear of the bizarreness, wildness and irrationality inside ourselves if we are going to get what we want most for ourselves in our living. For without doing that there is no possibility of testing out our inner craziness. And such testing out is the very crux of our living.

It is the crux of our living because what we are doing is bringing forth the ultimate of our imagination to bear on the severe problems before us. Out of our inner craziness we will find something that works in reality. And when that happens we gain the great reward for doing so: a pride in ourselves. We take a special pride in our ingenuity, our resourcefulness, our own very special creativity. Nothing else in our living is comparable.

The basic task we face in living is to turn our craziness into creativity. In doing so, we develop what is so unique about ourselves — our individuality — to its highest expression and reap the great gratification from being able to do just that.

What, then, is the starting-point for bringing forth our imagination to bear on the problems before us?

That starting point is what I set forth in the first chapter: It is to see the most difficult problems before us as challenges to our ingenuity rather than as oppressive burdens.

We must recapture the great curiosity and fascination we had as small children for everything that happens within ourselves and outside ourselves. Seen in this light, the craziness inside each of us, instead of being something terrifying, becomes something fascinating, something to explore, something to make sense of. It is that selfsame curiosity and fascination so obvious in small children that draws forth from deep inside ourselves a resourcefulness that we usually are only vaguely aware of.

The path to developing our creativity, then, is to be found in our attempts to test out our wildest ideas. It is just such testing out of those crazy — potentially creative — ideas that is the key to getting the whole process of vitality in living going. It is that curiosity and fascination that makes the whole of our living an exciting challenge.

All of which raises this question: How, then, does one actually go about such testing out?

My answer stems from what I saw worked in my helping efforts. I can sum up the essence of that testing-out in two words: dreaming and daring.

It is the dreamer in us that frees our imagination and our ambition. It is the darer in us that frees our power, self-mobilization and self-assertion. When we are dreamers and darers we are our own, unfettered man or woman.

It is out of our wildest dreams for ourselves that we get the inspiration to get what we want most out of our living. It is out of our daring that those dreams are turned into reality. The potential of imagination we are born with must, after being left free to roam, be worked on, tested and refined. Our craziest ideas to be creative must, in the end, work in our outside world.

This is what people needed to hear from me:

- Reach for the moon.
- Go out and take the risk of making a first class fool of yourself.
- If you succeed, you can smile with satisfaction.
- If you fail, you can have a good laugh at yourself and start over again.
- You have then learned something about yourself that doesn't work — at least that is out of your system.
- It's no big thing to look like a fool, that's part of living.
- As long as you do no harm to others, you have the right to live your life precisely as you wish.
- Forget those who ridicule and condemn; they do so because they themselves fear to dream and dare.

Such words of encouragement are what a person should hear to get the courage to test out one's imagination. Such words, as I see it, are the key to facing one's desperation and turning it into vitality. Seen this way, my job was to help a person find a way to bring his or her dreams within reach.

When we are troubled we need the help of someone who is not fearful of the craziness, rage, panic, violence, hopelessness and self-destructiveness within himself or herself, someone who is not put off when these elements burst out in others, someone who can see that there is an admirable quality at the core of such seemingly negative features.

Seeing a linkage between craziness and creativity this way is admittedly far different from what is usual. There is another way of looking at such a linkage that is far more common.

That perception holds that some people have to suffer the worst states of craziness to be truly creative. The image of the mad genius comes to mind.

One thinks of Vincent Van Gogh, of his exquisite paintings, of his deep depressions and mental hospitals stays, of his cutting off his right ear because of the teasing jest of a young woman. How does one explain such a combination of craziness and creativity? Is such craziness essential to creativity?

My answer is that the ability to dream and dare can be quite different in the different spheres of our living. Success in dreaming and daring in one sphere of living does not necessarily apply to all the other spheres of living. One may do wonderfully well at turning craziness into creativity in one's work yet fail miserably in doing so in one's loving, the sphere of living which is invariably the most difficult one for us. One's creativity in work may be breathtaking but at the same time one's desperation in loving may seriously undermine one's living.

That is how I explain the fact that many individuals who are highly successful in their work often suffer a tormented existence in their love life. That is how I explain the appearance of the worst aspects of craziness combined with creativity. That is why I see it is wrong to think that one must suffer the worst states of craziness to be truly creative.

However, that there is a connection between success in loving and success in work.

That connection depends upon knowing what the real rewards in each sphere of living are and using one's imagination to pursue those rewards. Success in either loving or work can enormously bolster one's confidence in the other area. The more one feels like a mature man or woman the more self-confidence one will have to dream and dare in one's work. The more one develops a unique, personal, expertise in one's work the more self-confidence one will have to dream and dare in one's loving.

The focus of this chapter has been on our living as adults. The next chapter concerns the growing up years. In it I set forth my answers to these questions: How does the ability to turn craziness into creativity develop in those years? What in growing up makes for the great wonder in living? What is the pitfall that makes things go wrong? What is needed during the growing up years to get the best out of one's future life?

CHAPTER 11. THE WONDER AND THE PITFALL IN GROWING UP

At the heart of growing up ought to be the ability to turn craziness into creativity. That means the ability to test out one's wildest, craziest ideas to see what works and what doesn't work. Small children reveal that ability in a striking way.

I still find it fascinating to see small children test themselves out, use their imagination, master difficulties on their own, learn for themselves and, then, take pride in their ingenuity. The ability to call forth such ingenuity is what I see is the great wonder in growing up.

That is what should be central to growing up — and, indeed, to the whole course of living. Mastering small difficulties should lead to the ability to mastering increasingly harder difficulties — and to deriving in ever-increasing degree a pride and confidence in oneself for doing that. That is the key to getting what one wants later on out of one's adult living. It is likewise the key to dealing effectively with problems facing one and to preventing the development of crippling psychiatric handicaps.

Seeing things that way raises these two questions: What is it that fosters such development in children and youth? What is it that gets in the way?

My answers to those questions came out of my efforts to help children, youth and parents.

Parents sought help, or were referred for help, because their children were seen as having serious difficulties. Such difficulties were wide-ranging:

temper tantrums, immaturity, poor learning at school, truanting, disobe-dience, psychosomatic symptoms, eating difficulties, tension, depression, withdrawal, fearfulness, wildness, fighting, crazy behavior, delinquency, substance abuse. Parents were at a loss as to how to help their children. De-spite the best of intentions their efforts were ineffective.

I came to see that what underlay those difficulties was the inability of children and youth to get what they wanted most for themselves in such areas as friendship, learning and recreation. It was in equal measure the in-ability of parents to help their children do that. When I was successful in my helping efforts it was because I could help both parents and their children bring forth that ability.

As a result of those helping efforts I came to some conclusions about what children and youth need from their parents and how their parents could give them just that.

In Chapter 5, "The ABCs of Successful Helping," I set forth three prin-ciples that I saw underlay my helping efforts as a psychiatrist. Those three principles are equally central to how parents can effectively help their children.

Affection. It might seem obvious that children ought to hear words of praise from their parents. Unfortunately such praise is too often taken for granted by parents. Too often children would say to me they never heard a word of praise from their parents. They had to hear such words from their parents and from me. Such words were an open expression of an underlying affection. They were basic to a child's developing sense of self-confidence.

Putting-Oneself-In–Another's-Shoes. One of the main reasons parents go astray in their helping efforts is that they have forgotten how they them-selves felt when they were children, they have forgotten what they wanted from their own parents and did not get. It is as though after becoming im-mersed in their adult life they have put their childhood years completely be-hind themselves. Inadvertently they often repeat what they disliked about their parents' approach just because that parenting approach is the one they have experienced most intimately. In my helping efforts with parents I saw it important to bring forth that memory of their childhood. Such bringing-forth gave them a far better sensitivity to what their children needed.

The-Asking-For-Help-And-The-Giving-Of-Help. I had to learn the hard way, both as a psychiatrist and as a parent, that one should not offer help until help is asked for, that one should not give an answer until one has heard a question. The major problem undermining most parents' efforts is that they offer advice when no advice is asked for. In the minds of such parents they do so to spare their children frustration, disappointment or failure. The unintentional result, though, is that one's child feels dominated. The message that comes through is: Do things this way, Do things my way. Such helping is resented. Either one shuts out the words of one's parent or one obediently does as one is told but without much enthusiasm. A child is then seen as either stubborn or passive. To make things worse, when a child does things his or her own way and fails in that effort the message that often comes through from one's parent is: I told you so, Why don't you listen to me?

Where did such a perception come from? It came from what children and youth often told me when they felt they could speak freely. They would say that they could never ask their parents for help, that their mother or father was the last person they would ask for help, that their parents did not understand them. They felt intimidated. They saw their parents as critical and demanding. In the end I came to see that that matter of a parent's giving help when it is not asked for is the greatest pitfall in a child's growing up.

It is such a pitfall because it deprives a child of learning for oneself how to deal with frustration. It deprives a child of the enthusiasm that comes from tackling and overcoming difficulties on one's own. Such difficulties, instead of being seen as personal challenges, are seen as oppressive obstacles which one cannot master on one's own. As I have come to see things, a child's ability to deal with difficulties on one's own is the preparation needed to deal well, later on in life, with the frustrations that are part and parcel of living.

Unfortunately parents often compound the undermining of their good intentions in a particularly harmful way. When they see their children doing or saying things that seem outlandish they might remark: Don't be silly *or* Don't be ridiculous *or* Be realistic. It is not easy to keep quiet when one sees one's child doing or saying things that one sees is wrong. The effect of such comments, though, is that a child or youth is afraid to take chances, is afraid of looking silly or ridiculous. Such remarks are experienced as put-downs. The result is a fear of ridicule, of doing things wrong, of looking foolish. That result is the opposite of what is needed.

What, then, does one do when one's child makes clear that help *is* wanted and needed?

What children need from their parents is the encouragement to test themselves out, to find things out for themselves, to risk failure, to succeed on their own in what they do. That is how they learn to utilize their imagination to get what they want in learning, friendship and recreation.

Such encouragement means a child's hearing that one shouldn't be afraid of looking silly, foolish or ridiculous. It means hearing words such as: I'm sure you can do it, go ahead and give it a try. Children need to feel that their parents have confidence in their ability to do just that. That is how children learn to deal effectively, early on, with the frustrations and setbacks involved in growing up. That is how children learn, early on, to dream and dare.

Nevertheless, there are times when one's child feels totally blocked, when he or she cannot think of any possible way to deal with a particular problem. One's child then asks for help. How should such help be given?

When a child asks for help he or she is open to receiving such help. What I have found effective is for a parent to say something such as: What would you think about doing things this way? Put in such words, one's opinion comes across as a suggestion. One's child feels that he or she still has the right to decide whether such a suggestion is good or bad.

Such an approach may seem obvious or elementary but, in my experience, it is often overlooked in the particular circumstances involved in helping one's own child. I can only say that that is what I have done in my helping efforts, that that is what I have suggested to parents and that that is what has usually worked.

Given parental encouragement, a child will learn in increasing degree to deal effectively with the frustrations in living. That need for encouragement increases as a child grows older. For, as aspirations become higher and problems become more complicated, frustration increases in intensity. As frustration increases in intensity it becomes, at times, desperation. There, thus comes a time when a child must learn to deal with the elements of desperation: crazy thoughts, feelings of rage, panic, violence, hopelessness and an impulse to self-destructiveness.

One has to come to grips with those elements within oneself. One has to test oneself out. One has to learn to turn craziness into creativity, rage into courage, panic into initiative, violence into dynamism, hopelessness into achievement, self-destructiveness into self-fulfillment. That, as I have tried to make clear in the previous chapter, is what all of us must do. The trick is to see such desperation as a challenge to one's ingenuity.

Children will learn that trick if their parents encourage them to see things that way. For parents to do just that means that they themselves must live their own lives according to such a principle. They then are not panicked when their children reveal such elements of desperation.

What children need to hear from their parents is that experiencing those elements of desperation are part of growing up, that such elements arise in everyone when things are going really rough. What should come through clearly is the parental conviction that their children can deal effectively with the obstacles facing them and when they do so their desperation will disappear.

How then does one deal with such obstacles? What is it that parents can give their children to do that?

What one's children need, first and foremost, is a clear idea of the real and false rewards in loving, friendship, learning, work, idealism and a private life. Such a clear idea of the real rewards in living is, as I have tried to make clear earlier in this work, what imbues one with an enthusiasm to tackle the inevitable obstacles that arise in each sphere of living. It is those real rewards that spell out what one should be getting out of one's living. Such a perception is what parents ought to convey to their children. There are two ways that parents can do that.

The first way arises when a child asks a parent for advice about a difficulty being experienced in a given area. Help is being asked for and has a high chance of being accepted. The second way is far more telling. Parents reveal, by the way they live their own lives, an enthusiasm to tackle obstacles in those different spheres of their living. They set an example of how one can turn desperation into vitality. One's children pick up by a kind of emotional osmosis what the real rewards are in loving, friendship, learning, work, idealism and a private life and how to pursue those rewards.

It is just such a perception of real rewards that I have conveyed to those children, youth and parents whom I have helped. And, as I see it, by far the most important, is that which concerns loving.

In a previous section, on the real and false rewards of loving, I wrote about the effect of the loving between parents on their children. The point of view I set forth there bears repeating here since I see that such loving plays a crucial role in how children grow up. It, furthermore, makes clear why I see that the greatest asset of parents in bringing up their children is being able to show them that the sex–love–marriage linkage can work well.

The following three paragraphs sum up the essence of that point of view.

- Even though parents sought help because of a difficulty of their children, that difficulty often reflected a problem in the relationship between the parents. My helping efforts, then, involved improving that relationship. When that happened there was invariably a marked improvement in the well-being of their children.

- My efforts to help parents focused on their having fun together. When that happens children realize, often for the first time, that their parents greatly enjoy being with each other and doing things together. They realize that the difficulties between their parents are quickly and effectively resolved. They experience a living example of how loving works well. That example has a profound effect.

- This gives children a sense of security. A child experiences the family as strong and solid. The awareness of being a member of a strong and solid family gives a child the self-confidence needed to confront and deal with problems outside the family. And, in later years, that parental example provides a good model to emulate when one tries to get the best out of one's own loving as an adult.

That need for self-confidence becomes acute when one leaves childhood behind and becomes a youth. That is a great turning point in one's life.

Then, it is as though the whole exciting world of adulthood is about to open up. It is as though all the aspirations for an adult life that had been building up during childhood are now an imminent reality. One is ready to stand on one's own two feet independent of one's parents. For most youth there is an eagerness and enthusiasm to strike out on one's own. It is as though one is embarking on a wonderful new adventure in living. And part and parcel of that adventure is an intimate combination of both challenge and obstacle.

The challenge for youth lies in making critical decisions about the course of one's future adult life. Such decisions concern one's future occupation, one's long-term recreational interests, the kind of friendships one would have, one's idealistic orientation and, especially, what one wants out of loving. The obstacle lies in getting what one wants out of each of those spheres of living.

What I find so striking about youth is the enormous energy they put into trying to get what they want out of their living. That great input of energy would seem essential for making the transition from childhood to adulthood. For at just that time what comes to an unavoidable head is the need to test oneself out, to mobilize one's ability to dream and dare, to sort out from one's craziest ideas what works in getting what one wants and what doesn't work.

That need to test oneself out usually makes those youth years a time of great emotional flux. One can swing quickly from the height of elation, when one is succeeding in one's efforts, to the depth of despair, when everything seems hopeless. One can swing dramatically between supreme confidence in oneself to abject helplessness. Youth can appear completely crazy one moment and completely rational the next.

It is a time when desperation can be overwhelming and frightening. In such instances there is a bursting out of the most troublesome aspects of human behavior: gross bizarreness, uncontrolled rage and violence, complete withdrawal, suicidal depression.

Such outbursts are not at all uncommon. For those years are characteristically turbulent ones for youth. And those years are, also characteristically, difficult ones for parents. It is uncomfortable for parents to see the bursting-out of such behavior. It is not easy to remain calm and see such outbursts as part of the growing up process. Some parents are bewildered and turn to psychiatry for help. Some others react in ways that make things worse. Their reaction to rage or violence is often exasperation, expressed in such remarks as "Control yourself," or "Why can't you behave like everyone else." Their reaction to depression or withdrawal is often perplexity and such remarks as, "Come on, snap out of it," or "There's no reason to be so upset." Their reaction to bizarreness is often incomprehension and such remarks as, "You're not making sense," or "You must be crazy." Such reactions are experienced by youth as a lack of understanding of what they are going through. It is as though their parents would control them or trivialize their difficulty or ridicule them.

Why do parents react that way?

They react that way out of frustration and fear. Such behavior seems incomprehensible and scary. They don't know how to handle it. So they say such things in an effort to minimize the seriousness of such behavior. And it is just such seriousness that they fear. They fear that such behavior might be a sign of a deep-lying serious mental illness. More specifically, they fear that such outbursts might mean that their children might be losing their mind, might be going crazy. That fear is understandable.

For in most societies, gross bizarreness, uncontrolled rage and violence, complete withdrawal and suicidal depression are commonly regarded as signs of a seriously disturbed mental state, of an abnormal condition, of — in popular parlance — craziness. "Craziness" sums up in a word the fear and incomprehension such behavior evokes in most people.

How, then, does one explain such severe reactions?

Such outbursts are a direct expression of the high ambitions youth have for themselves and the seeming hopelessness they feel in not being able to realize such ambitions. I see that such outbursts stem from the special difficulty in testing oneself out during the turbulent and critical youth years.

For such testing out means finding the courage to do things in one's own way. It means daring to realize the dreams one has for oneself. It means daring to be different, to be a nonconformist, to make mistakes, to risk falling flat of one's face. It means freeing oneself from the authority of one's parents. It means living up to one's image of the adult man or woman. It means risking ridicule or condescension, even possibly condemnation or ostracism. And that testing out comes to a head during the youth years.

During childhood there is no urgency to come to grips with such ambition. It is during the youth years that that question becomes acute. It is during the youth years that desperation can become overwhelming and can burst out in craziness. The bursting out of such behavior brings to a head not only the need of youth to deal with the worst aspects of desperation but also the need for their parents to do so.

The great difficulty for many parents is that they see the seriousness and scariness of such outbursts but don't see what underlies those outbursts. They don't see the high ambition and seeming hopelessness of realizing those ambitions. They don't see the severe desperation such beyond-hope ambitions bring forth. That is why they react with bewilderment, fear or irritation. That is why I see that parents often feel a profound helplessness in knowing how to help their youth cope with such outbursts.

For to help their youth deal with such outbursts they would have to look once again at how they themselves dealt with the desperation and turmoil they experienced during their own youth years. That can be extremely pain-ful. That would bring to the fore their own lost ambitions for themselves. That would bring to the fore a deep-lying desperation in their own current living, something that they thought they had laid to rest. That would bring to the fore the scariest part of themselves.

I came to see that what youth act out in their extreme of desperation is what lies within people in general. It is the scariest part of ourselves, the part that is crazy, wild, bizarre, the part that comes forth in all of us during the worst of times, those times when we are faced with obstacles that appear insurmountable.

It is the craziness imbedded in our desperation that makes those worst of times so scary for us. It is as though there is a part of ourselves that is beyond understanding, beyond rationality, beyond control. One would avoid such craziness at all costs.

For the idea that there may be a craziness inside ourselves instills fear. There is the fear that one is not a healthy, normal, well-adjusted, competent person. There is the fear that one might be totally losing control over one-self and one's life. There is the fear that one might be — or might become — mentally ill, abnormal, maladjusted and incompetent, a psychiatric case. One fears that others will perceive one as such a psychiatric case and will treat one with ridicule, condemnation or condescension, just those attitudes which usually go hand-in-hand with such a perception. That fear was ex-pressed to me repeatedly by people who came to me for help. I saw that that fear made things worse. It paralyzed people.

It is that fear, more than anything else, which stands in the way of people being able to deal with the worst of desperation inside oneself so as to get what one wants most out of living.

All of which raises two questions that I see are central to our living: How does one come to grips with that scariest part of ourselves? What gets in the way of doing that?

CHAPTER 12. COMING TO GRIPS WITH THE SCARIEST PART OF OURSELVES

To come to grips with the scariest part of ourselves we must somehow make sense of the wildness, bizarreness and irrationality that comes to the fore when our desperation is at its worst. That making sense is the key to dealing well with our living.

What gets in the way of making such sense is that such wildness, bizarreness and irrationality would seem to defy commonsense explanation. It appears strange, weird, not normal. Indeed, it raises the fear that there might be something *really* crazy inside oneself. And that fear raises, in turn, the question of whether the wildness, bizarreness and irrationality people can experience is somehow connected to the craziness that psychiatrists deal with.

It may seem far-fetched to imagine that the wildness, bizarreness and irrationality people in general can experience at the worst of times is connected to such diagnoses as schizophrenia and manic depression (now called by psychiatrists "bipolar disorder"). However, I have come to see that such a connection not only exists but also pinpoints both the means for understanding ourselves and the obstacle to doing just that.

That obstacle is how psychiatrists diagnose craziness. They call it psychosis. They see such craziness as mental illness or mental disorder. It is assumed that such conditions are at root biological, hereditary or genetic in origin. They are thus beyond any commonsense comprehension that ordinary people could easily understand. Those conditions have nothing to do with the lives of those who are not mentally ill, those presumed to be mentally healthy.

My own perception is that such a division between mental illness and mental health is a fiction. Also that one can make common sense out of such conditions as schizophrenia and manic depression. Moreover, I feel that making common sense of those conditions is central to understanding how to deal with the worst states of desperation that all of us can experience.

Such a perception may well seem hard to believe. After all, the idea that there are such things as mental illness and mental health has been generally accepted and has been so for a long time. Thus, I see it as important for people to understand what those ideas are based on and why they are so strongly fixed in the public mind.

Weird obsessions, violent mood swings, bizarre behavior, convictions of persecution, delusions and hallucinations all seem to defy commonsense explanation. Furthermore, individuals suffering such difficulties often appear impossible to reach, as though they were beyond reasoning with. And since those difficulties usually incapacitate people it would seem reasonable to assume that what is at work is an illness. Psychiatrists, as physicians, approach such conditions as other physicians do.

Thus, at the heart of today's psychiatry is the making of psychiatric diagnoses of mental illness. A diagnosis is meant to give a clear idea of what is known about the causation and treatability of a given medical condition. It is assumed that in time an effective treatment specific to a given diagnosis of illness will emerge that will lead to cure. Gross bizarreness, uncontrolled rage and violence, complete withdrawal and suicidal depression would warrant a diagnosis of psychosis. The most common diagnoses of psychosis are schizophrenia and manic depression.

The central problem in that psychiatric approach is the assumption that there is such a thing as mental illness, illness of the mind.

Other physicians deal with bodily organs. Defects in such organs can invariably be shown that offer convincing proof that there is actual damage, actual illness, actual abnormality. But proof that there is an illness or abnormality of the mind is, as I see it, impossible.

It is impossible because of the great difference in opinion about pinning down what mind actually is, let alone defining what is normality and abnormality of the mind. If mind, generally seen, means thinking, then defin-ing what is normal and abnormal thinking leads one into highly treacherous waters. In the end, the evidence that abnormality of the mind actually exists lies solely upon the judgmental opinion of the psychiatrist making such a diagnosis — something which is a far cry from the evidence for abnormal-ity and illness in the rest of medicine. Such proof is also impossible because, assuming that mind is connected to brain functioning, there has never been any evidence of abnormalities of the brain itself in diagnoses of psychosis.

The concept of mental illness would not be so hard to accept, despite the impossibility of proving its validity, if today's psychiatry offered marked optimism to people diagnosed as suffering a psychosis. It doesn't.

What treatment is offered is medication that holds symptoms in check and usually must be continued over a lifetime. There is the constant risk of a new outbreak of the original severe condition. Utilizing such medications only reinforces the impression that individuals exhibiting such behavior must be suffering from a permanent serious medical disability. That rein-forcement is further augmented by the designation of such medications as being "anti-psychotic" — as though they were specific only for craziness even though they aren't.

The end result of that psychiatric orientation is to set forth a great ob-stacle to making optimistic common sense of craziness.

Craziness becomes something only crazy, mentally ill, people suffer from. Craziness becomes a concept filled with fear. It defines bizarre conditions that are deemed irreversible and beyond commonsense understanding. Thus, when people who are extremely desperate experience a wildness, bizarreness and irrationality within themselves what is evoked is a fear that they may be going crazy — rather than a search for making sense of such craziness.

Such a search would seem futile. For if the craziness that psychiatrists deal with is beyond the comprehension of ordinary people it would seem clear that so is the wildness, bizarreness and irrationality that comes to the fore when one's desperation is at its worst. It is psychiatry's premise that there is such a thing as mental illness — typified by psychosis — that stands in the way of our dealing with the scariest part of ourselves.

All of which raises the question of why the idea that there are such things as mental illness and mental health is so deeply rooted in public opinion.

They are so deeply rooted because psychiatrists are generally considered the ultimate experts on the worst, most troubling, states of individuals.

Psychiatry has amassed a vast amount of research in studying the diagnoses of psychosis: elaboration of different kinds of psychosis, the incidence of such difficulties in different populations, comparison of the effect of different medications in ameliorating symptoms, the course of such conditions, testing biochemical hypotheses of possible abnormality. The great weight of that research in professional journals would seem to testify that there are, indeed, illnesses of the mind. The problem in all that research is that it is an elaborate superstructure of seeming science built upon a foundation of quicksand.

To define an abnormal condition one must, first of all, define what is normal functioning. Psychiatry has never come up with a definition of mental health — except that mental health is the absence of mental illness. More to the point, psychiatry has never defined a fixed demarcation line between mental illness and mental health. Having such a definition would be a great consolation to those who, when deeply troubled, would know they are on the healthy side of that line. In short, the idea that there is such a thing as mental illness is a myth.

A pioneering work that spelled out the nature of that myth is Thomas Szasz's book, *The Myth of Mental Illness*.

Szasz and others offer a well-grounded, trenchant, critique of today's psychiatry. Nevertheless, such critique has not taken root in the public perception of craziness; people still accept the idea that there are such things as mental illness and mental health. That situation led me to ask just why that is so. The answer I came up with is that what is needed, and is lacking, is a commonsense understanding of all the different pictures of craziness — its weird obsessions, violent mood swings, bizarre behavior, convictions of persecution, delusions and hallucinations.

By "a commonsense understanding" I mean one that makes clear just how to be completely rid of such difficulties so that individuals can get the best out of their living. Such an understanding would make clear why people in such states are so hard to reach and how to reach them. Such an understanding would also dispel the fear of craziness that is so widespread and would offer a practical way for people in general to deal with the wildness, bizarreness and irrationality that comes to the fore when one's desperation is at its worst.

As I came to see things, there is no separating the craziness inside all of us and the worst appearing states of psychiatric craziness. Those states are simply the bursting out and engulfing of a person by the craziness that exists inside of all of us. To come to grips with the scariest part of ourselves it is necessary to see that those extreme states are not incurable mental illnesses, that they are completely reversible, that one can, indeed, make logical common sense of the most bizarre— seemingly most incomprehensible — pictures of craziness. To come to grips with that scariest part of ourselves it is necessary to see that there are no such things as schizophrenia and manic depression.

Out of my helping efforts I had arrived at what I saw was a way of making common, optimistic, sense of craziness.

The pictures considered typical of psychiatric craziness are the result of how one, at the extreme end of one's desperation, lets one's fantasy life take over most — but not all — of one's daily living.

When one sees one's living as almost beyond hope or meaning, when one sees the world around oneself as so threatening or meaningless one would escape from that world without killing oneself. A final way out is to withdraw inside oneself into a fantasy world. One escapes inward, into one's own private inner world. One tries to shut out what one doesn't want to look at. One lets one's imagination blow out of proportion one aspect of oneself. It is like living out one's life in a dream world, a dream world that one makes up to fit how one would like to have things. And just as with dreams one can find a measure of gratification in such fantasies.

One can take comfort in knowing that one possesses a fantastic amount of energy and ingenuity, a resource that propels one into great bursts of activity and afterwards, as with all super-human efforts, a sense of despair and exhaustion at the enormous problems one is still facing. Or one can imagine oneself as enormously courageous in defying the enemies who would thwart or persecute one. Or one can glory in the idea that one is the most important person in the world.

I see that all of us at times indulge in such fantasizing as either escape, dream or ambition. What happens in the worst of situations is that one blows out of proportion one facet of one's imagination, which, if one could mobilize and utilize it better, would be an obvious and powerful resource.

Ideas of grandeur are only called that if they don't succeed; otherwise it would seem clear that early in their lives those individuals who have attained great renown must have had some such image of themselves and of their own potential.

Ideas of persecution are only called that when they appear terribly out of proportion; otherwise, when put in the perspective of those who are socially successful, the same ideas are the source of an exquisite sensitivity to the ulterior motives of others.

The idea of possessing immense energy, central to the highs and lows of conditions called manic-depression, is, in the successful, the germ of that capacity needed to mobilize one's energy towards achieving one's great ambitions interspersed with necessary periods of rest and even self-doubt.

The idea of super-human control over, or total detachment from, one's body is central to the immobility of conditions called catatonia; in the successful, that same idea can be seen as the source of that enormous capacity for inner reflection and bodily control exemplified in the expertise of practitioners of some Asiatic religions.

If one can see the above connections, one can see that what is so dramatically revealed in those who are most desperate are only exaggerations of what we all have thought and felt at times. Those thoughts and feelings could, if conditions were otherwise, be a distinct asset.

For those who use such fantasies as an escape from living in the outer world, those fantasies may be experienced as the height of either pleasure or terror — just as we experience such emotions in the best of our dreams and the worst of our nightmares — but there is, nevertheless, a security in both such fantasies and such dreams. For, when one lives out such withdrawal it is like being protected by living in a cocoon.

One is shielded from an outside world that appears threatening, a world in which one is faced with perpetual anxiety and hopelessness. And yet there is a consolation in that cocoon world: In the back of one's mind there is the thought that one could come out into the outside world once again if life seemed really worth living. For, one knows, even as one lives out such fantasies and as one experiences such dreams, that they are just that, only fantasies and dreams. One knows that such fantasies are not real and one could dispel them if one wanted to — just as one knows that one will eventually wake up from a dream even while it seems so real and so gripping during one's sleep.

At least that is how one feels when such fantasy living starts. That is the reason why the great majority of people with the diagnosis of schizophrenia or manic-depression recover spontaneously after their first visit to a psychiatric hospital. However, the problems of living in the outside world do not go away during that respite in living — and one usually retreats again to living out a fantasy life.

What happens is that the longer one lives out that fantasy life, the more difficult it is to remember that one could come out of it if one wanted to. One loses track of how things started. The outside world becomes more and more terrifying and the fantasy world becomes more and more a great security. The picture of craziness solidifies.

When that solidified picture of craziness is seen by others it is easy to assume that the individual is basically abnormal and has always been so. It is easy to assume that such a condition is the result of some basic genetic-hereditary-biochemical abnormality a person was born with. What makes such an assumption even easier is that people who appear so troubled often see or hear things that others don't.

Psychiatrists call that phenomenon "hallucinations". Adding hallucinations to delusions — crazy ideas — would seem to pin down the diagnosis of psychosis. However, for me, there is a logical explanation even for such experiences. For, when one withdraws into a fantasy world of one's own it is quite reasonable to expect that a person sees and hears things which others don't. One doesn't need to think in terms of an abnormal mental process to explain them.

Such imaginings occur even in everyday life. Even when there is no severe distress in our lives, our mind sometimes plays such tricks with us.

When we are falling asleep or, more often, when just waking up, it is often impossible to recall, just then, whether what we heard or saw was real, an actual occurrence, or fantasy. When we are at times deeply sunk in daydreaming the same experience can befall us. And at dusk in strange surroundings, such as a dark forest, it is easy to imagine hearing and seeing things that aren't there. In all these situations it takes a decided effort to discriminate reality from fantasy.

One can deliberately bring about such experiences. The abuse of alcohol and drugs, such as LSD, can evoke them in anyone. And it is well known that in solitary confinement there is a point in time when such imagined hearings and sights will come forth regardless of who is confined. The shock of exposure to severe battle conditions during warfare can do the same.

Furthermore, hearing and seeing things that others don't is a phenomenon great numbers of people share. Whole peoples believe in literally talking with and seeing God, Jesus, spirits, long dead parents or others. In such instances those experiences are widely considered as something decidedly, and obviously, positive.

Our ability to think and to perceive things is highly adaptable. We do so when such activity helps us in the living of our lives. For me, such experiences are understandable as solely psychological processes. In very great measure we think and perceive things as we want them to be. Thus, when an individual would withdraw into his or her own fantasy world and block out the rest of the world, such imaginings are understandable and make good common sense.

Delusions and hallucinations are aspects of the living of all of us that are blown way out of proportion when one is at the extreme of desperation. There is no need to explain them in terms of a basic genetic-hereditary-biochemical abnormal process.

That conclusion was brought home to me when I looked at the lives of individuals before such craziness burst forth.

There was no possibility of predicting beforehand just which individuals would react that way. The first of such outbursts typically occur during youth and early adult years. Even those who seemed somewhat strange during earlier years were not necessarily predestined to such a reaction. Such a reaction could occur equally well in those who seemed markedly well-adjusted.

When I took the time to go into a person's previous life story that period was always unpredictable and flexible. I always found that something had happened to precipitate an extreme sense of desperation in one's living, something that a person found impossible to deal with, something that caused that person to withdraw into his or her own inner fantasy world.

In previous chapters I have described several of those situations: the young woman whose parents objected to her love affair and was brought to the psychiatric hospital mute; the young woman who was enamored of a young man, could not accept the fact that her love wasn't reciprocated, and was brought to the hospital in part because she heard his voice talking to her; the man whose marriage had turned for the worse and imagined that his wife was poisoning him.

What I gained from those helping efforts were answers to these two questions: How does one help those who seem so hopelessly beyond help? What gets in the way?

The central helping problem is to be able to help those caught up in such fantasy living see that the outside world need not be threatening and can yield just the meaningfulness they are seeking.

The task of helping, simply put, is to be able to help a person make one's craziness work in the world around oneself instead of walling oneself off from that world. To help a person do that, a helper must, first of all, look inside himself or herself to see how he or she has been doing on that score. One must be willing to share with another person one's own way of turning craziness into creativity.

That need of the helper to look inside oneself is the reason why the most extreme psychiatric conditions appear so inaccessible. There are far too few within psychiatry who see the helping problem in this light and, consequently, there are far too few prepared to make such an effort. The reason why this is so is that such helping requires a perception into one's own living that can be frightening.

That need requires a great sensitivity to one's own inner desperation, turmoil and futility in living. Only such sensitivity will yield an understanding that the wall of craziness that those in such extreme situations throw up hides admirable qualities and genuine strengths. Indeed, psychiatric symptoms in general, because they usually have such a negative effect on others, make such sensitivity and such understanding very difficult. People, including psychiatrists, are put off by surface appearances.

That matter of being put off by the outward picture of extreme craziness epitomizes a major problem standing in the way of effective helping in most situations.

For people who are desperate usually put their worst foot forward. Despite wanting and needing help they are very apprehensive that such a want and need identifies them as a person who is in a significant way inferior to others, those who don't need help. That thought is threatening. And when one is threatened one protects oneself by exaggerating and distorting one's real strengths. Thus, for example:

- self-confidence becomes arrogance
- caution becomes evasiveness
- reaching out becomes clinging
- industriousness becomes obsessiveness
- imaginativeness becomes bizarreness
- self-sufficiency becomes selfishness
- spontaneity becomes uncontrollability
- organization becomes compulsiveness.

Seen in this light, trying to reach and help those who seem most unreach- able — those in the throes of craziness — goes to the heart of how one helps another person who is desperate. The problem for the helper in all those situations is to be able to perceive that the most admirable of resources lie hidden behind the most negative, most repelling, of surface pictures.

If one has such a perception one can offer the praise, encouragement and affection that is so essential to helping another. Therein lies the great prob- lem for the professional helper.

For such praise, encouragement and affection must come from what the helper himself or herself has wanted and needed at the worst of times in living. It comes from the helper's being extremely aware of his or her own underlying desperation in living and how he or she is dealing with that des- peration. It comes from the helper's being extremely aware of the wildness, bizarreness and irrationality within himself or herself. It is just such an awareness that makes a helper particularly sensitive to the deep desperation of another person.

Unfortunately in psychiatry, where one is continuously confronted with those who are most desperate, it is far too easy for the professional helper to shut one's eyes to such an awareness.

There is a sense of security that comes from seeing craziness and extreme desperation as not a part of one's own life, from seeing oneself as an objective, distant, well-adjusted, observer of those so troubled. That self-perception may well work for people in general but it stands directly in the way of help- ing those so sorely in the need of help.

Without such sensitivity to a shared deeper desperation, attempts at affection will be sensed as condescension, even criticism. For those in the throes of craziness are acutely aware at how incapacitated they are — even if they would often deny it. They have suffered a great blow to their self-image of being a mature, competent, independent adult. One feels oneself a failure in living. One would wall oneself off from the hurts of others. One fears condescension and criticism.

The great problem I faced in my helping efforts was that most of those caught up in craziness feared that they were, indeed, a hopeless case. What I had to do was to dispel that fear.

To counteract that self-image of being a hopeless case I had to say: "My only aim is to help you get what you want for yourself. As I see it, you have all the capacity in the world to do that. If you want, we will work on that together."

I could say those words because I could make sense of what that cocoon of craziness meant to people. People cling so tenaciously to their fantasies because those fantasies are like a lifebuoy, a last desperate hope against sinking to the bottom of the sea, against committing suicide. Effective helping may be likened to convincing another to let go of that lifebuoy and try swimming again, with all the guidance, encouragement and confidence I could muster.

When I could do that, there was an excellent chance that the individual I would help would emerge tentatively from that cocoon, would begin to use imagination not to escape but to find what he or she could get out of living, and would test out his or her own ideas in that pursuit. When that happened, an individual would gain a newfound sense of pride.

I have seen that happen. When I have been able to help those individuals who were deeply enmeshed in their craziness make such an effort, I saw a successive fading away and disappearance of their fantasized escape world.

Others who have done the same kind of helping know instinctively what I am talking about. They also have experienced the two special rewards in such work: first, the immense satisfaction of helping another, seemingly hopelessly lost in the depths of desperation, to achieve a new, vital, rewarding, life; and second, the great insight one gains into one's own inner life and personal resources.

It was just that helping experience that brought home to me the message that craziness contains for the living of all of us, and it bears repeating: To find vitality in our living, we must start with the craziness inside ourselves; we must see the positive potential in that craziness. We must see it as the wellspring of our imagination. All the effort we might bring to bear on our endeavors won't yield self-fulfillment if we don't, first and foremost, see vitality in our living in terms of turning craziness into creativity.

That scariest part of ourselves is at the heart of our most private world, that world of both great uncertainty and great ambition. What we must do in our living is continuously test ourselves out. To do that we must see that there is a good side to craziness, that which is the source of our creativity and ingenuity. To do that, we must be able to confront and understand the fear that our craziness brings with it.

When I could help people do that, I could help them give up all the different means they were utilizing to escape from dealing with desperation: excessive drinking, smoking, overeating, burying themselves in work, living for passive entertainment, being dependent upon psychopharmaceuticals and narcotics. Seen this way, at the heart of understanding and dealing with our desperation is understanding and dealing with our craziness.

All of us must have this perception to get the best out of our living. It goes to the heart of dreaming and daring, of not fearing ridicule or failure. To get what we want out of our living, we must make sense of the craziness inside ourselves, what is seemingly beyond understanding, beyond rationality, beyond control. Testing out our craziest ideas is the key to our self-reliance, self-confidence and self-pride.

That point of view is the source of my optimism about how to help people and about how people can help themselves. It is the key to reversing the worst states of desperation. It stems from the idea that one can, indeed, make optimistic common sense of the scariest aspects of ourselves, that one need not fear that those aspects of ourselves are signs of a grave, incurable, mental illness.

My perception of craziness, desperation in living, and a psychiatrist's expertise is the polar opposite of what is generally accepted within psychiatry. That polarization, as I came to see things, pinpoints the prime problem in how we perceive and deal with our living — both as discrete individuals and as a whole people. It also raises a key question in our living: How can one prevent the development of severe psychiatric conditions?

In 1962, five prominent American psychiatrists and social scientists at the Cornell University Medical College published the results of a remarkable research project, one that even today stands as a unique contribution to understanding the presence of psychiatric problems in society. They made a survey of a population segment in the center of mid-town New York City. They interviewed a large sample of adults from a population of 175,000 people. This is what they found: 81% had out-and-out, clear-cut, psychiatric symptoms, only 19% were symptom free. There was a sliding scale in the severity of those symptoms but a rough classification indicated that 23% of that total population had the severest of psychiatric symptoms, 30% moderately severe symptoms and 30% mild symptoms. What is of particular importance in that study is that only a minuscule number of those surveyed had any contact with psychiatry.[2]

Since then, subsequent surveys in different countries have also indicated the widespread presence of unequivocal severe psychiatric difficulties in populations — with only a minute number of those so troubled seeking help. Those results, as I see it, speak tellingly against the commonly-held assumption that only very few in the population have the severest of psychiatric difficulties and that those so troubled come to and are taken care of by psychiatry. They speak *for* a serious, widespread and unrecognized problem in

2   Rennie, T.A.C., L. Srole, S.T. Michael, T.S. Langner and M.K. Opler, *Mental Health in the Metropolis: The Midtown Manhattan Study.* New York: McGraw Hill, 1962.

societies. That conclusion has important consequences for both individuals and society as a whole. [3]

For individuals those results mean that a great many people live out their lives seriously handicapped, that they get far less out of their living than what they could and should be getting. Many give up completely and take their lives. For society it means that a significant part of the population maintains itself by means that bring with them a host of serious psychological, medical and social problems.

Such problems include an inability to work or work well, the abuse of tobacco, alcohol and psychopharmaceuticals, psychosomatic difficulties, theft, outbursts of violence. The toll those problems takes from society is great. That toll comes in the form of considerable costs for social and economic supports, medical care and police measures. It also comes in the form of markedly impaired work efficiency. All of which raises this question: How does one get at that presence of widespread hidden severe psychiatric difficulties?

That question raises, in turn, what I see as a key question in how we live our lives: Can we prevent the development of the worst states in living? The key word in that question is *prevention*. For, as I see it, preventing the worst of states would mean knowing how to deal with the most difficult problems in our living so as to get the best out of living — instead of being locked into the worst of states. Seen this way a good, practical, idea of prevention would be the key to markedly diminishing the presence of the worst of states of individuals in society.

Such an idea of sweeping, society-wide, prevention might well sound like a pie-in-the-sky ambition. Could there really be such a thing? What would it look like?

There was, indeed, a highly promising beginning made in the 1960s. A number of prominent psychiatrists were then engaged in the area of prevention. Gerald Caplan, then of the Harvard School of Public Health, pulled together what was known about that subject in a seminal work, *Principles of Preventive Psychiatry*. He offered concrete suggestions for the development of

---

3   Jablensky A., "Epidemiological Surveys of Mental Health of Geographically Defined Populations in Europe," in *Community Surveys in Psychiatric Disorders*. M. Weissman, J. Myers, C. Ross and A. Slaby (editors), New Brunswick: Rutgers University Press, 1986.

psychiatric prevention. His own primary focus was on psychiatric engage-ment in the community, particularly in schools. [4]

Unfortunately, however, interest among psychiatrists in prevention pro-gressively decreased in later decades. At present it is far out on the periph-ery of mainstream psychiatry's concerns. Moreover, the basic orientation of today's dominant psychiatry leaves little prospect for the development of psychiatric prevention.

I see that the prime reason for that situation was the explosive develop-ment of the psychopharmaceutical industry and its effect in forwarding a biological-physiological approach within psychiatry. Theories about the ac-tions of medications seemed to make good scientific sense. Results in terms of symptom alleviation seemed scientifically measurable. That development greatly reinforced a medical perception of a psychiatrist's expertise.

Psychiatrists saw that their work was, in essence, making the appropri-ate diagnosis of mental illness or mental disorder and then applying a spe-cific treatment when that was available. They usually saw that their treat-ment expertise was, at bottom, having a refined knowledge of how different psychopharmaceuticals acted on the body. They saw their work as rooted in science.

The possible prevention of mental illness or mental disorder was com-monly seen as a nebulous area, one of possible interest to psychologists but beyond the scope of psychiatry. It was often assumed that a genetic or hered-itary factor was a significant causative factor underlying diagnoses of psy-choses, neuroses and character disorders. Such a factor would speak strongly against the possibility of effecting prevention.

Such a perception might be acceptable if one assumed that all those with severe psychiatric difficulties actually did come to psychiatry for help. If psy-chiatric expertise was delimited in such a way then psychiatrists' perception of causation and prevention might well be valid.

However, the reality of things spoke strongly against such a perception and its validity.

Given the widespread presence of severe psychiatric difficulties in soci-ety it seemed to me untenable to assume that all or most of those people suf-fered from a genetic-hereditary disorder. It would be as though most people in society suffered from such disorder and only a minority did not.

---

4   Caplan G., *Principles of Preventive Psychiatry*, New York: Basic Books, 1964.

Furthermore, given the fact that only a minuscule number of those with severe difficulties came to psychiatry, it seemed clear to me that the usual psychiatric expertise had little relevance to the living of the great number of people that did not come to psychiatry. Thus, any psychiatric assumption about the impossibility of psychiatric prevention needed to be taken with a large grain of salt.

How, then, does one make a start in tackling the sweeping problem of psychiatric prevention? Why was it that previous attempts to forward prevention within psychiatry rarely took hold? Let me share my own thinking about answers to those two questions.

It seems self-evident to me that any idea of the prevention of psychiatric difficulties must be grounded on a concept of causation. Prevention must block such causation.

The central problem in arriving at such causation is the great overlapping of difficulties that people experience at the worst of times: crazy thoughts, anxiety, depression, impulses to self-destructiveness and violence. Those difficulties are mixed together; they are not isolated problems. That same overlapping is characteristic of psychiatric diagnoses, of the different neuroses, psychoses and character disorders. Such overlapping makes it impossible to tease out a special causative factor presumably underlying one or another specific psychiatric difficulty. It speaks strongly against the possibility of finding a preventive approach specific to one or another psychiatric difficulty.

It speaks compellingly for the idea that what is essential for psychiatric prevention is a causal conceptual foundation that encompasses *all* psychiatric difficulties. More specifically, such a conceptual foundation would have to explain the causation and reversibility of all psychiatric difficulties. For reversibility is the key to preventing being locked into a severe psychiatric condition. It seems to me that only such an approach could lead to sweeping psychiatric prevention.

That conclusion, to my mind, goes to the heart of what was wrong with earlier attempts at psychiatric prevention.

There was in those earlier attempts no such encompassing conceptual foundation.

One utilized the concept of mental illnesses or mental disorders as though those terms described discrete conditions. One utilized the term treatment as though there were specific measures applicable to one or another mental illness or mental disorder. One utilized the term mental health as a preventive approach without defining what it was and how it worked.

I came to see that the idea of a sliding scale between desperation and vitality in living offered just such an encompassing conceptual foundation. Desperation was a mixture of the different elements of psychiatric difficulties. The idea of a sliding scale went to the heart of the matter of reversibility.

The great numbers of people with severe psychiatric difficulties constitute a vast hidden reservoir of human desperation in society. That reservoir constantly feeds new cases into psychiatry. That reservoir is replenished by those, increasingly desperate, who have come to see their living as hopeless. The problem of psychiatric prevention is to turn desperation into vitality on a societal scale.

How does one get at that reservoir? How does one prevent new people from falling into it? How does one help those in it to get out?

Over a period of seven years, from 1976 and 1983, I carried out a pilot project in psychiatric prevention in Malmö, Sweden. During the course of those years I found my own answers to those questions. Although I have mentioned that project in the introduction, let me repeat its basic premise here.

The central idea was that personnel outside of psychiatry and psychology could offer effective help to people who were troubled early on — before they might need to come to psychiatry — if they received backup supervision from me in how to do that. Such personnel included neighborhood police, social workers, immigrant counselors, teachers, judicial referees in child custody disputes, recreational center leaders, outreach workers in delinquency, and workers in the areas of narcotics and alcohol abuse.

When I first met with such personnel I described what I had in mind. I offered them the opportunity to meet with me once a week in an ongoing group session, on a voluntary basis. I made it clear that we would discuss only difficulties they experienced in reaching individuals whom they saw as a problem for them in their work. The idea was that instead of trying to refer such individuals to psychiatry or psychology, they would try to offer help themselves.

At the start of that project I had no idea how such personnel would react to such a proposal coming from a psychiatrist. I made it clear that we would continue meeting only as long as we felt that such meetings were fruitful. I was greatly encouraged by how things developed. Most such personnel were eager to participate in such a group discussion. There invariably was no other ongoing group meeting to discuss such problems. Almost all the groups met for many months; participants were rarely absent because of other work obligations. Motivation was uniformly high. Over those seven years, there were forty such groups.

That project gave me a special insight into the broader aspects of effecting psychiatric prevention.

Central to that insight was how highly-experienced personnel saw their work role. Let me begin with the work role of teachers, work supervisors and recreational instructors, since those spheres of living are important elements of one's day-to-day reality. Teachers saw their role as presenting a body of knowledge in a clear, easily understood way; work supervisors saw their role as making clear just how work can be done effectively and efficiently; recreational instructors saw their role as making clear how to acquire recreational skills. All those perceptions centered on clarity, and they were valid — but of secondary importance.

What was primary was to arouse a burning enthusiasm for learning, work, and recreation. That matter was invariably overlooked. It depended, first and foremost, on one's own great enthusiasm for one's work, to see work as a challenge, and to communicate enthusiasm for that challenge to others. For me, the greatest challenge in work was to reach out and motivate those who appeared least motivated. That motivational work is how I saw my job when children, youth and adults were referred to me.

That challenge was rarely a central focus in the education and training of such personnel. That, to my mind, pinpointed a way to build psychiatric prevention into society itself. What was at issue was communicating what I saw as the real rewards in those spheres of living, and doing so on a sweeping scale. That is what counteracts the pursuit of false rewards in living.

Such an approach to work roles might appear, at first glance, both simple and easily done. It isn't. Changing work roles means a radical change in the focus of an entire social institution, its method of education and training of personnel. Let me give two examples from the worlds of education and recreation that typify that problem.

- In a group of teachers, one long-experienced teacher brought up a problem she had with her class: they weren't paying attention and were unruly. I asked her what subject she was teaching. She answered: ancient history. I asked her what was so interesting about ancient history. She said, "nothing special." I then asked why she was teaching that course. She said because it was assigned to her. It seemed clear to me that if she had no great enthusiasm for what she was teaching it would be difficult for her students to muster such enthusiasm and attention.

- In a group of recreation center leaders, the problem came up of youth who were lackadaisical about coming to the center. Eventually the discussion came around to what those leaders were actually doing in their work. For them it was a job to be done efficiently.

I suggested that each of them only instruct in some activity that they themselves were greatly enthusiastic about. That brought about a significant change. They simply had not thought about their work in that way. It was only the exceptional person who placed such a great emphasis on communicating enthusiasm for her or his work. Asking that this be a central day-in-and-day-out focus appeared to be asking too much; indeed, it often seemed like asking the impossible.

Yet such a change is essential to effect broad scale psychiatric prevention. That is the way to markedly diminish the flow of new cases into that reservoir of desperation. That is the key to revitalizing a society's social institutions.

Such a revitalization is equally applicable to helping those great many who have slipped into that reservoir of desperation.

Many of those so caught up, although they didn't come to psychiatry, were well known to other personnel. Indeed, they often constituted a significant part of the problems such personnel had to deal with. But it was usually difficult to refer such individuals to psychiatry.

Many refused such a referral, considering that psychiatry was for "crazy people" and that they were not crazy. Others were often considered by psychiatry as unsuitable for its helping methods; the problems of such individuals were often combined with social or criminal problems such as narcotic abuse, multi-problem families, violence and theft. The end result was that personnel usually had a great deal of difficulty referring people to psychiatry. It seemed clear to me that the way to reach those in that reservoir of desperation was to offer them effective help.

What I suggested to those in my groups was that they take time to talk one-to-one with those who seemed troubled. I realized that that wasn't part of their usual duties. Nevertheless, I saw that not only could their helping efforts be effective but that the reward they got out of such helping could be great. Because I had boiled down my own helping efforts to three basic elements I felt I could give such personnel the backup support they needed. Only when those efforts failed was a further referral necessary. That was my idea of building better helping supports into society. That was also my idea of how to reduce the great reservoir of desperation in society.

It seemed clear to me that personnel outside of psychiatry and psychology can have a great helping impact on people to change the course of their lives for the better. One example of such impact that I had read about has remained present in my mind.

> [Kermit] felt he could not do well at anything. He received uniformly poor grades in all classes. Then one day in biology class the students were dissecting frogs and the teacher, Mrs. Joan Thomas, watched him and said, "Kermit, you're doing an excellent job." He was terribly embarrassed and he was sure she was making fun of him. All the other kids began to laugh too, sure that she was mocking him. After all Kermit was the boy who had never been praised before and who was often the butt of a teacher's frustrated criticism. "No," she corrected them, "I mean it. Kermit is doing an excellent job." That was the first time anyone had ever told him that he was good at anything in his entire life. With that he began to feel confident in biology and he began to study and get good marks. Soon he had good marks in biology and poor marks in everything else. Then Mrs. Thomas became his homeroom teacher and she looked at his report card and told him that he ought to try to do better in other courses too. "You know, Kermit," she said, "you're intelligent and you could get good marks if you wanted to." He was stunned by that, by the idea that she thought he was intelligent. In his last year at Calvin Coolidge he made the honor role. He was very proud of that.[5]

That paragraph tells about a turning point in the life of Kermit Washington who went on to be one of the premier stars in the National Basketball Association.

I would like to think that most teachers have that same capacity as Joan Thomas. I still remember from my own early years the handful teachers who had such a great impact on me. Also, as I have noted in Chapter 5, there were mentors who profoundly changed the way I saw my work. I would like to imagine that within societies there is a great reserve of human capacity to

---

5   Halberstam, David. *The Breaks of the Game*. New York: Ballantine Books, 1981, pages 258-259.

help others which has barely been tapped — in large part because it is not seen as part of one's work role.

That perception applies in equal measure to the work roles of psychiatrists and psychologists, many of whom have a great deal to offer to those working in other fields, as I sought to do and as Gerald Caplan imagined was the way to effect wide-scale prevention. The problem is that this approach departs greatly from the education and training of psychiatrists and psychologists. It departs, too, from the self-image of such specialists who work almost exclusively in private practice, clinics, mental health centers and hospitals.

This approach, however, is a good way to get at the great reservoir of desperation in society. This is a way to build effective helping into the fabric of society. And of key importance to doing so is the need to change psychiatry. For psychiatry defines what the worst of states are and has the ultimate responsibility of helping those who are worst off.

However, the resistance to effecting prevention and changing the role of the psychiatrist cannot be overestimated. That resistance is something I ran into personally with my preventive project.

After the first two years of my project, I organized a day-long symposium to set forth its results. Two members from five different groups described briefly how they had experienced those groups. Those ten constituted one panel. The other panel, those who listened to the reports and commented upon them, were the heads of the different administrations involved: schools, police, social service, education, recreation, psychiatry. The two political leaders responsible for health and welfare in the city were invited but did not come. Reporters from the two newspapers were present.

My intention was to use that symposium as a springboard to form a small team — a social psychiatric unit — to expand what I had been doing alone up to that point. I had the support of the professor of social medicine who agreed that such a unit would be part of his department. However, there was marked resistance from psychiatry. And it became clear to me that without psychiatric support, heads of other administrations would be reluctant to support such a proposal. The key to effecting such a proposal rested, in the end, with the political leaders responsible for health and welfare since they had the ultimate responsibility for such a decision. They were silent. That was understandable.

For as long as I was some kind of maverick psychiatrist working on my own with interested personnel, that was all right. But to formalize such an activity in the face of resistance from psychiatry was too much to expect from either heads of other administrations or political leaders. The enthusiastic endorsement of group participants, who were at the grassroots level within those administrations, did not carry much political weight. Neither did the articles in the newspapers reporting on that symposium. When I sought support from the teachers' union, their reaction was confusion, as though improving the effectiveness of teachers was not a union concern.

Looking back, I can now make better sense of what happened. I can see that that result stemmed from an incompatibility between how I see psychiatry and how most psychiatrists, even today, see their specialty. What I was doing was seen as outside the competence and expertise of psychiatrists.

That matter of incompatibility goes to the heart of both the ideas set forth in this book and what is wrong with most of today's psychiatry. It pinpoints the prime problem in our living, namely, how we perceive the most troubled states of human beings.

- Either those states are what psychiatrists define as mental illnesses or mental disorders, or they are the extreme of the same desperation we all have experienced.
- Either they are as yet incurable conditions, or they are completely reversible.
- Either they have no bearing on the lives of most people, or they have great significance for the living of everyone.

If my perception is right, it brings optimism to how we see the worst of states and goes to the heart of the living of everyone.

I would like to think that the ideas set forth in this book — the real rewards in living, desperation as challenge to one's ingenuity, how to give effective helping, the encouragement to dare to test out one's craziest ideas, the key to prevention — bring a new clarity and optimism to how we live our lives. I would like to think that they are of practical use in "getting a kick out of living." I would like to think that they spell out the bottom line in our living, what vitality is and how to get that.

There is a great wonder in living life. My hope is that this book will help people experience that wonder in each successive day.